DATE DUE

MAY 1 1 199		JAN 1 7 2012
Stull 5/8		
SEP 3 0 1987		
APR 2 1988		
MAY 1 3 1988		
DEC 1 4 1988		
MAY 0 9 1991		
MAY 1 2 1992		
APR 0 6 1995		
FEB 0 9 2000		
NOV 1 5 2002		
MAY 0 7 2004		

DEMCO 38-297

Employing the Handicapped

Employing the Handicapped

a practical compliance manual by Arno B. Zimmer

amacom a Division of American Management Associations

To my dear mother,

for her continued love and affection

Library of Congress Cataloging in Publication Data

Zimmer, Arno B
   Employing the handicapped.

   Includes index.
   1. Handicapped—Law and legislation—United States.
2. Handicapped—Employment—United States. I. Title.
KF3469.Z55   344.73'0159   80-67967
ISBN 0-8144-5525-5

First Printing

Foreword

Handicapped people and disabled veterans are a minority against whom employers have historically discriminated. It's infuriating, but it's a fact of life. That discrimination continues as we enter the decade of the 1980s.

The drive for a new era of civil rights for handicapped people has already begun, and we can expect the 1980s to bring large-scale improvements in the rights of handicapped people. This movement began during the second half of the last decade as groups of handicapped people and several veterans' organizations grew more vocal in demanding that their rights as citizens of our country be recognized. Handicapped people are, perhaps, the last minority—the last group of people who have been prevented from participating in those activities of daily life that so many nondisabled people take for granted. They have been kept out of the mainstream by unnecessary barriers in architecture and transportation systems. That much is obvious. But movement of the handicapped into the mainstream of American life has also been needlessly slowed by harmful attitudes toward them among Americans generally—and employers specifically.

The groups of handicapped people and the veterans' organizations that have pushed the issue of civil rights for the handicapped into the foreground have provided the impetus to amend Title VII of the Civil Rights Act of 1964 to assure handicapped people the place in our society that they, as American citizens, have a right to enjoy. If the act is amended to include this segment of our population, virtually every employer in our country will be prohibited from discriminating against handicapped people and disabled veterans on the basis of handicapping conditions. Hundreds of thousands of employers doing business with the federal government are already prevented from doing so under existing laws and regulations. Employers should be prepared for an onslaught of complaints if their policies and procedures are not modified to assure equal opportunity for the handicapped. Such preparation can help avoid and eventually eradicate discrimination against the handicapped, whether that discrimination be conscious or unconscious. We, America's disabled citizens, also have a dream. And, like the followers of that great American leader, Dr. Martin Luther King, Jr., we will not slow the pursuit of our dream until we have achieved it.

This book addresses—and interprets in layman's language—a very complex issue: the employment rights of America's disabled citizens. I believe every employer should read it, even those not covered by current laws and regulations. There has been a growing willingness—even a desire—among employers to bring handicapped workers into the mainstream of our society's worklife. However, many don't know what they're expected to do. Others fear large-scale expenses in adapting the workplace that probably aren't necessary. Still others are having difficulty identifying the issues as they affect potential employees in their organizations. This book is designed to help these employers.

The hurtful biases that handicapped people and disabled veterans face in the job market are unjustified. And this book will help bring about a total dissolution of those biases.

Ronald W. Drach
National Employment Director
Disabled American Veterans

Acknowledgments

My thanks to the many individuals, in the government and in the private sector, who provided information and resources during the research process. My particular gratitude to Dick Comer at the Department of Health, Education and Welfare's Office for Civil Rights, Dave Brigham at the Department of Labor's Office of Federal Contract Compliance Programs, and Ron Drach of the Disabled American Veterans, all of whom contributed ideas and constructive criticism. Finally, my very special thanks to Donna, Cindy, and Jackie Hughes, three erudite ladies who spent endless, laborious hours poring over and then typing this manuscript.

Contents

Introduction

In 1957, President Dwight D. Eisenhower presented the Handicapped American of the Year Award to Hugo Deffner of Oklahoma. But before the President could give him his award, Deffner had to be hoisted onto the stage by two marines. During his visit to Washington, D.C., Mr. Deffner was unable to enter the U.S. Department of Labor building in which the annual meeting of the President's Committee on Employment of the Handicapped was being held, due to a number of architectural barriers. These cruel ironies didn't go unnoticed by high government officials, and the above events led, in part, to the passage of a series of federal, state, and local laws designed to bring equal rights in all phases of American life to the disabled.

There was a time when helping the handicapped individual or the disabled veteran secure gainful employment could be a gratuitous gesture. The year 1973 changed all that for the business community with the passage of the Rehabilitation Act.

Since that time, myriad laws and regulations have been promulgated which require specific action by federal contractors and subcontractors—in fact, by any organization that receives or benefits from federal financial assistance. It has been estimated by the President's Committee on Employment of the Handicapped that one-half of the businesses in America (some 3 million) are covered by various laws mandating nondiscrimination, affirmative action, or equal employment opportunity for the handicapped.

A number of major corporations have shown that employment of handicapped people makes good business sense. In effect, they have made a virtue of necessity. Thousands of employers, however, either waiting for the government's impetus or relying on antiquated employment practices, have done little if anything to hire and train the handicapped.

A number of observers in government and the private sector have seen a distinct trend in the late 1970s toward more activism by the handicapped, many of whom view themselves as the latest minority in this country. Any businessman who remembers the passage of the Civil Rights Act and the ensuing push made by racial minorities in the 1960s for equal employment opportunity should not underestimate the commitment now being made by individuals, special-interest organizations, and the federal government to ensure equal rights for handicapped persons. Federal investigators will be investigating employers not only for gross violations of the law but also for more subtle forms of discrimination.

Businessmen bristle at the mere mention of additional regulatory burdens on their companies; yet the scope of federal government requirements seems to be ever expanding. Early in 1979, one large corporation declared that it spent approximately $268 million in 1977 to comply with federal regulations. This figure does not seem so staggering when one considers the General Accounting Office's estimate that 116 government agencies and programs now regulate business.

Since 1973, a series of employment regulations have been put forth by the Department of Health, Education and Welfare*

---

*HEW has recently been reorganized into two new departments: the Department of Health and Human Services and the Department of Education. Readers are requested to translate all subsequent references from "Department of Health, Education and Welfare" to "Department of Health and Human Services."

and the Department of Labor. These new regulations are adding to what the private sector considers an already monumental regulatory cost. To some employers, these new regulations are vague and confusing, but to the federal government and a number of activist organizations the message is clear: companies doing business with the federal government in any capacity must end discrimination and/or take affirmative action to hire and accommodate qualified handicapped individuals.

The evolution of federal regulations mandating equal employment of the handicapped has been gradual and rather indirect. It began four decades ago when President Franklin Roosevelt established a committee in the White House Office of Production Management to enforce nondiscrimination in all defense contracts. The year was 1941, and no mention was made of coverage for handicapped persons.

In 1943, Congress stepped into the picture with passage of the Barden-LaFollette Act, which required that blind persons be given rehabilitation to improve their chances of securing gainful employment. The gains by blind people were meager at the start, but a precedent had been established. Also in 1943, President Roosevelt established a larger White House committee on fair employment, which focused on the prevention of discrimination in war industries. This Committee's authority expired in 1946. Not until 1951, with the formation of President Harry Truman's Committee on Government Contract Compliance, did the White House renew the general effort against discrimination in private employment.

In 1953, President Dwight Eisenhower formed a new committee with authority to receive and review complaints of federal contractor noncompliance. However, the committee had no authority to impose sanctions on violators. Instead, it had to rely on persuasion and conciliation to end employment discrimination.

The 1960s marked the turning point in actually requiring equal employment opportunity and affirmative action from federal contractors and subcontractors. In 1961, President John Kennedy issued Executive Order 10925, which, in addition to creating the President's Committee on Equal Opportunity, imposed specific obligations on government contractors and subcontractors. This

Committee was the first one with enforcement authority, since it could assess penalties for noncompliance. Under this executive order, a nondiscrimination clause had to be included in each government contract. Further, contractors were required to take affirmative action to ensure that employees and applicants were treated equally without regard to race, color, creed, or national origin. Cancellation of a contract or disbarment from future government contracts could be imposed for noncompliance. In 1962, President Kennedy extended coverage of his executive order to include federal and federally assisted construction projects.

In 1965, President Lyndon Johnson issued Executive Order 11246, and the federal government moved a step closer to including handicapped persons in the nondiscrimination obligations of contractors and subcontractors. This executive order paralleled President Kennedy's in coverage while delegating primary compliance authority to the Secretary of Labor. At the same time, the Office of Federal Contract Compliance (OFCC) was created within the White House to administer the new executive order. Day-to-day enforcement authority was delegated to several federal agencies. In 1967, the President amended the executive order to include sex as a protected category. Still, there was no mention of the rights of handicapped persons.

In 1971, the Employment Standards Administration was established within the Department of Labor, and the Office of Federal Contract Compliance was moved there from the White House. With the passage of the Rehabilitation Act of 1973 and the Vietnam-Era Veterans Readjustment Assistance Act of 1974, OFCC gained primary responsibility for ensuring nondiscrimination against handicapped persons, disabled veterans, and Vietnam-era veterans. In 1975, OFCC's name was lengthened to Office of Federal Contract Compliance Programs (OFCCP).

In an effort to streamline and consolidate enforcement of equal employment opportunity and affirmative action requirements of contractors and subcontractors, President Jimmy Carter gave total responsibility for enforcing Executive Order 11246 to OFCCP on October 1, 1978. The effect was startling, for the business community witnessed a wholesale transfer of staff and budgets from a number of federal agencies dealing with contract compliance to one superagency with unquestioned authority—OFCCP.

There should no longer be a question in the minds of business owners about the federal government's intent with regard to equal employment opportunity for the handicapped, disabled veterans, and Vietnam-era veterans. Not only are the regulations becoming more expansive, they are becoming more specific and demanding as well. Special-interest activities of these protected groups are growing, too. When the federal government's compliance efforts fall short or are perceived as inadequate, several advocacy organizations for the handicapped or veterans will step in to initiate administrative complaints and even litigation on behalf of their constituents. In addition to federal statutes, all 50 states and some municipalities now have laws requiring employers either to take nondiscriminatory action to employ the handicapped or to remove architectural barriers to the mobility-impaired. Advocacy groups are also making sure that these state and local statutes will be enforced.

For a federal contractor or subcontractor, the consolidated authority of OFCCP might seem to be a blessing, and for the astute employer it will prove to be so. The arm of OFCCP extends to every government contractor (and subcontractor) who wins a procurement contract through the competitive bid process. By OFCCP's estimate, its authority now extends to 400,000 contractors and approximately 3 million subcontractors employing over 12 million handicapped workers.

Although OFCCP's jurisdiction is restricted to companies involved in the federal government contractual process, what if a company receives federal funds, or benefits from them, outside the contractual process? If a business participates in a federally funded training program sponsored by the Department of Labor or undertakes a research study under a grant from the Department of Transportation, then it is *not* governed by OFCCP regulations but is instead subject to a separate set of compliance guidelines for handicapped workers and applicants. As a beneficiary of federal financial assistance in any form, an employer can be investigated for discrimination against the handicapped by the Office for Civil

Rights in one of 30 federal agencies that now dispense federal funds on a noncontractual basis.

What if a business is occupying a building constructed after 1968? If it was constructed with the assistance of federal funds, the business might be investigated by the Architectural and Transportation Barrier Compliance Board, a federal agency with authority to prohibit architectural barrier discrimination against handicapped citizens. In short, federal requirements to protect the rights of handicapped citizens are pervasive. Almost every financial or business transaction entered into with the federal government (and many state governments) brings with it certain requirements for compliance with legislation to aid the handicapped.

Without question, the era of "good faith" efforts to aid the handicapped is long past for federal contractors, subcontractors, or any business benefiting directly or indirectly from federal financial assistance. Any business owner who has lived through the years of compliance inspections by the Occupational Safety and Health Administration, for instance, should be keenly aware of the kinds of problems a company can face for noncompliance with legislation protecting the rights of workers.

Many observers are saying that the civil rights movement for the handicapped has just begun, and there is copious evidence to support this opinion. Physical barriers to buildings have been called "threshold discrimination" by one activist. Another leader of the antidiscrimination movement is said to have touted his constituency as "the newest minority on the block." Many handicapped persons view inaccessibility to buildings as an issue of the same importance as "white only" was to a black person trying to enter a restaurant during the early days of the civil rights movement.

If a business owner decides not to acquiesce to all these demands of the federal government to give special consideration to handicapped persons, or if he feels that the demands pose "undue hardship" (which is a legal exemption from the requirements discussed later), what can be done? From a historical and legal perspective, the encouragement is scant at best, especially if the Civil Rights Act of 1964 is viewed as an accurate barometer of how Congress, the courts, and the federal government intend to enforce all antidiscrimination statutes, including those protecting handicapped individuals.

Business owners have been less than successful in resisting the demands of the government and the courts for equal employment opportunity and for the redress of past deficiencies in employment practices. Experts in the emerging field of personnel law have pointed out that seemingly narrow decisions by the courts are often couched in language that encourages their use as a precedent in other cases. Thus a decision on age discrimination against an employer by one court might be used in another court to bolster a case against an employer charged with discrimination against a handicapped worker.

Particular case law dealing with discrimination against the handicapped is meager and inconsistent. One U.S. District Court declared that a city government's employment practices discriminating against the handicapped were unconstitutional, violating the equal protection clause of the Fourteenth Amendment. The court even encouraged a class action suit to remedy past and future abuses. Another U.S. District Court ruled that the private right of action is inconsistent with the intent of Congress to resolve discrimination disputes through conciliation initiated by the appropriate federal agency.

The Supreme Court of one state ruled against a major defense contractor in the application of its antidiscrimination law, upholding the reasonable-accommodation requirement for a worker with cerebral palsy. The appeals court in another state ruled in favor of a one-armed taxicab driver, emphasizing that the state's antidiscrimination law was more pressing than other state laws and even a federal law governing the operation of motor vehicles.

Some legal experts view the potential for strict enforcement of laws and regulations protecting the handicapped as quite strong, in light of a number of U.S. Supreme Court decisions in the early 1970s which established that employers can be subject to significant financial exposure for discrimination even if the discrimination is unintentional.

It is because of these formidable obstacles at the federal and state level that most employers have chosen to back away from prolonged defenses and, instead, to seek the settlement of discrimination charges with administrative agencies such as OFCCP. As will be seen later, however, some employers are fighting back and have pursued their cases all the way to the U.S. Supreme Court.

Perhaps two events, one in 1977 and the other in 1979, best sum up the new atmosphere in favor of equal employment rights for the handicapped. The first event was the 1977 White House Conference on Handicapped Individuals. One senator in attendance declared that "1977 is the year of the handicapped." President Carter stated that recognition of the rights of handicapped Americans was long overdue. The Secretary of Health, Education and Welfare made the strongest statement to attendees (and delivered an implicit warning to employers) by pronouncing that "we are now entering a new era of civil rights for the handicapped individuals of America. And we will not be turned back."

The second event occurred in February 1979 in the Senate of the United States, where Harrison Williams (D., N.J.) introduced a bill to amend Title VII of the Civil Rights Act of 1964. Entitled the "Equal Employment Opportunity for the Handicapped Act of 1979," this bill, if enacted, would prohibit discrimination against *all* individuals because of a handicap. Enforcement of this proposed legislation would be placed with the Equal Employment Opportunity Commission, the federal agency which now regulates antidiscrimination statutes against most employers.

Whereas existing federal law covers only federal contractors and subcontractors and recipients of federal financial assistance, this proposed act would require *all* private employers to eliminate discrimination against qualified handicapped individuals and take affirmative action to hire them. As will be seen, all the precedents which grew out of enforcement of the Civil Rights Act of 1964 and deal with the hiring and promoting of minorities, females, and older Americans will have a direct impact on the status of any handicapped individual seeking to enter the private-sector job market if this new Congressional bill is passed.

With the battle lines drawn clearly, employers must decide either to make the effort to comply in an economical and timely fashion or to fight back through the federal and state courts.

Part One
The Law

1
Federal Laws Affecting Employers

There are a number of federal laws protecting the rights of the handicapped which, directly or indirectly, affect the daily operation of companies doing business with the federal government. Two laws, the Rehabilitation Act of 1973 (Sections 503 and 504) and the Vietnam-Era Veterans Readjustment Assistance Act of 1974 (Section 402), are of primary concern, since they mandate distinct employment and affirmative action efforts. Other federal laws, such as the Freedom of Information Act, foster the enforcement of legislation pertaining to the handicapped.

All the federal laws discussed in this chapter apply to companies that fall into one or more of three categories: federal contractors, federal subcontractors, and recipients (directly or indirectly) of some form of federal financial assistance.

Rehabilitation Act of 1973 As Amended—Section 503

Businesses and Contracts Covered

Section 503 of the Rehabilitation Act, enforced by the U.S. Department of Labor and amended in 1974 and again in 1978, requires federal contractors and subcontractors "to take affirmative action to employ and advance in employment qualified handicapped individuals" if the value of the contracts and subcontracts is $2,500 or more annually. A contract or subcontract (written or unwritten and including any modifications) as defined under Section 503 can be for the furnishing of supplies or services or for the use of real or personal property, including construction. Not covered are agreements in which the parties stand in the relationship of employer and employee. As a federal contractor or subcontractor, an employer must make his facilities accessible to handicapped workers, whether he leases the facilities or owns them. Federally assisted agreements are covered under the separate Section 504 requirements discussed later in this chapter.

For the purposes of the act, contractual services provided the federal government (or provided other parties on behalf of the federal government) include utility, construction, transportation, research, insurance, leasing arrangements, and fund depository activities. For these contracts to be covered by Section 503, the federal government need not be the purchaser or seller.

Construction is defined as the construction, rehabilitation, alteration, conversion, extension, demolition, or repair of buildings. Construction also covers changes or improvements to real property, including facilities providing utility services. The supervision, inspection, and other on-site functions pertaining to the actual construction are covered as well. Highways are *not* included in the definition of construction.

As already noted, contracts and subcontracts for less than $2,500 are *not* covered by the act. However, with respect to indefinite delivery-type contracts (for example, open-end contracts) the act applies unless the contracting agency has reason to believe that the amount to be ordered in any year under the contract will be less than $2,500. No contractor or subcontractor (or government agency) can procure supplies in less than usual quantities to avoid the applicability of the affirmative action clause of the act. If any federal agency anticipates signing a contract valued at $1 million or more, a pre-award survey will be conducted to verify compliance with handicapped and veterans laws unless the contractor received a satisfactory affirmative action review in the prior 12 months.

Affirmative action requirements may be waived, at the option of the federal government, for facilities separate and distinct from those at which the contractor or subcontractor performs his work under federal contract. Also, the affirmative action requirement is waived with respect to contract and subcontract work performed outside the United States by employees who were not recruited within the United States.

Waivers, formerly available only through the direct intervention of the president (in the interest of national security), can be granted also by the director of the Office of Federal Contract Compliance Programs at the Department of Labor if it is felt that such a waiver will not interfere with fulfilling the overall provisions and intent of the Rehabilitation Act. As will be shown, however, the government intends to enforce the act vigorously with few exceptions.

The 1978 Amendments

In November of 1978 President Carter signed the Rehabilitation Comprehensive Services and Developmental Disabilities Amendments, which changed the original act and placed even more stringent requirements on the business community. These amendments affect both Section 503 and Section 504 enforcement. Among other things, they:

- Expand the coverage of Section 504 of the act (discussed later in this chapter) to any program or activity conducted by a federal executive agency as well as to any organization receiving federal financial assistance.

- Establish an Interagency Coordinating Council to improve efficiency and to reduce duplication in antidiscrimination enforcement by numerous federal agencies.

- Allow a court to award reasonable attorneys' fees to prevailing parties, other than the United States, in cases of discrimination, thus encouraging private lawsuits as an alternative or supplement to administrative remedies.

- Extend the remedies, procedures, and rights set forth in

Title VI of the Civil Rights Act of 1964 to handicapped individuals with regard to federal employment and access to benefits from programs receiving federal assistance. (For example, companies participating in federally funded training programs must comply with handicapped legislation.)

- Specify that only those active alcoholics or drug abusers who can perform the essential functions of a job in question or who do not present a danger to life and property are covered by the employment provisions of Sections 503 and 504.

- Permit the Department of Health, Education and Welfare, under its Projects with Industry Program, to enter into agreements with employers to provide training and employment services to physically and mentally handicapped persons in realistic work settings, with the maximum share of federal financing to be set at 80 percent of the project's cost.

Who Is Handicapped?

The federal government has a tradition of issuing complex definitions to redefine previously issued definitions that were themselves confusing to the business community. Already, over 600 medical conditions have been identified as possible handicapping conditions covered under federal law. The legal definition of handicapped, however, while raising a number of puzzling questions, does provide some clarification of whom the employer must serve.

Under the act, a handicapped individual* is a person who (1) has a physical or mental impairment that substantially limits one or more major life activities; or (2) has a record of such impairment; or (3) is regarded as having such an impairment. A handicapped individual is substantially limited if he or she is likely to experience difficulty in securing, retaining, or advancing in employment because of a handicap. Traditionally, employers have thought of the handicapped as persons with severe physical limitations. However, Section 503 also protects individuals with "hidden handicaps" such as diabetes, epilepsy, heart disease, and cancer.

*This basic definition applies to both Sections 503 and 504 requirements. As will be seen, however, subdefinitions of who is a "qualified" handicapped individual are different under the two sections.

Under Section 503, a *qualified* handicapped individual is a person who is capable of performing a particular job with reasonable accommodation to the handicap.*

For an employer trying to determine which applicants and workers are handicapped as defined under the act, the following explanation of the key phrases in the above definition should be of assistance.

"Substantially limits" refers to the degree to which the impairment affects employability. For example, an amputee, an epileptic, or a facially disfigured person are all handicapped individuals likely to experience difficulty in securing, retaining, or advancing in employment.

"Life activities" include communication, ambulation, self-care, socialization, education, vocational training, employment, transportation, and adaptation to housing. Employers will obviously focus on life activities affecting employability.

"Record of impairment" means that a person may be completely recovered from a previous physical or mental impairment (for example, mentally retarded persons, heart attack or cancer victims, erroneously classified individuals, or those misclassified as mentally retarded).

"Regarded as impaired" refers to individuals who are perceived as having a handicap, whether an impairment exists or not. The reason for including this class of individuals is that the attitudes of employers or supervisors may have an adverse effect on the individual's ability to secure, retain, or advance in employment. Thus the able-bodied applicant is protected from being discriminated against simply because the interviewer thinks the person is handicapped (that is, a person who has recovered from cancer or one who is aesthetically offensive owing to extreme obesity).

Employers required to comply with the Rehabilitation Act should pay particular attention to the above definitions when revamping their personnel policies and practices. As can be seen from these statutory definitions and clarifications, the test of who qualifies as a handicapped individual is a broad and imprecise one. Employers should keep in mind that it is *not* discriminatory to apply

---

*Compare this Section 503 definition of a qualified handicapped individual with the Section 504 definition discussed later in this chapter.

valid intellectual as opposed to physical or mental criteria when selecting new employees. The cautionary reminder, though, is to make sure that all criteria are job-related and can be proved as such through statistical validation or other reliable means.

Labor Union Influence

If affirmative action necessitates a revision in a collective bargaining agreement, then affected labor unions must be given adequate opportunity to present their views. The Secretary of Labor has the authority to urge labor unions (as well as subcontractors, training agencies, or any other representative of workers) to cooperate with and assist in the implementation of affirmative action plans for the handicapped.

Major international unions have taken an active interest in handicapped legislation and are urging their local union affiliates to cooperate with the federal government in enforcing the law. For instance, the AFL–CIO, through its Human Resources Development Institute (HRDI), is briefing affiliated unions throughout the United States on Section 503 regulations as well as on other laws affecting the handicapped. HRDI is also setting up training programs in key cities to help implement the Rehabilitation Act. Thus the business community must contend not only with federal enforcement activity and surveillance but also with union participation in the affirmative action process. For a description of HRDI activities, see Chapter 6.

What Is Affirmative Action?

Since passage of the Civil Rights Act of 1964, affirmative action in every phase of employment is an obligation of all businesses. In doing business with the federal government, an employer automatically agrees to employ qualified handicapped individuals. Rather than wait for handicapped people to apply for work, employers must recruit these candidates actively for all levels of employment, including executive positions.

The concept of affirmative action requires detailed outreach procedures in the recruitment of new workers as well as in the design of specific internal procedures to ensure that all handicapped applicants and employees receive the same benefits and opportunities as other workers.

Affirmative action must extend to all handicapped workers, not just job applicants, in the areas of upgrading, transferring, training opportunities, demotions, layoffs, and terminations. In the area of compensation, an employer must pay the handicapped individual on the same level with other employees in comparable positions, notwithstanding outside sources of income such as disability or pension payments.

What Will an Acceptable Affirmative Action Plan Cover?

As stated earlier, affirmative action for federal contractors and subcontractors cannot be left to chance or relegated to an insignificant management goal. Specific action must be taken and documented.

Within 120 days of a contract's commencement, a company with 50 or more employees and with a contract of $50,000 or more or a series of contracts totaling $50,000 or more (at least one of which exceeds $1,500) in a 12-month period must prepare and maintain an affirmative action plan at each covered establishment. Smaller employers with smaller contracts still have to take affirmative action but need not have a written plan available for inspection by the federal government. Each covered contract or subcontract must include an affirmative action clause, as shown in Chapter 7. The plan for handicapped applicants and workers need not be separate but can be integrated with an existing affirmative action program at the company.

The affirmative action plan must be reviewed and updated annually and must cover all employment practices at all levels, including but not limited to the following areas:

Hiring.
Upgrading.
Demotion.
Transfer.
Selection for training (including apprenticeship).
Rates of pay (or any forms of compensation).
Recruitment.

Layoffs.

Termination.

Recruitment advertising.

If there are any significant changes in the affirmative action plan with regard to procedures, rights, or benefits that result from a company's mandatory annual review, then these changes must be communicated to employees and to applicants for employment.

Effective communication is a key element in the effectiveness of an affirmative action plan. Employees or applicants who might be covered by the law and who might benefit from the plan must be invited to identify themselves. In the view of federal compliance officials, the application for employment can include a letter or a telephone inquiry—in fact, almost any communication connected with seeking employment. Employers must be alert to the informal aspects of their own application processes. One way to monitor these informal inquiries is to maintain a *permanent* log of all requests for employment information.

If the employee or applicant identifies himself, then the employer must seek the individual's advice with regard to proper job placement and appropriate accommodations. If an employer has "actual knowledge" of an employee's or applicant's handicap, then he must take affirmative action as outlined in the plan. However, an employer need not search the medical files of employees or applicants to determine the existence of a handicap. As one way of improving the application process, OFCCP has suggested that the following written or oral statement be used by employers:

> As an affirmative action employer, subject to Section 503 of the Rehabilitation Act of 1973, we invite you to inform us of any mental or physical handicap you may have. This information is not required by law, and will be handled in a nondiscriminatory and confidential manner.

One acceptable way of informing employees and applicants of an affirmative action policy is to post an announcement on various bulletin boards throughout the company's facilities. The full affirmative action plan of the company must be available upon request for inspection by any employee or applicant. The location and hours during which the plan may be reviewed must be posted at each facility.

In developing an affirmative action plan, employers should consider the following areas for review and coverage:

Job qualifications. Review all personnel processes to determine whether they assure thorough and systematic consideration of the job qualifications of known handicapped applicants and employees for job vacancies filled either by hiring or promotion, and for all training opportunities offered or available at the company.

Physical and mental qualifications. Review, according to an established schedule, all physical or mental job requirements that tend to screen out qualified handicapped individuals, are not job-related, and are not dictated by business necessity or the safe performance of the job. Qualifications that screen out qualified handicapped individuals must be related to the specific job or jobs for which the individual is being considered. Contractors can require applicants or employees to document their claims of disability and can require physical examinations at the company's expense. Any documentation required must be based on the American Medical Association's "Guide to the Evaluation of Permanent Impairments," which is discussed below. However, the *Guide* can be used only to determine the existence of the impairment without regard to its degree. The company, not the worker or the applicant, has the burden of demonstrating compliance with this requirement.

Medical examinations. Comprehensive medical examinations can be conducted by the company prior to employment. However, when an inquiry is made into an employee's or applicant's physical or mental condition (or if a medical examination is conducted prior to employment or before a change in employment status), these inquiries or examinations must be kept confidential, except that:

- Supervisors and managers can be informed regarding job restrictions and accommodations.
- First-aid and safety personnel can be informed to the extent appropriate (for example, to provide emergency treatment).
- Government compliance officials conducting investigations under the law must be informed.

As mentioned earlier, if a company physician is not sure whether a worker or applicant meets the definition of a qualified handicapped individual, he should rely on the American Medical Association's *Guide* (see Appendix O for ordering information). If an applicant's or worker's impairment is listed in the *Guide*, then the employer should consider the person as handicapped, since OFCCP will most likely concur. In 1979, OFCCP established a new procedure to settle medical disputes. When third-party *medical* opinions are necessary, OFCCP will rely on the *Directory of Medical Specialists* to locate a specialist to arbitrate disputes between handicapped individuals and employers. Each OFCCP regional office maintains a copy of the *Directory,* which is published by Marquis's *Who's Who* for the American Board of Medical Specialists.

Accommodations to physical and mental limitations. Reasonable accommodation must be made to the physical and mental limitations of an employee or applicant unless it can be demonstrated that such accommodation will cause undue hardship to the company. In determining the extent to which such accommodations must be made, a company may take into account business necessity and financial cost.

Employers are *not* expected to lower productivity in their efforts to provide reasonable accommodation. In effect, the maintenance of reasonable productivity standards constitutes a legitimate qualification for a job.

Deciding when to make reasonable accommodation can present perplexing problems for employers. An employer might be in the situation, for instance, of considering a one-armed individual for a typing position requiring a speed of 55 words per minute. Reasonable accommodations could be made by purchasing a special one-handed typewriter that would permit the handicapped individual to meet the company's 55-words-per-minute standard. However, if it is felt that the minimum typing standard couldn't be met even if the special equipment were secured, then it can be presumed that the handicapped individual needn't be hired. At the same time, the employer might want to consider the handicapped individual for another position in which typing is not a major task, thereby avoiding both an unnecessary confrontation with the handicapped individual and a challenge to the company's overall compliance efforts. In effect, employers must continually make creative efforts to comply with the reasonable-accommodation requirements of the law.

Examples of reasonable accommodation include reassigning secondary delivery chores of a mobility-impaired keypunch operator to another worker; eliminating rotating-shift responsibilities for an epileptic worker who needs a regular schedule; providing air-conditioned workspace to a worker with a respiratory ailment; and allowing a worker with leg braces to park close to the building entrance. For additional recommendations on achieving reasonable accommodation, consult the Section 504 discussion later in this chapter as well as Chapter 4.

Compensation. With regard to initial employment or promotion, a company cannot reduce the amount of compensation offered because of any disability income, pension, or other benefit the individual receives from another source. For example, a veteran receiving disability payments cannot be paid less than other employees in comparable positions.

Positive recruitment and outreach activities. After reviewing its personnel program to determine whether it includes an adequate affirmative action plan for handicapped people, the company must undertake positive outreach and recruitment activities in the community. Some suggested outreach activities are included in the model affirmative action plan in Chapter 7.

Testing. An employer's tests must be shown to clearly yield a score that is a valid predictor of success or competence in the job for which the individual is being tested. If a test screens out applicants without any relationship to success in the particular job, then it may be deemed discriminatory.

Internal policy. To ensure that the recruitment and outreach plan is effective, an employer must institute a strong internal policy which has the support of managers, supervisors, and even workers who may have had limited contact with handicapped people in the past.

Responsibility for implementation. An executive of the company should be appointed as the manager or director of affirmative action, designated as such on all relevant company communications (both internal and external), given top management support, and provided the staffing necessary to carry out his functions.

Development and execution of the plan. It is one thing to have an affirmative action plan and quite another to see that it is carried out adequately. Constant evaluation of all phases of the plan is required.

Sheltered workshops. Contracts with sheltered workshops do *not* constitute affirmative action in lieu of employment and advancement of qualified handicapped individuals in the employer's workforce. However, such contracts with sheltered workshops can be included as part of an affirmative action plan if the workshop trains employees especially for the company and if the company is obligated to hire the sheltered-workshop trainees at full compensation when they become "qualified handicapped individuals" as defined under Section 503 of the Rehabilitation Act.

Enforcement

Enforcement of Section 503 of the Rehabilitation Act of 1973 has been placed with the director of the Office of Federal Contract Compliance Programs (OFCCP) in the Department of Labor. Whereas in the past a contractor or subcontractor might have been confronted with enforcement by one or more federal agencies, OFCCP now has complete authority over the compliance process. Thus an employer's affirmative action plan originally approved by the General Services Administration or the Department of Defense may be outmoded and not meet the ever changing requirements of OFCCP. The director of OFCCP can undertake the investigations of complaints and the evaluations of contractors as well as other activities deemed necessary to ensure compliance with the law. Designees of the director, which can include other federal agencies, may also participate in enforcement. For complete information on OFCCP's enforcement and investigatory powers, see Chapter 3.

Recordkeeping

With passage of the 1974 amendments, the period for preserving records under Section 503 of the Rehabilitation Act was reduced from three years to one year. Records must include complaints and the actions taken to resolve them plus employment or other records required by the director of OFCCP. Failure to maintain records, have them available for insepction, or update them annually constitutes noncompliance with the act and can be grounds for the imposition of sanctions. Employers must permit OFCCP to examine these records during normal business hours. To the consternation of some employers, records include computer tapes and printouts as well as general personnel files.

Rehabilitation Act of 1973 As Amended—Section 504

Businesses and Agreements Covered

Section 504 of the Rehabilitation Act is administered and enforced by the Department of Health, Education and Welfare, acting as the lead federal agency, and 30 additional federal government departments that dispense federal funds. The decentralized enforcement of Section 504 is described in detail later in this chapter. Section 504 of the act mandates that no qualified handicapped individual, as a result of his handicap, may be denied participation in, or benefit of, any program or activity that receives federal financial assistance.

Coverage of Section 504 is *not* extended to federal contractors and subcontractors, since these firms are already subject to the Section 503 regulations. Since the requirements of Sections 503 and 504 are not identical, however, an employer who is a contractor (by virtue of selling equipment to the federal government) as well as a recipient of federal funds (by virtue of participation in a government-funded training program) would be subject to two different sets of regulations. The confusion and the problems that arise out of this dual responsibility will be discussed in detail later in this chapter.

Recipients of federal funds are defined under the law as any state, any instrumentality of a state, any public or private agency, institution, or organization, or any other entity to which federal financial assistance is extended either directly or through another recipient. Typical organizations covered under Section 504 include colleges, public school districts, hospitals, and public or private employers benefiting from federal funds. Private employers should note that even though the Section 504 regulations seem to have been prepared primarily with hospitals, universities, and similar institutions in mind, they apply whenever one is a recipient of federal financial assistance.

Who Is Protected by Section 504?

As mentioned in the discussion on Section 503, the general definition of "handicapped individual" under the act focuses on physical or mental impairments that limit the opportunity to secure and retain a job. In other words, the basic definition of handicapped individual is the same under Sections 503 and 504. However, whereas Section 503 defines a qualified handicapped individual as a person who is capable of performing a particular job with reasonable accommodation to the handicap, Section 504 defines such an individual as someone who, with reasonable accommodation, can perform the *essential* functions of the job.

The Section 504 definition, with its emphasis on essential job functions, places a greater burden on the employer to define precisely the essential and nonessential responsibilities of each job. For a company subject to both 503 and 504 regulations, the various possible interpretations of "qualified handicapped individual" and "essential functions" are causing considerable consternation and frustration. This problem, along with other apparent conflicts between Section 503 and Section 504 regulations, is discussed later in this chapter.

Some employers have difficulty comprehending how two sections of the same federal law can have different definitions for qualified handicapped individuals. Part of the answer lies in Congressional intent. Since HEW was given primary jurisdiction over recipients of federal funds and since OFCCP was granted authority over federal contractors and subcontractors, employers can expect differing bureaucratic interpretations of Congressional intent. Any time two large and autonomous federal agencies are granted parallel jurisdiction, it should not be surprising when they respond differently.

As we saw in the discussion on Section 503, OFCCP provides little clarification of the physical and mental impairments protected by the Rehabilitation Act. HEW suggests, however, that the following handicapping conditions are covered under the law:

- Alcoholism.
- Cancer.
- Cerebral palsy.
- Heart disease.
- Mental retardation.
- Developmental aphasia.
- Diabetes.
- Drug addiction.
- Epilepsy.
- Multiple sclerosis.
- Muscular dystrophy.
- Orthopedic, speech, or visual impairment.
- Perceptual handicaps (for example, dyslexia).
- Minimal brain dysfunction.
- Mental or emotional illness.
- Deafness or hearing impairment.

This expanded Section 504 definition of who is protected under the law, although set forth by HEW, should be of help to federal contractors and subcontractors (as well as recipients of federal financial assistance) in determining who might be a "qualified handicapped individual" under Section 503.

HEW's Interpretation of Congressional "Intent"

In summarizing its statutory role, HEW has stated that the Secretary "intends vigorously to implement and enforce" the mandate given HEW by the language of Section 504. What HEW means is that it will take the basic definitions in Section 504 of the act and proceed to promulgate its own interpretative definitions as a logical extension of Congressional intent. HEW has been joined by a number of activist organizations in calling Section 504 the first federal law protecting the civil rights of handicapped persons. A number of experts view Section 504 as comparable to the nondiscrimination provisions of Title VI of the Civil Rights Act of 1964. What the views of these activists and even HEW officials indicate is that employers should be prepared for stringent if not "imaginative" enforcement of 504 by HEW and other federal agencies.

Thus HEW has clearly forecasted its intent to interpret its Section 504 authority in broad terms. While admitting that the scant legislative history of the enactment of Section 504 provides little guidance to employers on how to resolve complex issues like the burdens and costs of compliance, HEW has emphasized that major compliance burdens provide no basis for an employer's exemption from either Section 504 itself or HEW's interpretative regulations.

In interpreting "federal financial assistance," for instance, HEW's interpretative guidelines for Section 504 specifically exclude procurement contracts covered already under Section 503. Contracts of insurance or guaranty are also excluded. HEW views federal financial assistance under Section 504 as "any grant, loan, contract (other than those exempted above), or any other arrangement by which the Department provides or otherwise makes available assistance. . . ." Assistance can include funds, the services of federal personnel, real or personal property (including transfers or leases on such property), or the use of facilities such as buildings, structures, equipment, roads, walks, parking lots, and perhaps any other related property which HEW might from time to time deem to be covered.

In short, HEW puts practically no limit on what it considers federal financial assistance. Employers must keep this open-ended definition in mind when they accept federal funds or assistance in any form.

Earlier, we examined HEW's definition of the types of impairments covered under Section 504. One HEW interpretive guideline expands on this basic definition by describing physical or mental impairment as any physiological disorder or condition, cosmetic disfigurement, or anatomical loss affecting one or more of the following body systems: neurological; musculoskeletal; special sense organs; respiratory, including speech organs; cardiovascular; reproductive; digestive; genitourinary; hemic and lymphatic; skin;

and endocrine. Also covered are mental or psychological disorders (such as mental retardation, organic brain syndrome, and emotional or mental illness) and specific learning disabilities.

By "major life activities" covered under Section 504, HEW means functions such as caring for one's self, performing manual tasks, walking, seeing, hearing, speaking, breathing, learning, and working.

It is important for employers to note that the handicapped individual's impairment must result in a "substantial limitation" of one or more major life activities before it constitutes a handicap under Section 504. HEW has declined to offer an interpretive definition of the phrase "substantial limitation" but has indicated that severe handicaps will be the focus of its enforcement action.

The inclusion of drug addicts and alcoholics in the definition of qualified handicapped individual warrants particular mention because of the special responsibilities faced by and exemptions available to employers. The Secretary of HEW obtained a legal opinion from the Attorney General of the United States supporting the view that drug addicts and alcoholics are handicapped if their impairment substantially limits at least one of their major life activities. While this ruling would seem to place unlimited burdens on employers, HEW has advised recipients of federal financial assistance that they may hold drug addicts and alcoholics to the same standard of performance and behavior to which other workers are held—*if* unsatisfactory performance or behavior on the job is related to the person's drug addiction or alcoholism. In other words, the behavioral manifestations of these conditions may be taken into account in determining qualifications for the job and performance on the job. If it can be shown that drug addiction or alcoholism prevents successful job performance, then the individual need not be provided the employment opportunity in question.

In addressing the unique problems of employing drug addicts and alcoholics, HEW has clarified just what a recipient of federal funds may ask all other handicapped job applicants. According to HEW, legitimate inquiries can be made about past personnel records; absenteeism; disruptive, abusive, or dangerous behavior;

violations of rules; and unsatisfactory work performance. In addition, employers can enforce workplace rules prohibiting the possession or use of alcohol or drugs against employees who are alcoholics and drug addicts, *provided* that such rules are enforced against all other employees as well.

Grievance Procedures

If a business employs 15 or more people, it must adopt grievance procedures that incorporate due-process standards and that provide for the prompt and equitable resolution of complaints by existing employees alleging noncompliance with Section 504. However, these grievance procedures need not be established with respect to complaints from applicants for employment.

Notices

If a business employs 15 or more people, it must notify (within 90 days of the date Section 504 coverage is effective) all participants, beneficiaries, applicants, and employees, including those with impaired vision or hearing, that it does not discriminate on the basis of handicap. Unions or professional organizations holding collective-bargaining or professional agreements must be similarly notified.

Notification may take the form of posting of notices, publication in newspapers and magazines (although no longer encouraged as productive), placement of notices in internal publications, distribution of memoranda, and other written communications.

HEW has stated that it intends to undertake a major public effort to inform people of their rights under this regulation in particular and Section 504 in general.

Employment Practices

Under Section 504, a recipient of federal funds may not limit, segregate, or classify applicants or employees in any way that adversely affects their opportunities or status because of handicap. In addition, a recipient may not participate in a contractual or other relationship that has the effect of subjecting qualified handicapped applicants or employees to discrimination prohibited by the act. In defining "relationships," HEW is referring to those relationships entered into with employment and referral agencies, labor unions, organizations providing or administering fringe benefits to employees, or organizations providing training and apprenticeship programs. HEW makes it clear, in language stronger than Section 503, that the obligation to comply with Section 504 is not reduced by the inconsistent terms of any collective-bargaining agreement to which the recipient is a party.

In referring to employment practices, however, HEW is consistent with Section 503 guidelines by extending Section 504 coverage to the following practices:

- Recruitment, advertising, and the processing of applications for employment.
- Hiring, upgrading, promotion, award of tenure, demotion, transfer, layoff, termination, right of return from layoff, and rehiring.
- Rates of pay or any other form of compensation and changes in compensation.
- Job assignments, job classifications, organizational structures, position descriptions, lines of progression, and seniority lists.
- Leaves of absence, sick leave, or any other leave, and fringe benefits available by virtue of employment, whether or not administered by the recipient.
- Selection and financial support for training, including apprenticeship, professional meetings, conferences, and other related activities, including selection for leaves of absence to pursue training.
- Employer-sponsored activities, including social or recreational programs.
- Any other term, condition, or privilege of employment.

In examining their recruitment and employment processes, employers will want to look at creative methods of serving the handicapped. A taped telephone message that lists job openings for blind persons or special assistance in filling out application forms for physically impaired individuals are just two examples of imaginative ways to serve handicapped job applicants.

Reasonable Accommodation

In defining "reasonable accommodation," HEW has indicated that a slight difference in 504 phraseology should not be construed as inconsistency with 503 regulations. In making reasonable accommodation to qualified handicapped individuals, employers are advised to consider (1) the overall size of the federally subsidized program with respect to the number of employees, number and type of facilities, and size of budget; (2) the nature and cost of the accommodations needed; and (3) the type of operation, including the composition and structure of the workforce. With these factors in mind, typical reasonable accommodations could include:

- Providing accessible and convenient parking opportunities.
- Making facilities readily accessible to and usable by handicapped persons.
- Job restructuring and part-time or modified work schedules.
- Equipping a telephone for use by a secretary with impaired hearing.
- Acquisition or modification of equipment and devices.
- Providing readers or interpreters.
- Relocation of jobs and offices to accessible buildings.
- Providing a blind employee with a cassette recorder.
- Providing an adequate workplace (and access to it) if the worker uses a wheelchair.
- Allowing time off for a worker to receive treatment at a methodone or alcoholic care clinic.

Program Accessibility

In the view of many, program accessibility is the key provision of Section 504, since it requires that handicapped persons be afforded equal opportunity for *full participation* in an employer's programs. What does program accessibility mean to the average employer? First, it must be remembered that many of the Section 504 requirements were established with hospitals and universities in mind, since they are the principal beneficiaries of federal financial assistance. Thus a college would be expected to make its courses and extracurricular activities accessible to the handicapped.

For the private employer, however, accessibility might be achieved by such things as the installation of ramps leading to the workplace, the adaptation of elevators, or the purchase of special equipment for the handicapped worker or applicant. Additional suggestions for achieving program accessibility are provided in Chapter 4.

In accessing the viability of their program accessibility efforts, employers should apply six major principles:

1.   Handicapped persons or their representatives must be involved in the planning process.

2.   Communication with handicapped representatives must be open and regular, and there must be a formal grievance procedure.

3.   Separate programs or services for the handicapped are illegal except when equal opportunity necessitates them.

4.   Barriers to certain work activities may require modification to structures and the study of alternative access methods.

5.   Structural changes should be made only after it is determined that there are no feasible alternatives to achieving accessibility (that is, program accessibility and barrier-free environment are *not* synonymous terms).

6.   Common sense, creativity, and a thorough knowledge of both legal requirements and alternative compliance methods will eliminate unnecessary and costly errors. HEW has given the practical example of making a water fountain accessible to a person in a wheelchair, not by changing the height of a fountain, but simply by installing a paper cup dispenser within easy reach.

Employers should establish priorities when trying to achieve program accessibility for handicapped workers and applicants. Ongoing evaluation and even a transition plan can be used to determine which worksite changes need to be given preference. The ultimate goal, however, should be complete program accessibility.

Testing

With few exceptions, no employment test or selection criteria can be used that screen out or tend to screen out handicapped persons in general or any particular class of handicapped persons (for example, all blind people). However, if a test is genuinely job-related, then it can be used even if handicapped persons are screened out. In some cases, HEW will recommend alternative tests that don't screen out the handicapped. Employers are obligated to use these alternative tests.

Tests can be used only to indicate performance of essential job functions and not nonessential tasks. For example, if a position requires regular lifting of 50 pounds, then a test of the handicapped applicant's ability to lift 50 pounds would be valid provided that all other applicants were subject to the same test and standard. However, if only occasional lifting was required, then the 50-pound requirement, as well as the test itself, would be considered *nonessential* and the employer would probably be expected to hire the handicapped person and assign the lifting responsibilities to another worker.

In selecting and administering tests, employers must make sure they do not discriminate unfairly against individuals with sensory, manual, or speaking impairments. HEW is concerned that tests reflect actual job skills and aptitude rather than a handicap. The test cannot reflect the handicap except where those impaired skills are factors that the test purports to measure. For example, a person with a speech impairment may be perfectly qualified for a job that does not (with or without reasonable accommodation) require ability to speak clearly. Yet, if given an oral test, the person with a speech impairment will be unable to perform satisfactorily on the test. The test results would not, therefore, predict job performance but instead would reflect impaired speech. In such cases, HEW expects employers to utilize alternative testing or evaluation techniques.

Pre-employment Inquiries

An employer cannot conduct a pre-employment medical examination or make a pre-employment inquiry to determine whether the applicant is a handicapped person. In addition, an employer cannot ask an applicant about the nature or severity of a handicap.

However, if an employer is taking remedial action, either voluntarily or for other reasons, to overcome past discrimination, then applicants can be invited to reveal whether or not they are handicapped and, if so, to what extent, provided that the employer makes clear in a written questionnaire or orally (if no written questionnaire is used) that (1) the information being requested is intended solely for remedial action or for use in developing and implementing an affirmative action program; and (2) the information is being requested on a voluntary basis, will be kept confidential, and refusal to provide such information will not subject the applicant or worker to adverse treatment.

If information is obtained about the medical condition or history of the applicant, it must be collected and maintained on separate forms and on a strictly confidential basis, except that:

- Supervisors and managers can be informed about restrictions on the handicapped worker's duties or about necessary accommodations to be made.
- First-aid and safety personnel can be informed if the handicapping condition might require emergency treatment.
- Government compliance officials conducting an investigation can be provided with relevant information.

Quite clearly, HEW's intent is to limit pre-employment inquiries as much as possible. Unfortunately, HEW has given few hints as to what questions can be asked or how they can be phrased. Essentially, employers should restrict pre-employment inquiries to job-related tasks of clear-cut importance. For example, an employer might want to ask an applicant if he has a valid driver's license (if it is a necessary qualification for the job) but wouldn't want to ask if he has a visual impairment. Or an employer might want to ask an applicant if he can perform a certain job without endangering himself or other workers (for example, as a crane operator) but wouldn't want to ask him if he is an epileptic.

Often, the way an inquiry is phrased is as important as the information an employer is legitimately trying to gain from a handicapped applicant or worker. Employers shouldn't be timid about asking questions relating to safety, security, and productivity for fear of violating Section 504 requirements. For instance, from a practical viewpoint, an individual with a manual impairment who applies for a job that involves handling hazardous materials could be "guided" into another job at the company rather than be told flatly that he is not qualified for the particular job in question. In making pre-employment inquiries, careful and even sympathetic handling of delicate employment problems by the personnel staff can have a salutary effect for the employer.

Publications

Various employer publications used in recruitment or in dispersing general information about the company will naturally be made available to handicapped workers and applicants. In these instances, a clear statement of Section 504 compliance responsibility and policy must be made (and prominently displayed) either by inserts or by revisions to the publications. Typical publications covered include bulletins, promotional literature, department brochures, employee handbooks, orientation materials, and application forms. Broadcasts related to recruitment and employment should also contain a nondiscrimination message that includes a reference to the handicapped.

For new publications and announcements, employers can use the following statement:

> This Company does not discriminate on the basis of handicap in the recruitment and employment of its staff or in the operation of any Company activities, as required by federal law and regulations. The Coordinator of this Company's activities to achieve and maintain compliance with Section 504 of the Rehabilitation Act of 1973 is
>
> _____ .

Existing Facilities

An employer need not make every facility or even every part of certain facilities accessible to or usable by handicapped persons. In determining compliance with the law, HEW looks at an employer's facilities and programs in their entirety.

Facilities compliance can be achieved through redesign of equipment, reassignment of activities to accessible buildings, assignment of aides to assist handicapped workers, alteration of existing facilities, or construction of new facilities in conformance with HEW guidelines. However, structural changes are not required when equally effective methods of achieving compliance can be utilized. HEW does give priority, however, to methods that place handicapped workers in the most integrated setting possible.

In making facilities accessible, the employer must work within a specific time frame. Generally, accessibility must be achieved within 60 days of the date the employer begins to benefit from federal financial assistance, However, if structural changes are necessary, a three-year period is allowed.

If a business must make structural changes, it must also have a transition plan that sets forth the steps to be taken. The plan itself must be developed within six months of the date an employer is covered by Section 504 guidelines, and it must be prepared with the input of interested persons and organizations representing handicapped persons. At the very least, HEW will expect a transition plan to:

- Identify physical obstacles in facilities that limit accessibility to handicapped persons.
- Describe in detail the methods to be used to make the facilities accessible.
- Specify the steps to be taken during each year of the transition.
- Indicate which company official is responsible for implementation of the plan.

HEW has indicated that certain changes can be made to existing facilities immediately and should not be left for action during the transition plan period. For example, HEW feels that outside ramps to buildings can be constructed quickly and at relatively low cost. Employers can develop workable transition plans by following closely the "Self-Evaluation Guide" in the Appendix to this chapter.

New Construction

As will be discussed later in detail in Chapter 4, any employer who does business with the federal government in any capacity should be keenly aware of accessibility requirements for existing buildings and accessibility recommendations for new construction.

Under Section 504, HEW requires that new facilities be designed and constructed so that, either in whole or in part, they are accessible to and usable by handicapped persons. Building alterations made by recipients of federal financial assistance fall under the same guidelines.

Like many other federal agencies, HEW looks for conformance to the American National Standards Institute's specifications known as ANSI A 117.1-1961 (R1971). Many organizations feel that the ANSI specifications (now being revised) are antiquated, however, and HEW will allow alternative methods of new construction and alteration if they can be shown to ensure equivalent access to handicapped persons.

If an employer has commenced construction (that is, if groundbreaking has taken place), he will not be required to alter the design of the facility so long as he was not subject to Section 504 regulations prior to groundbreaking.

If a facility is being altered and accessibility can be improved by the manner in which the alteration is made, then the employer should choose the method that will enhance accessibility. For example, if a doorway or wall is being altered, then the door or other wall opening must be made wide enough to accommodate wheelchairs.

Policy Determinations

One way in which HEW interprets its statutory authority is by means of a "policy determination." Through its enforcement arm, the Office for Civil Rights (OCR), HEW has issued a number of policy determinations which can assist employers in their Section 504 compliance efforts. These determinations, which can also be viewed by employers as strategic guides to handicapped individuals and activist organizations, will be published in the Federal Register and fall into one of three categories:

1. Policy interpretations designed to clarify and explain regulatory provisions.
2. Procedural announcements designed either to outline the specific actions employers must take to achieve compliance or to specify the procedures OCR will follow to obtain compliance.

3. Decision announcement designed to illustrate how OCR has applied regulatory provisions to specific fact patterns developed through investigations.

As of May 1 1978, OCR had issued six policy determinations, which are discussed below.

Policy interpretation 1. This determination deals with discrimination that occurred prior to the effective date of the handicapped regulations. Although Section 504 became law on September 26, 1973, OCR will *not* normally investigate charges of discrimination prior to June 3, 1977, which is the date the 504 regulations officially became effective. The exception to this general rule would normally involve a discrimination case in which a clear-cut violation of the statute occurred *before* June 3, 1977, and OCR perceived a pressing need to investigate.

Policy interpretation 2. This determination deals with the application of the 180-day limitation period for filing and investigating complaints of discrimination that occurred prior to the June 3, 1977, effective date. Basically, the limitation will *not* apply, and the 180-day period will begin to run on June 3, 1977. However, the complaint must allege a clear-cut statutory violation.

Policy interpretation 3. This determination deals with the several requirements for program accessibility (discussed earlier in this chapter) by stating that "the absence of mobility-impaired persons residing in a given geographical area cannot be used as a test of whether programs and activities must be made accessible." OCR's objective here was to classify as "unworkable" the establishment of arbitrary geographical boundaries for each area, the identification of all handicapped persons in the area, or the use of periodic surveys to determine whether handicapped individuals had moved into or out of the area. The determination also reaffirms the employer's option to use effective alternative methods of program accessibility in lieu of structural changes. Finally, OCR reaffirms that there will be no waivers to the program accessibility requirements.

Policy interpretation 4. This determination deals with the carrying of handicapped persons to achieve program accessibility. Due to the humiliating nature of carrying a handicapped person, OCR views it as unacceptable except under two circumstances: when it serves as a temporary expedient where structural changes are being made, and when under manifestly exceptional circumstances the carrying of a handicapped person is provided in a reliable manner by properly trained personnel. Although program accessibility is not required during construction, OCR encourages it and even permits the carrying of handicapped persons as an "interim expedient."

Policy interpretation 5. This determination deals with the participation of handicapped students in contact sports and has little application to most employers. OCR points out, however, that it applies to all private institutions, affirming that an otherwise qualified individual who has lost an organ, limb, or appendate (for example, kidney, leg, or finger) cannot be excluded from contact sports. Also, if athletes are provided with medical care insurance for sickness or accident, then such coverage must be made available to handicapped athletes.

Policy interpretation 6. This determination affects private as well as public institutions with school board members who might be used as hearing officers in discrimination disputes. Basically, school board members cannot serve as hearing officers in resolving disputes between parents of handicapped children and officials of the school system.

Employers would be well advised to monitor the *Federal Register* for future policy determinations by OCR as well as for additional rulings affecting the entire gamut of evolving compliance regulations.

Enforcement

If compliance with Section 504 cannot be encouraged by informal means, HEW has the authority to take appropriate enforcement action against employers, including referral to the Department of Justice for court action, refusal of federal financial assistance, and termination of federal financial assistance.

Enforcement of Section 504 is under the jurisdiction of HEW's Office for Civil Rights (OCR).* Complaints can be filed on an

*As discussed later in this chapter, HEW's formerly exclusive enforcement authority under Section 504 is being spread among a number of federal agencies that provide financial or other assistance.

individual or class action basis either with HEW or with a federal district court. If filed with HEW, a complaint may be dealt with according to the agency's administrative guidelines or it may be referred immediately to the Justice Department. HEW maintains an OCR in each of its ten regional offices listed in Appendix C. The OCR regional office will accept complaints within 180 days of the alleged violation and initiate investigations where necessary. Where possible, conciliation through negotiation is sought by OCR.

Within OCR, there is a Handicap Discrimination Branch, which has developed a multifaceted enforcement program, including a computerized "tracking system" for civil rights cases under investigation. In addition to investigating charges of discrimination, OCR responds to literally thousands of telephone calls and letters each year asking for help in defining Section 504 regulations.

To further compliance efforts, OCR investigators in HEW's regional offices will drop in on employers and institutions in much the same way OFCCP conducts the Directed Compliance Reviews discussed in Chapter 3. In the first nine months of 1978, OCR received almost 2,000 complaints alleging violations under Section 504. OCR indicates that the number of complaints it receives increases dramatically each month. Having doubled its staff, however, OCR is confident that all future complaints will be processed and settled expeditiously. For interested employers, OCR will aid in the resolution of perplexing compliance problems through its Technical Assistance Unit.

Although the Section 504 regulations were passed in September of 1973, OCR has decided not to investigate complaints that allege violations *prior to* June 3, 1977 (which is the effective date of the regulation), unless special circumstances dictate that it do so. What the business owner must keep in mind is that regulations like Section 504 are not static but evolving continually as HEW evaluates the intent of Congress and issues interpretive guidelines and policy determinations such as those discussed earlier in this section.

On a few issues of recurring interest to the business community, HEW decided in 1978 that:

■ Active drug addicts are not qualified handicapped persons for jobs that require direct access to drugs (OCR has not made a decision with regard to former drug addicts).

- It will not require exhaustion of a recipient's grievance procedures before accepting a complaint for discrimination.
- It is not necessary for a complainant to exhaust HEW's administrative enforcement procedures before pursuing court action.

HEW can be expected to release new policy interpretations from time to time covering such matters as accessibility, structural changes to facilities, and alternatives to traditional methods of integrating handicapped persons into the workforce. It seems likely that other federal agencies enforcing their own Section 504 guidelines (a subject discussed later in this chapter) will also issue policy interpretations, particularly during the process of standards development now in the seminal stage.

Self-Evaluation

HEW's regulations require that all recipients of federal funds evaluate their current policies and practices with the assistance of interested persons, including handicapped individuals and their organizations. After such consultation and evaluation, policies and procedures not meeting the requirements of the Rehabilitation Act must be modified. In addition, steps must be taken to remedy the effects of any discrimination.

If a business benefiting from federal financial assistance employs 15 or more people for at least three years after such self-evaluation, it must designate at least one person to coordinate compliance efforts and maintain a file for examination by either HEW or any other federal agency having enforcement authority for Section 504. This file must also be available for public inspection and include:

- A list of interested persons consulted.
- A description of areas examined and any problems identified.
- A description of any modifications made and remedial steps taken (for example, providing services to persons discriminated against or reinstatement of employees who were terminated improperly).

To assist employers with this internal review process, a self-evaluation guide has been included as an Appendix to this chapter.

1978—The Year of the Expanded Section 504

In 1978, with the publication of what were called "implementation guidelines" for Executive Order 11914 (signed two years previously by President Ford), the enforcement of Section 504 took on added significance. Executive Order 11914 extended Section 504 coverage beyond HEW grant programs to all activities utilizing federal funds. Consequently, Section 504 enforcement authority was assumed by the 30 federal agencies listed in Appendix C.

In 1979, each of these federal agencies began setting up an Office for Civil Rights not unlike HEW's enforcement arm discussed earlier. In structuring their own nondiscrimination programs, these agencies were directed by Executive Order 11914 to set up enforcement guidelines consistent with those established by HEW but *not* inconsistent with the Department of Labor's Section 503 guidelines. According to a number of employers, interagency enforcement guidelines are inconsistent if not contradictory, making it almost impossible to comply with Section 503 and Section 504 at the same time. This problem is discussed later in this chapter in the section titled "The 503/504 Flap."

The significance of Executive Order 11914 for the business community can be understood by looking again at the broad application of Section 504 enforcement guidelines—in short, these guidelines apply to almost any activity in the public or private sector benefiting directly or indirectly from federal financial assistance. Thus a business receiving a study grant from the Department of Transportation (DOT) and a contract from the Department of Defense will need to study the specific Section 504 guidelines of DOT as well as the general Section 503 rules affecting all federal contractors and subcontractors. An additional federal grant from, say, the Department of the Interior (DOI) would obligate this same business to comply with DOI's Section 504 guidelines.

In effect, HEW will be yielding its former monopolistic Section 504 authority to the federal agency dispersing the funds. If a business receives federal funds from more than one federal agency, it could be subject to more than one set of Section 504 guidelines. Even though Executive Order 11914 directed all federal agencies to develop Section 504 guidelines not dissimilar from HEW's, it is not difficult to imagine varying degrees of enforcement emphasis.

Since HEW has received the presidential mandate to assist other federal agencies in establishing their own Section 504 guidelines, let us look at the HEW interagency rules as a model, keeping in mind that each agency will have flexibility in establishing its own rules.

HEW's Governmentwide Section 504 Guidelines

In signing Executive Order 11914, President Ford directed HEW to coordinate the implementation of Section 504 for "all federal departments and agencies empowered to extend federal financial assistance to any program or activity." Employers must keep in mind that these implementation rules have no effect on the separate and distinct enforcement rules for contractors and subcontractors covered under Section 503. Also, these rules have no impact on what HEW might do itself to enforce 504. Rather, they are guidelines, general in nature, for other federal agencies to follow in formulating their own rules for Section 504 coverage. Because HEW's implementation rules are not inflexible, employers can expect some variations in how different federal agencies interpret their Section 504 authority. Obviously, this situation could add frustration and confusion to the compliance effort.

On June 24, 1977, HEW specified procedures for the promulgation and enforcement of Section 504 regulations by all federal agencies providing financial assistance to any organization, public or private. HEW made it clear that its guidelines were not meant to be exhaustive and that other federal agencies might wish to consider additional requirements to meet the particular needs of their programs. What follows is a discussion of the interagency Section 504 guidelines and their intended application by agencies other than HEW.

During the interagency discussions on 504 rule making, a

number of federal agencies made it clear (and HEW agreed) that cooperation on enforcement was essential, particularly when a complainant filed a discrimination charge with the wrong agency. In a signal to the business community, most agencies pledged close cooperation, especially on issues dealing with employment discrimination against handicapped persons. While not endorsing a rule making the Department of Labor the primary enforcement agency on employment discrimination cases, HEW acknowledged that the Labor Department would be the natural lead agency for a federal contractor who got nominal Section 504 financial assistance from another agency. However, where a major HEW grantee is also a nominal federal contractor, HEW has indicated that it prefers to take the primary enforcement role with respect to employment discrimination complaints. With HEW's position in mind, it is not inconceivable that other federal agencies will take the same independent tack as that exhibited by HEW. The worst conceivable dilemma for a business would be subjection to conflicting employment criteria by two different federal agencies, one trying to enforce Section 503 and the other Section 504.

Thus the business community can look forward to some overlapping and possibly inconsistent enforcement of Section 504 throughout the federal government, depending on the aggressiveness displayed by the lead federal agency—or agencies, as the case may be. Frequently, HEW has made it clear to other federal agencies that its basic Section 504 compliance guidelines are minimal and can be expanded by the enforcing agency. For example, other federal agencies can supplement HEW's basic definition of qualified handicapped persons when setting forth qualifications for specific grant programs.

On the question of medical examinations, HEW has left the door open for certain qualifications to the general prohibition against pre-employment inquiries. First, while employers may not, during the application process, inquire about the existence of a specific handicap (for example, epilepsy), they may ask about the applicant's ability to perform duties necessary to the job in question. Second, an employer can solicit information on a voluntary basis regarding an applicant's handicap if the employer is subject to remedial or affirmative action obligations or if the employer is undertaking voluntary action to increase employment of handicapped persons. Third, an offer of employment can be conditioned on the successful completion of a medical examination, provided that no offer is withdrawn on the basis of medical conditions that are not job-related. In the above three examples, HEW has issued governmentwide guidelines consistent with its own intra-agency rules.

It is important to emphasize here the distinction between Section 504 and Section 503 requirements on medical examinations, because under the 503 regulations, examinations and inquiries can be made *before* an offer of employment. HEW has firmly ruled against such pre-employment procedures. Several federal agencies objected to the 503/504 distinction on pre-employment inquiries, but HEW, in its authoritative lead role, has ruled that its standard makes it possible to determine whether the reason for not hiring a handicapped person is the handicap. HEW further argued that this restriction does not prohibit an employer from taking job-related conditions into account in making employment decisions and does not preclude an employer from obtaining necessary medical information. According to HEW, it merely affects the time at which and the manner in which this information can be obtained.

The term "program accessibility" received considerable attention during interagency discussions, with HEW urging other agencies to set forth in their own regulations illustrative types of actions that employers may take as alternatives to structural changes in their facilities. In establishing program accessibility guidelines, HEW has directed federal agencies to give priority to methods that offer programs and activities to handicapped persons in the most integrated setting appropriate. For private employers, program accessibility affects activities such as training programs and company-sponsored social events and not just daily working conditions.

Employers should keep in mind that "program accessibility" is a term that implies a prohibition against the exclusion of handicapped persons from programs by virtue of architectural barriers to such things as buildings, vehicles, and walkways. However, program accessibility does not require that existing facilities be completely barrier-free.

HEW, in looking at its own requirement for companies to achieve program accessibility within a three-year period from the time federal funds are received, has recognized that other agencies may find difficulties with such a schedule. For instance, the Department of Transportation has been given the authority to establish its own time period for making various transportation systems accessible, and the Department of Housing and Urban Development has been granted an extension to draw up accessibility standards in public housing projects.

In dictating enforcement procedures for Section 504, HEW has directed each federal agency to adopt enforcement and hearing procedures as specified in Title VI of the Civil Rights Act of 1964 and to require recipients of federal funds to sign assurances of compliance with Section 504. Each agency has also been directed by HEW to have recipients (1) notify employees and beneficiaries of their rights under Section 504; (2) conduct a self-evaluation of their compliance under Section 504 with the assistance of interested persons, including handicapped persons or organizations representing handicapped persons; and (3) consult with the above groups in achieving compliance with Section 504.

To ensure interagency cooperation and minimal enforcement conflict, HEW has directed that in cases where a substantial number of recipients are receiving federal financial assistance for similar or related purposes from two or more agencies, the agencies involved must coordinate Section 504 compliance efforts. Also, any federal agency conducting a compliance review or investigating a complaint of an alleged Section 504 violation is required to inform other affected agencies (if they have jurisdiction as well) of its findings. Further, HEW has authorized joint reviews or investigations by different agencies.

Finally, all federal agencies have been directed to cooperate with the Office of Federal Contract Compliance Programs in enforcing Section 504 employment discrimination requirements with respect to recipients of federal funds if the recipients are also federal contractors subject to Section 503 compliance. Many businesses fear that this cooperation won't occur or, worse yet, that conflicting employment requirements will be developed and therefore preclude the possibility of cooperation.

Employers doing business with any of the federal agencies listed in Appendix C, on other than a contractual basis, should carefully study the Section 504 enforcement guidelines of those agencies. For many agencies, Section 504 rules are still in the draft stage. However, some agencies have finalized their regulations, a few of which are discussed in the following pages.

Community Services Administration

The Community Services Administration (CSA) Section 504 rules follow substantially the HEW guidelines, although there are important differences. For instance, CSA has emphasized strongly the basic principles of barrier-free design, initially setting forth "performance" as opposed to rigid "prescriptive" standards. All existing facilities under CSA authority must meet performance standards, while new facilities must conform to prescriptive standards set forth by the American National Standards Institute (ANSI). CSA is developing additional compliance guidelines regarding transition plans and the serving of the approximately 7.5 million low-income handicapped persons who benefit from CSA programs.

In defining reasonable accommodations to a job applicant, CSA suggests making vacancy announcements available in a form readily understandable to mentally, visually, and auditorily impaired persons. CSA also suggests providing readers and interpreters where necessary during the application testing and interviewing processes.

Department of Transportation

The Department of Transportation (DOT), through its Office of the Assistant General Counsel for Regulation and Enforcement, has published final rules for enforcement of Section 504. In defining "federal financial assistance," DOT refers to any grant, loan, contract (except procurement contracts or contracts of insurance or guaranty), or "any other arrangement by which the Department provides or otherwise makes available assistance" in the form of funds, services, personnel, or real or personal property. In short, DOT's basic definition of covered agreements is identical to the one promulgated by HEW.

DOT's primary concern is to ensure an accessible transit system for the handicapped. Airport terminals, railroad stations, highway rest area facilities, and adjacent areas must be made accessible on an interim and eventually permanent basis. Calling it a "significant" rule, DOT emphasizes that recipients of its funds can't discriminate in employment against qualified handicapped persons.

In making accommodation to qualified handicapped individuals, employers are not expected to make unreasonable adjustments to the job. For example, placement of a handicapped person in a job is not automatically required if the individual can't perform capably and safely. Also, if an individual becomes handicapped after being hired, an employer needn't pay the individual at the pre-handicap level if adequate performance can't be achieved. DOT also points out that recipients of its funds aren't required to create surplus job openings to accommodate the handicapped, even though job restructuring is encouraged. At the same time DOT expects employers to "go the extra mile" in their efforts to achieve reasonable accommodation.

In defining the broad range of its Section 504 coverage, DOT cites the obligation of a third party who obtains personal property from the initial grant recipient. According to DOT, if a small airport buys a snowplow with federal aid, it continues to be bound by Section 504 regulations even if it sells the snowplow to the county government, provided the government, in turn, uses the snowplow to clear the airport's runways of snow. In all likelihood, DOT and many other federal agencies will be seeking to establish extensive authority over *indirect* beneficiaries of federal funds when preparing Section 504 regulations.

Department of Energy

The Department of Energy (DOE), through its Office of Equal Opportunity, has issued proposed regulations concerning nondiscrimination in its own federally assisted programs.

On the subject of employment practices, DOE has taken the position favored by the business community, stating that they will be scrutinized by DOE only when the primary purpose of the federal financial assistance is to provide employment or when the delivery of services under the grant is affected by the grant recipient's employment practices. If this position is taken by other federal agencies, and sustained by DOE and the federal courts, then grant recipients will find that Section 504 employment provisions will normally be enforced only when federal funds are used to conduct on-the-job training and related programs.

DOE has adopted HEW's policies in most other areas. In particular, it has (1) encouraged voluntary affirmative action in the absence of a finding of discrimination (even though *not* statutorily mandated); and (2) requested that recipients search for alternative employment selection methods and test validation procedures if existing techniques appear to discriminate.

Department of Agriculture

The Department of Agriculture (DAG) will enforce Section 504 through the Civil Rights Division in its Office of Equal Opportunity.

In its proposed rules published in January 1979, DAG made it clear that the difference between its rules and those promulgated by HEW will be "minor." The primary difference is that DAG will require *all* recipients of funds to keep records of their self-evaluation (to achieve compliance) whereas HEW requires such recordkeeping only by recipients with 15 or more employees.

DAG emphasizes in its proposed rules that all its departmental units will coordinate and consult with the Department of Labor in enforcing the employment provisions of Section 504 *if* the recipient is also a federal contractor subject to Section 503.

Finally, DAG expects recipients who also receive funds under the Education of the Handicapped Act (a law discussed later in this chapter) to take positive steps to employ qualified handicapped persons and advance them in employment.

Department of Defense

The Department of Defense (DOD) was hard-pressed in January of 1979 to even give an example of how it would enforce

Section 504 in the private sector, since it does business with employers almost exclusively on a contractual basis, which defers enforcement to OFCCP.

Department of Commerce

The Department of Commerce (DOC) published proposed Section 504 rules in the *Federal Register* in November 1978. These rules are expected to take effect after a public-comment and final-review period.

In defining recipients of federal financial assistance, DOC includes a category called "other parties" with a "direct or substantial participation in any federally assisted program." Examples of "other parties" are contractors, subcontractors, employers, users of facilities or services, and commercial or industrial organizations located in a federally assisted industrial park. Covered facilities include buildings, ships, equipment, roads, parking lots, parks, and industrial parks.

DOC follows HEW's definition of prohibited discrimination and, in warning that information about recipient activities must be available and accessible to the handicapped, suggests the use of braille and tapes for the visually impaired. DOC also advises recipients of federal funds *not* to select the location of a facility if the choice discriminates against the handicapped.

In the area of employment, DOC states that discrimination will not be tolerated "regardless of the recipient's intentions." Areas of prohibited employment discrimination parallel those outlined by HEW. With regard to reasonable accommodation, DOC also follows HEW's lead by recommending job restructuring, part-time or modified work schedules, acquisition or modification of equipment or devices, and furnishing readers or interpreters for the handicapped.

Employment on ships is an area of special concern to DOC. Accepting as a fact that few handicapped individuals will meet U.S. Coast Guard requirements, DOC exempts from its Section 504 coverage all cargo ships. However, passenger ships are not exempt, and DOC expects that reasonable accommodation will be made, on an individual basis, for qualified handicapped persons meeting

Coast Guard requirements as set forth in 46 CFR 10.01-1 et seq.

In mandating structural changes to existing facilities, DOC adapts the guidelines prescribed by the American National Standards Institute (ANSI). Structural changes to achieve program accessibility must be made within three years of the date DOC's Section 504 regulations affect the recipient.

DOC will be seeking written assurances from recipients that they are complying with its Section 504 regulations. Similar assurances may also be sought from other organizations participating in federally assisted programs sponsored by the recipient.

DOC requires recipients to conduct an initial self-evaluation within one year of the effective date of the regulations. Follow-up self-evaluation must be conducted at least every two years thereafter. The unit within DOC that extends federal financial assistance will review the recipient's self-evaluation.

Small Business Administration

The Small Business Administration (SBA) set forth its Section 504 regulations in June 1979, following closely the agencywide guidelines issued by HEW. In defining covered businesses, SBA emphasized that compliance will be expected of recipients and "subrecipients" of federal financial assistance. Subrecipients are considered secondary beneficiaries of the funds. Regulations do *not* apply to financial assistance extended by way of insurance or guarantee.

If an employer receives financial assistance from either an SBA development or small business investment company, SBA expects advance assurances and regular written reports verifying compliance.

SBA regulations prohibit discrimination in the extension of credit to the handicapped applicant by a recipient creditor if, for instance, the handicapped individual derives all or part of his income from a public assistance program or exercises his rights under the federal Consumer Credit Protection Act.

In cases of noncompliance, SBA can suspend or terminate assistance, refuse financial assistance approved but not yet disbursed, or refuse to make further disbursements in the case of a loan that has been partially disbursed. Legal action by SBA under its Section 504 regulations can include demands for accelerated loan repayments and referral to the Department of Justice for prosecution. SBA has indicated that it will even encourage legal action under applicable state and local statutes.

General Services Administration

At the General Services Administration (GSA), little application of Section 504 to private companies is foreseen by the agency, unless the employer is somehow the recipient of surplus goods (for example, furniture, vehicles, or other materials) outside the federal contractual process. GSA has a small investigative staff and hasn't even finalized its Section 504 guidelines for the initial HEW review.

Department of Labor

The U.S. Department of Labor (DOL) presents employers with the most interesting example of Section 504 coverage. It might seem natural for DOL's OFCCP to assume responsibility for Section 504 enforcement along with its duties under Section 503. However, DOL is setting up a separate office (in another agency division) to handle Section 504 enforcement, which raises the possibility that cooperation will not always take place with OFCCP in the event of simultaneous intra-agency investigations under Section 504 and Section 503. How can this apparent double jeopardy occur within one federal agency?

First, it has been established that a contractor or subcontractor can be investigated by DOL's OFCCP under Section 503 no matter what federal agency signs the contract. Second, if the same contractor or subcontractor participates in a training program funded under the Comprehensive Employment and Training Act (CETA), a federal training law discussed later in this chapter, then the company is in receipt of the kind of federal financial assistance that subjects it to Section 504 enforcement by DOL's Office for Civil Rights as well. DOL had not finalized its Section 504 regulations by the Fall of 1980, but indications are that they will not parallel OFCCP's Section 503 regulations. Some cynical observers ask how DOL can possibly comply with Executive Order 11914's mandate to develop Section 504 guidelines consistent with those promulgated by HEW but not inconsistent with its own Section 503 guidelines when the basic definitions under each section are inherently different. For the employer, it is hoped that this question will be answered through intra-agency compromise.

Various programs to assist the unemployed, the Vietnam-era veteran, and the disadvantaged population are funded by DOL under CETA, one such program being the HIRE program. Programs like HIRE, which is cosponsored by DOL and the National Alliance of Business, are promoted in the business community as a way of providing a community service while reducing training costs for new workers. Rarely is the employer's liability under Section 504 mentioned.

The preceding discussion of Section 504 regulations now being promulgated by select federal agencies indicates the necessity for employers to stay current on all Section 503 and Section 504 regulations. Any contractor (or an employer who is not a contractor) who is in receipt of any kind of federal financial assistance should secure the Section 504 guidelines of the agency dispensing the aid. The differences between Section 503 and Section 504 extend beyond pre-employment physical examinations and employment discrimination standards. As we have seen, Section 504 regulations can vary from agency to agency. Finally, initial Section 504 regulations are likely to change as agencies reinterpret the law over the next years.

The 503/504 Flap

Many federal contractors or subcontractors attempting to comply with Section 503 regulations are particularly disturbed by the necessity to comply with a separate set of Section 504 requirements if they are recipients of federal funds as well. For this reason, many contractors are refusing to participate in any federally funded activities, such as the training programs sponsored under the CETA legislation discussed later in this chapter. The basis of this refusal is that the employment provisions of Section 504 apply to recipients when the primary purpose of the federal assistance is either employment and training or the providing of services that are affected by employment practices. As we will see in Chapter 6, however, advocacy organizations are urging OFCCP and the federal courts to authorize broad Section 504 coverage.

The concern about Section 503 vs. Section 504 requirements goes beyond the question of HEW/OFCCP compliance authority, however, since 30 federal agencies have established or are in the process of establishing separate Section 504 regulations under Executive Order 11914 and with the guidance of HEW. Many employers feel that HEW has either misinterpreted or intentionally exceeded its own mandate under Section 504 and, in attempting to guide other federal agencies in their rule making, has heaped confusion upon confusion.

Under Executive Order 11914, federal agencies were directed to establish Section 504 guidelines consistent with those promulgated by HEW but *"not inconsistent with,* or duplicative of," other federal regulations governing handicapped persons (emphasis mine). Clearly, the Executive Order 11914 had the Department of Labor's Section 503 requirements in mind when it gave HEW explicit instructions to avoid conflicts. The battle lines were drawn, however, when HEW made it clear that its guidelines *were* consistent with Section 503 while employers said the guidelines were clearly inconsistent. Caught in the middle of this debate are the other federal agencies still trying to devise reasonable Section 504 guidelines for the financial-assistance programs they administer.

Before compliance authority can be established by a federal agency, it must be ascertained what form of federal financial benefit the employer is receiving. For a clear definition of the difference between contracts and other forms of federal financial assistance consult the discussion on the Federal Grants and Cooperative Agreement Act later in this chapter. This act should be used by employers as the final arbiter in determining whether they have a contract subject to Section 503 regulations or some other form of federal financial assistance subject to Section 504 regulations.

Although there is some legislative and judicial history supporting the contention that the employment provisions of Section 504 should apply only when the primary function of the federal funds directly involves employment or the employment practices (a view which a federal contractor supplying the General Services Administration and also conducting a study under a Defense Department grant, for instance, would embrace heartily), there is no conclusive evidence at this time that the dispute will be resolved by federal agency directive, presidential executive order, or Congressional action. Eventually, the conflict may need to be resolved by the federal courts.

As discussed earlier in this chapter, the Section 503 and Section 504 requirements are similar in many respects. Nonetheless, there are some important distinctions in requirements that must not be ignored, for they can have a critical impact on covered employers. For some observers, the two regulations are more than duplicative; they are confusing and contradictory. The key areas of conflict between 503 and 504 are discussed in the following subsections.

Qualified Handicapped Individuals

Under Section 503, a qualified handicapped individual is defined as a "person capable of performing a particular job with reasonable accommodation to [the] handicap." For most people, this definition is straightforward and easily understood. Under Section 504, however, a qualified handicapped individual is someone who, with reasonable accommodation, can perform the "essential functions" of the job. The flap arises when one tries to define what is essential.

Unfortunately, HEW has given little guidance in this confusing area, expecting employers to make reasonable determinations on an individual occupational basis. It is clear, however, that HEW expects employers to omit occupational tasks that bear only a marginal relationship to a particular job. For example, HEW feels that if a secretary in a wheelchair spends most of her workday—say, 80 percent—pounding away at the typewriter or answering the telephone, essential filing tasks or mail delivery responsibilities could be assigned to someone else in the office.

The difficulty is more acute when the dissection of the job tasks cannot be made clearly along essential/nonessential lines. For instance, an all-purpose worker at a small company may spend 30 percent of his day driving a truck, 30 percent assisting at the loading dock, and another 30 percent stocking supplies in the warehouse, with the remaining 10 percent spent on miscellaneous duties. For his employer, the obstacles to analyzing job tasks may seem insurmountable; perhaps the only solution (short of terminating federal contractor and/or grantee status) is a wholesale realignment of job functions throughout the company.

Reasonable Accommodation

Under both Section 503 and Section 504, reasonable accommodation to handicapped applicants and workers must be made if no "undue hardship"—taking into account business necessity—is created for the company. The language of Section 503 seems to allow more flexibility to employers in determining whether or not business security and financial costs eliminate the requirement for reasonable accommodation. Under Section 504, however, and amplified through HEW's policy determinations, the thrust is toward explicit action. One way to achieve reasonable accommodation, according to HEW, is for a recipient of federal funds to hire two individuals, or one individual and an aide, to perform what would normally be the tasks of one person. OFCCP guidelines are conspicuously vague on this subject, as on many other key areas, whereas HEW frequently chooses to be illustrative in assessing Congressional intent.

Collective-Bargaining Agreements

In looking at the definition of a qualified handicapped individual in terms of essential and nonessential job tasks, it is evident that problems can arise with collective-bargaining agreements if a company tries to unilaterally realign job responsibilities to comply with a vague federal requirement.

Under Section 503, employers are instructed to consult with bargaining agents to determine where compliance efforts would result in disruption of or conflict with existing collective-bargaining agreements. The implication is that time will be given to work out difficulties and thereby ensure a smooth transition from noncompliance to compliance.

Under Section 504, however, an employer is told that his

compliance requirements will in no way be reduced by terms in a collective-bargaining agreement that are inconsistent with statutory responsibilities. The implication here is that employers must take immediate action to resolve conflicts regardless of the consequences. Supposedly, employers are expected to expeditiously renegotiate labor agreements to remove inconsistencies with Section 504. One area of HEW concern is the apparent lack of apprenticeship opportunities for handicapped persons.

Pre-Employment Medical Examination

Under Section 503, an employer is *not* prohibited from giving an applicant a comprehensive medical examination prior to employment, provided that the examination does not discriminate against a qualified handicapped individual who should be hired with reasonable accommodation.

Under Section 504, except under certain restricted circumstances discussed earlier in this chapter, an employer *cannot* conduct a pre-employment physical examination unless employment has been offered and only when all other new employees in the same job classification are given the same examination.

Medical Information

Under Section 504, medical information must be collected and maintained on separate forms and *cannot* be comingled with general personnel information. Also, such information must be kept confidential.

Under Section 503, an employer need not collect or maintain medical information on separate forms. However, Section 503 requires that medical information be kept confidential.

Affirmative Action

Under Section 503, contractors and subcontractors are required to take affirmative action to employ and advance in employment qualified handicapped persons. Under Section 504, there are no affirmative action requirements and, by implication, no goals and timetables for integrating handicapped individuals into the workforce. However, Section 504 does outlaw discrimination in employment, and the 504 regulations do suggest affirmative action as a means to end discriminatory actions and policies. Thus the distinction in requirements can be seen as a slight or nonexistent gain for employers subject to Section 504 rather than Section 503 requirements.

In May 1979, acknowledging the problems many employers are facing with separate 503 and 504 requirements, the Department of Labor announced that it was considering changes in Section 503 that would eliminate the dual-coverage problem. The major thrust of the Section 503 revisions would be to declare that where overlapping occurs, federal contractors or subcontractors already meeting Section 503 requirements automatically would comply with Section 504 requirements. However, a federal contractor who is also a federal grantee would still be subject to both sets of regulations in all other areas where conflict doesn't exist.

As the Department of Labor views it, the key areas of conflict, and the possible resolutions, are as follows:

Accessibility. DOL recognizes that Section 504 accessibility requirements were developed by HEW primarily with hospitals and schools, not industrial settings, in mind. Thus DOL is considering a Section 503 change that would eliminate the employer's obligation to make all facilities barrier-free and concentrate instead on those things needed by disabled persons to get their job done. Thus, attention would focus on the parking lots, restrooms, cafeterias, and the handicapped individual's work area.

Accommodation. DOL recognizes that radical accommodation requirements present a formidable obstacle to employers with collective-bargaining agreements. Thus DOL may encourage alternative working arrangements such as staggered hours, compressed work weeks, and job sharing to accommodate disabled workers. DOL may even view the existence of a collective-bargaining agreement as a reasonable restriction on the employer's ability to accommodate the handicapped.

Pre-employment inquiries. A modified DOL standard governing pre-employment inquiries will probably focus on medical examinations. The new requirement may permit the medical exam to be given at any time before the job selection *as long as* it is the last factor rated before the selection. The employer could ask questions regarding the applicant's ability to perform the job safely, for instance, but couldn't inquire about specific handicapping conditions. In short, the employer would have the responsibility of proving that a hiring decision based on medical information was totally separate from other factors in the employment selection process. Until DOL and HEW officially resolve their differences, however, employers will have to contend with the compliance inconsistencies created by the 503/504 "flap."

Vietnam-Era Veterans Readjustment Assistance Act of 1974, Section 402

Who Is Covered?

As if the Rehabilitation Act of 1973 didn't place enough of a burden on the business community, there is an additional federal law which in many respects mirrors Section 503. Section 402 of the veterans law, also administered and enforced by the Department of Labor, applies to all government contracts or subcontracts of $10,000 or more (including those below the first tier) for the furnishing of supplies or services or for the use of real or personal property (including construction).

A contractor's or subcontractor's obligations under Section 402 are quite similar to those promulgated under Section 503 of the Rehabilitation Act of 1973. However, there are some differences with which employers should be familiar. The following definitions should be helpful in determining Section 402 requirements and coverage.

Key Definitions

Disabled veteran. A person entitled to disability compensation under laws administered by the Veterans Administration for a disability rated at 30 percent or more, or a person whose discharge or release from active duty was for a disability incurred or aggravated in the line of duty. (Note: OFCCP is urging its field staff and local veterans representatives to advise complainants *not* meeting the 30 percent requirement to consider the possibility of their coverage under Section 503 instead of Section 402.)

Qualified disabled veteran. A person who is capable of performing a particular job with reasonable accommodation to his disability. Consult the Section 503 discussion for definitions of "reasonable accommodation" and other key terms.

Veteran of the Vietnam era. A person who served on active duty for more than 180 days, with any part of the service occurring between August 5, 1964, and May 7, 1975. The individual must have been discharged or released from active duty with other than a dishonorable discharge, *or* have been discharged or released from active duty for a service-connected disability if any part of such active duty was performed between the above dates, *and* must have been discharged or released within 48 months preceding an alleged violation of the act or any regulations issued pursuant to this act. Failure to meet any of the above criteria may disqualify a veteran from Section 402 coverage. Because of the 48-month requirement, and because the Vietnam era officially ended on May 7, 1975, relatively few of the 9 million veterans who served in the military between August 5, 1964, and May 7, 1975, are still covered by this act. However, it is possible that some Vietnam-era veterans may be covered as late as May 7, 1975. Covered employers are still required to maintain an affirmative action program for these veterans.

As mentioned in the Introduction, it is important for employers to recognize that veterans of the Vietnam era are eligible for substantially the same benefits and special considerations in employment as the two primary protected classes—handicapped persons and disabled veterans.

Unique Section 402 Requirements

An employer making an effort to comply with the requirements of Section 402 should be guided by the requirements of Section 503, as already discussed, with the important exceptions discussed below.

1. Affirmative action plans under Section 402 need to be developed and maintained if the contractor has 50 or more employees and a contract or series of contracts totaling $50,000 or more in a 12-month period. (Note: at least one of the contracts must be valued at $10,000 or more.)

2. Affirmative action plans under Section 402 must incorporate the mandatory listing of suitable job openings with the state employment service. Suitable openings include the following occupational categories: production and nonproduction; plant and office; laborers; mechanics; supervisory and nonsupervisory; technical; executive, administrative, and professional openings with compensation of less than $25,000 per year, including full-time and temporary employment of more than three days duration; and part-time employment. Suitable job openings do *not* include jobs to be filled either from within the organization or through a traditional union hiring arrangement. Employers should note that an exemption from the mandatory job listing requirement can be secured for independently operated corporate affiliates not subject to Section 402. Eligibility for exemptions will be determined by the national office of OFCCP, to which employers should submit their requests.

3. Veterans' complaints will be filed normally with the Veterans Employment Service, which is traditionally located within the local employment service office of the authorized state agency. However, complaints can be filed directly with OFCCP as well.

4. State employment service offices are required to give veterans priority in job referral for employment openings listed with them.

5. Contractors are required to maintain at each location records of jobs listed with the state employment service and to file quarterly reports regarding employment practices. These reports must list the number of individuals hired during the quarter, the number of nondisabled and disabled veterans hired, and the total number of disabled hired.

6. Section 402 limits the uses for which an employer may consider a covered veteran's military papers. Employers can use the papers only if the individual received a dishonorable discharge and cannot use a discipline problem in the military as an excuse for not hiring the veteran. In any hiring decision, consideration of a veteran's military record should be job-related, except that a dishonorable discharge is a valid reason for not considering the veteran for employment.

7. A specific affirmative action clause must be put in each covered government contract or subcontract, different from the clause required under Section 503 (for an acceptable clause, see "Contractual Clause on Affirmative Action for Disabled or Vietnam-Era Veterans," which appears in the model affirmative action plan at the end of Chapter 7.

Outreach and Positive Recruitment

In recruiting qualified veterans, and veterans of the Vietnam era, Section 402 recommends much more specific measures than does Section 503. For example, employers are encouraged to enlist the assistance and support of the local veterans employment representative or his designee in the state employment service office nearest their businesses. These representatives can recruit job-ready veterans and can even develop on-the-job training opportunities for covered veterans.

Employers should also contact the nearest regional office of the Veterans Administration and the nearest office of the National Alliance of Business (NAB) in order to cooperate with the Department of Labor's Jobs for Veterans Program. For a listing of the VA offices, see Appendix J. Local NAB offices can be found in the white pages of the telephone book.

Similar recruitment efforts should be made with the following:

- Veterans counselors and coordinators on college campuses.
- Service officers with national veterans groups.
- Local veterans groups and veterans service centers.
- Veterans service organizations that service disabled veterans or veterans of the Vietnam era.
- The Veterans Administration's newly established career development centers.
- Vietnam-era veterans outreach centers established by the White House, the Veterans Administration, and the Disabled American Veterans.

For a listing of some veterans organizations that can assist employers, see Appendix B.

Complaint Procedures

Complaint procedures under Section 402 differ from those under Section 503 as follows:

■ The complaint is filed in writing with the Veterans Employment Service of the Department of Labor through the local veterans employment representative or his designee at the state employment service's office nearest the employer.*

■ The local veterans representative assists the veteran in preparing complaints and maintaining records.

■ The local employment service office assists the OFCCP in the investigation of the veteran's complaint.

■ The complaint is accompanied by a copy of Veteran's Form DD-214 and, where applicable, VAL-5 or similar VA certification. The reason for this condition is that these forms indicate the degree of disability updated within one year prior to the date the complaint is filed.

In notifying employees and applicants of its obligations under Section 402, an employer should utilize bulletin board announcements and other acceptable forms of communications. For a suggested announcement, see the model affirmative action plan in Chapter 7.

In revamping personnel practices to ensure compliance, employers should look carefully at the suggestions made in the discussion of Section 503 and at the model affirmative action plan contained in Chapter 7.

Architectural Barriers Act of 1968

Who Is Covered?

This act requires that any building designed, altered, constructed, or leased in whole or in part with federal funds after August 12, 1968, must be accessible to and usable by the handicapped. This law was buttressed by Section 502 of the Rehabilitation Act of 1973, under which the Architectural and Transporta-

---

*As discussed earlier, veterans can bypass this local process and file complaints directly with OFCCP. Veterans organizations such as the Disabled American Veterans are assisting complainants with this expedited procedure.

tion Barriers Compliance Board was established. The board was given the legal power to "conduct investigations, hold public hearings, and issue such orders as it deems necessary to ensure compliance." The board potentially has jurisdiction over approximately 390,000 federally owned and 52,000 federally leased facilities. According to many, the board is just beginning to flex its muscles as increased Congressional appropriations allow it to strive for its goal of equal building access to all citizens.

It is generally agreed that this legislation was initially passed to eliminate barriers in federal government buildings. Although application to the private sector seems rather minimal, if a business owns a building and then leases it to the federal government or if construction or renovation of a building is achieved through the use of federal funds, then the requirements of the act apply. These requirements on accessibility also extend to federal contractors as defined under Section 503 and Section 402 and to recipients of federal financial assistance as defined under Section 504, provided the building is under construction during the agreement period or the contractor or grantee is the owner of a federally leased building. In these instances, private businesses (whether they are employers or not) must comply with the law. This requirement takes on added significance in light of the definitions of "reasonable accommodation" and "barrier-free" in the Rehabilitation Act of 1973, from which the board was spawned.

Businesses need to pay increased attention to barrier-free renovation, alteration, or construction because of the fact that every single state has now passed legislation against barriers to the handicapped. The Developmental Disability Service and Facilities Construction Act, in fact, required all states (beginning in October 1977) to set up advocacy offices to investigate complaints by individuals with disabilities such as epilepsy or cerebral palsy. Complainants have the option of filing complaints directly with the Department of Health, Education and Welfare rather than with the state agency. In either case, however, HEW or the state is empowered to take necessary legal or administrative action to eliminate barriers. A majority of local building codes include accessibility provisions for a variety of structures, reaffirming the trend toward more stringent government regulations in all areas protecting the rights of the handicapped individual. All businesses should take a careful look at all short- and long-range plans in the areas of renovation, alteration, and construction of facilities. Barrier-free accommodations for the handicapped are much less expensive if planned before construction begins. The National Center for a Barrier Free Environment (NCBFE), listed in Appendix B, acts as a clearinghouse for information on barrier-free design.

How Are Complaints Filed?

Any individual, handicapped or not, can file a confidential written complaint with the Architectural and Transportation Barriers Compliance Board if he or she feels that a building does not meet federal minimum standards for accessibility and usability. The complaint process is kept as informal as possible by the board to encourage handicapped people to take action. The following information should be provided with a complaint:

- An exact description of the barrier-related problem (for example, narrow doorway or lack of raised numerals on an elevator for a blind person).
- Exact location of the building.
- Name and telephone number of the person responsible for the building.
- Names of the building owner and tenant.
- Suggestions for solving the barrier problem.

Investigations and Hearings

The board has vowed to investigate every complaint it receives. Once responsibility and jurisdiction are determined, a copy of the complaint is sent to the parties involved. Much like the OFCCP or HEW's Office for Civil Rights, the board will attempt to negotiate a settlement. If the board decides that the complaint is valid, then 60 days will be allowed for reconciliation, even though corrective action might take longer. If the contractor or grantee does not choose to settle informally with the board, a citation will be issued as the prelude to legal proceedings.

A special warning: the Architectural and Transportation Barriers Compliance Board has its own investigatory staff, which is now conducting random on-site inspections. Formerly, the board responded only to complaints.

The board will prepare the citation for the complainant and then submit it to an administrative law judge. The board may seek documentation of noncompliance from employers, asking for architectural drawings, building specifications, and key correspondence. A business owner will have 15 days to respond to the charges and file documents with the board supporting his case. Then formal hearings will take place with testimony, cross-examination, and submission of evidence. If the administrative law judge rules against the building owner, then remedial action must be taken within a specified period of time. If such action isn't taken, then federal funds may be suspended or withheld. Ultimately, a business can seek judicial review of the administrative law judge's ruling. The board had new power granted in 1978 to bring civil actions in U.S. District Court to enforce a final order of the board.

In every case brought before the board, a file is established with all documents, except for the complainant's name, available for public inspection.

Technical Assistance

Through a special technical assistance unit separate from its compliance unit, the board is supposed to provide consultation to the private sector in overcoming architectural, communication, and transportation barriers to handicapped persons. Business owners can request help by contacting the Architectural and Transportation Barriers Compliance Board, 330 C Street, S.W., Washington, D.C. 20201. The board's telephone number is 202-245-1591.

Compliance Board Standards

The board is in the process of establishing minimum standards for making facilities accessible to and usable by handicapped persons. Like other federal agencies, the board has of late endorsed the American National Standards Institute (ANSI) standards as acceptable on an interim basis. However, the board may adopt different standards from ANSI's, which are themselves still being revised. Among other sources, employers should look to the ANSI standards and the standards set forth by the National Center for a Barrier Free Environment as well as to state and local building codes for guidance on all construction and renovation projects.

Comprehensive Employment and Training Act of 1973 As Amended

The CETA legislation was amended in 1978 to expand the number of private-sector programs designed to encourage the hiring and training of "protected categories" of citizens. Handicapped persons, disabled veterans, and Vietnam-era veterans are three of these special categories. In fact, the 1978 amendments make special mention of the need for "increased participation of qualified disabled and Vietnam-era veterans" in training programs supported by CETA. Where discrimination is found to take place against handicapped persons (as well as other protected classes), the Labor Department is authorized to take enforcement action under the authority of the Civil Rights Act of 1964 until the agency finalizes its own Section 504 requirements.

The 1978 CETA amendments also direct the Labor Department, in cooperation with other federal agencies, to use federal funds to meet the employment-related needs of handicapped persons through training and other supportive services. In particular, the federal government is directed to inform veterans, both disabled and of the Vietnam era, about job training and educational opportunities under the act.

As a signal to employers doing business with the federal government, the 1978 CETA amendments include a section directing that federal contractors and subcontractors be informed "of their statutory responsibilities toward such veterans." In a later section of the 1978 CETA amendments, approximately the same coverage is extended to handicapped persons, with special mention made to the need to remove architectural barriers to protected classes.

In the CETA legislation, particularly the 1978 amendments, employers can see the kind of pervasive emphasis in all federal government activities on the concept of complete civil rights for handicapped persons. If a contractor decides to participate in a CETA-funded training program to help a disabled veteran or to document his affirmative action efforts in accordance with Section 503 and Section 402 requirements, he suddenly finds himself subject to the additional Section 504 requirements of the Department of Labor now being promulgated.

Also, by participating in a CETA training program and performing poorly (in terms of integrating the handicapped individual or Vietnam-era veteran into the workforce), an employer could face Labor Department prosecution under its Civil Rights Act of 1964 authority. But if a federal contractor decides not to participate in a CETA program because of a desire to avoid the additional Section 504 compliance requirements, then pressure might be forthcoming from the Department of Labor to meet implicit statutory obligations. In addition, pressure may be put on employers by the veterans representative in the local employment service office to hire more veterans, since the president has directed that veterans be given preference for all jobs created through federally funded activities.

What the alert employer quickly discovers is the quintessential "Catch 22" dilemma. How does the employer reconcile Section 503 and Section 504 requirements with veterans preference laws, nondiscrimination provisions under the Civil Rights Act, a valid community goal to help special classes of citizens, and overriding business necessity? The dilemma underscores the need for all contractors and subcontractors to improve their employment practices for all protected categories of employees and applicants and to monitor carefully their participation in any federally funded training programs.

For employers interested in trying to meet their affirmative action requirements through CETA-subsidized training programs, a description of these programs is included in Chapter 5.

Veterans Administration Programs Extension Act of 1978

Section 6 of this act provides that *any* disabled veteran who is entitled to disability compensation under laws administered by the Veterans Administration may file a discrimination complaint with the Department of Labor against a federal contractor who fails to set up an affirmative action plan. Covered employers are still required to take affirmative action under Section 402 for disabled veterans rated at 30 percent or more disability.

Although it does not impose new legal obligations on employers, this act reaffirms the trend in federal law and regulation toward strengthening the rights of handicapped persons and disabled veterans seeking private-sector employment. Such laws are also increasing the burden on employers to document their compliance efforts.

Federal Grants and Cooperative Agreement Act of 1977

FGCAA was enacted to define the difference between federal grants, cooperative agreements, and contracts. Although the act does not impose additional obligations on employers, it does set forth the circumstances under which Section 504, 503, or 402 compliance requirements should be enforced by federal agencies. The act points out that the various legal instruments used by the federal government have caused inconsistency, confusion, inefficiency, and waste for recipients of federal funds and for the agencies distributing these funds.

Many employers obligated to comply with handicapped legislation have been frustrated by attempts to get a clear definition of their requirements as contractors, subcontractors, or recipients of federal financial assistance. Accordingly, employers should be familiar with the following definitions, which are supposed to be used by federal agencies in dispensing funds.

Contract. An employer enters into a contract with the federal government when the principal purpose of the agreement is the acquisition by purchase, lease, or barter of property or services for the direct benefit of the federal government.

Grant. An employer accepts a grant from the federal government when the principal purpose of the agreement is the transfer of money, property, services, or anything of value in order to accomplish a public purpose of support or stimulation (rather than acquisition as defined above for the benefit of the federal government), *provided* that no substantial involvement is anticipated between the government and the grantee.

Cooperative agreement. An employer enters into a cooperative agreement under the same circumstances as a grantee except that substantial involvement between the federal government and the recipient *is* anticipated.

Although it does not alter compliance obligations, FGCAA does clarify the federal contractual status which subjects an employer to Section 503 and Section 402 of the handicapped and veterans legislation, respectively. At the same time, whether an employer is a grantee or a party to a cooperative agreement with the federal government makes little difference, for in either case he would be subject to Section 504 regulations. Obviously, a contractor who is also either a grantee or a party to a cooperative agreement is subject to *all* the handicapped regulations discussed earlier in this chapter.

This Congressional directive should benefit employers somewhat by forcing federal agencies to clarify the kinds of relationships they are proposing. By referring to the act, employers can ensure that compliance officials are applying the correct guidelines during an investigation. If an employer is alert to the distinctions in these definitions, he can be certain that he won't be subjected to unrelated compliance requirements

The Office of Management and Budget is empowered to issue interpretive guidelines under the act and to authorize exemptions for individual programs and federal agencies as it deems appropriate.

Freedom of Information Act of 1966

The Freedom of Information Act (FOIA) has posed problems for the business community in many areas, including equal employment opportunity. Under FOIA, federal agencies may be required to disclose to the public compliance information obtained during an investigation. Employers are not allowed to make the claim of confidentiality unless they can prove that the release of information would result in either an invasion of privacy or the endangerment of the company's competitive position (for example, exposure of business plans involving expansion or merger). Even if confidentiality can be established by the employer, only select information can be withheld from the public, with the remaining data in the government's files being subject to disclosure.

Federal courts have generally supported the release of compliance information and have even directed reluctant federal agencies, like OFCCP, to make this information available to the public. As can be envisioned by recalling the role of activist organizations representing the handicapped (discussed earlier), disclosure can be used to force companies in the public eye to either take affirmative action or suffer a deteriorating community image. The objective of handicapped groups is quite clear: more and better job opportunities for handicapped individuals or good reasons why these jobs aren't forthcoming.

One federal court, after requiring disclosure, went on to force OFCCP to stop approving inadequate affirmative action plans and to take enforcement action against contractors not in compliance with federal regulations. The use of FOIA to force compliance really saw its beginning for federal contractors in 1972, when a legal aid society in California obtained the affirmative action plans of banks and savings and loan institutions in the state over the objection of the employers and even the federal government.

In April 1979, the U.S. Supreme Court ruled against Chrysler Corporation in what has become known in many circles as a "reverse" FOIA case. In recent years, many companies had succeeded in preventing OFCCP and other agencies from disclosing what they considered confidential and sensitive information. Citing Congressional intent, however, the court ruled in the Chrysler case that FOIA exemptions could not be used as "mandatory bars to disclosure." The court directed a lower court to determine if disclosure of the information in question in whole or in part would be a violation of another federal law, the Trade Secrets Act. If not, it can be assumed that relevant affirmative action information will be released.

Chrysler does business as a federal contractor with the Department of Defense and has provided considerable equal employment data to the agency, including staffing patterns, pay scales, actual and expected changes in employment, and present as well as projected employment of minorities and women. Chrysler feels this information would be useful to competitors and therefore wants to protect it. The Department of Defense was asked for the personnel information by the plaintiffs in a series of private discrimination suits against Chrysler.

Even the Securites and Exchange Commission (SEC) has been drawn into the FOIA dispute on the question of protecting sensitive business information. Whereas in the past the SEC let businesses decide, through blanket requests, which information filed with the SEC was to be kept secret, it now requires companies to make formal, fully supported requests. However, since any request for confidentiality (no matter how justified) will itself be released under FOIA, the SEC has potentially placed business in a more public position than if no confidentiality request were made in the first place.

OFCCP now has specific regulations that require the disclosure of affirmative action plans and equal employment opportunity reports without prior notification to a federal contractor or subcontractor. However, trade secrets, the names of certain individuals, and information concerning ongoing investigations or enforcement proceedings are not to be released under FOIA. In fact, the Trade Secrets Act passed in 1848 makes it a criminal offense for a government employee to disclose trade secrets unless authorized by law.

If OFCCP decides to release information to a special-interest group or to the general public, it is supposed to give the employer a chance to show why the information shouldn't be released. If there is disagreement, employers can go to court and file suit to prevent disclosure. A few major corporations have succeeded on the grounds that their competitive positions would be endangered. Other companies (presumably less well prepared) have lost on similar appeals, which reaffirms the need for employers to pay careful attention to the design and content of their affirmative action plans.

Employers face an almost insurmountable obstacle in suppressing the release of information on equal opportunity efforts, affirmative action plans, and compliance deficiencies. Quite obviously, special-interest groups, such as those representing the handicapped, will seek information on affirmative action plans, not only with the intent of placing the employer's position squarely in the public eye, but also with the intent of improving their cases in court or with OFCCP. For these reasons, employers should be prepared for an almost total release of information on their affirmative action programs by OFCCP.

Rarely, and even then with little success, has OFCCP supported employers on the shielding of employment information. Court challenges and intra-agency policy disputes have made OFCCP reluctant to support the employer's request for confidentiality. In fact, as a matter of principle, OFCCP would seem to be in favor of such releases, since it uses FOIA itself to gain information from reluctant employers. At one time, OFCCP would "borrow" information from employers during compliance audits. Now OFCCP retains the information and has even adopted procedures that make it more difficult for employers to successfully oppose disclosure. The burden, then, is more than ever on the employer to "shelter" information related to his affirmative action plan which is of a legitimately confidential nature and which OFCCP or the general public therefore shouldn't scrutinize. Sheltering can't take place, however, at the expense of the affirmative action plan's responsiveness to the handicapped and to the requirements of federal law.

Fair Labor Standards Act of 1938 As Amended

Since 1938, the Fair Labor Standards Act has been amended several times. Some of the amendments have a bearing on how employers treat certain categories of handicapped workers, particularly in light of the Rehabilitation Act requirements for affirmative action, equal employment opportunity, and nondiscrimination.

Under the specific circumstances to be described, employers may be exempt from the minimum wage in hiring certain severely handicapped workers.

Part 524—Handicapped Workers in Competitive Employment

Under Part 524, employers can receive special certificates for individuals whose earning or productive capacity is impaired by age, physical or mental deficiency, or injury. Wages can be paid at less than the minimum required by law, but normally not less than 50 percent of the wage paid nonhandicapped workers for the same quality and quantity of work. Certificates are issued by the Department of Labor after consultation with the state vocational rehabilitation agency (see Appendix G for a state vocational agency listing).

In most instances, the state agency will not issue a certificate authorizing wages less than 75 percent of the minimum wage. However, depending on the severity of individual handicapping conditions, rates as low as 50 percent or even 25 percent of the statutory minimum can be approved.

Employers submit applications to the regional office of the Wage and Hour Division, U.S. Department of Labor. The application should describe the nature of the new worker's disability, the occupation at which the worker is to be employed, and the wage guarantee. The nature of the worker's disability must be set out in detail; vague descriptions may result in rejection of an application.

Before submitting the application to the Wage and Hour Division, employers must secure certification from the state rehabilitation agency, which verifies that the individual is either multihandicapped or so severely impaired that he is unable to engage in competitive employment. The application must be jointly signed by the employer and the worker. Obviously, the kinds of persons defined as qualified handicapped individuals under Section 503 and Section 504 will not be considered for certification under this special program.

Under certain conditions, temporary certificates can be issued rather quickly. Certificates for experimental programs can also be issued under special circumstances. Employers should contact the state rehabilitation agency or the Wage and Hour Division of the Department of Labor for details.

Records to be maintained by employers participating in Part 524 programs include:

Description of the nature of the worker's disability.
Productivity of the worker at periodic intervals.
Prevailing wage of nonhandicapped workers.
Certificate authorizing subminimum wages.

A number of activist organizations believe that the special exemptions in the Fair Labor Standards Act have allowed employers to establish "work ghettos" for the handicapped groups they are purporting to serve. In light of the clear Congressional intent contained in the language of Sections 503 and 504 of the Rehabilitation Act (that is, to require affirmative action toward and equal pay to qualified handicapped individuals), it seems likely that companies employing the handicapped under special wage exemptions will receive closer federal government scrutiny in the future.

Part 529—Employment of Patient Workers in Hospitals and Institutions

This part allows employers operating hospitals or similar institutions to employ at less than the minimum wage patients whose earning or productive capacity is impaired. Patient workers include resident workers as well as nonresident workers who are receiving treatment and care. The facility can *not* be a sheltered workshop, and at least 50 percent of its income must be attributable to providing residential care for the sick, the aged, or the mentally ill or defective.

Examples of qualifying facilities include nursing homes, intermediate-care facilities, rest homes, convalescent homes, homes for the elderly or infirm, half-way houses, and residential centers for drug addicts or alcoholics. These facilities need not be licensed to qualify for the wage exemption.

Other requirements and procedures under this section are approximately the same as those set forth under Part 524.

Part 525—Employment of Handicapped Clients in Sheltered Workshops

Although this part has no direct bearing on the private sector, employers should be aware that the kinds of individuals certifiable under Parts 524 and 529 are eligible for employment in sheltered workshops under the terms and conditions described above. Employers should also keep in mind that participation in sheltered-workshop programs is no longer a means of demonstrating affirmative action for handicapped individuals as required by other federal laws such as the Rehabilitation Act of 1973.

Conclusion

Under special circumstances, employers can and should utilize the exemptions discussed in the subsections on Parts 524 and 529. For instance, if a long-term employee gradually becomes infirm or is suddenly severely disabled, it might be impossible to justify continued employment. Under special minimum wage exemptions, however, an employer can perform a good deed, fulfill a community need, and even boost worker morale by retaining a marginally qualified worker who has served the company well over the years.

Employers should be aware that enforcement of Parts 524 and 529 of this act is handled by investigators in the Wage and Hour Division of the U.S. Department of Labor (see Appendix D for a listing of offices). These investigators have basically the same powers as auditors representing the OFCCP. Employers using the minimum-wage exemption should make sure that they have complied with all applicable 524 and/or 529 requirements and that all pertinent records are maintained and available for inspection.

A final warning to employers: it is *imperative* that the productivity of the exempt worker be gauged periodically. The Fair Labor Standards Act does *not* sanction slave labor. If the productivity level of an exempt worker, for instance, were to reach or approximate that of other workers (either within the company or in the general vicinity), the employer would be obligated to adjust the wage scale accordingly. If he didn't, and the worker or his representative complained, it is not inconceivable that an employer originally exempt from minimum wage requirements under the Fair Labor Standards Act could suddenly be faced with discrimination charges under the Rehabilitation Act of 1973.

Education for All Handicapped Children Act of 1975

This act is aimed at ensuring that handicapped children receive "a free appropriate education which emphasizes special education and related services designed to meet their unique needs." While focusing on public education, the act covers private schools as well by directing the authorized state agency to ensure through regular monitoring that handicapped children are provided proper services and protection.

The employment practices of private schools are governed by this act, which borrowed an enforcement provision from the Section 504 regulations of the Rehabilitation Act of 1973. Under this act, recipients are directed to take "positive steps" to employ and promote qualified handicapped individuals. Failure to do so can result in loss of federal funds along with the same full range of administrative and court sanctions that can result under Section 504 if a complaint is filed by an employee.

Under this act, handicapped children means "those evaluated as being mentally retarded, hard of hearing, deaf, speech-impaired, visually handicapped, seriously emotionally disturbed, orthopedically impaired, other health-impaired, deaf-blind, multi-handicapped, or as having specific learning disabilities, who because of those impairments need special education and related services."

This act is administered and enforced by the Bureau of Education for the Handicapped, HEW, 400 Maryland Avenue, S.W., Donohoe Building, Washington, D.C. 20202.

Appendix:
Self-Evaluation Guide under Section 504 of the
Rehabilitation Act of 1973

A company's transition plan will be effective only if self-evaluation involves a thorough and even critical assessment of existing operations and policies. Goals such as program accessibility, reasonable accommodation, and nondiscrimination cannot be achieved without careful self-evaluation and follow-through.

The following self-evaluation guide should assist employers in this endeavor, particularly since a detailed affirmative action plan is *not* required under Section 504 as it is under Section 503. Certain parts of the guide should be completed after careful review by executives, managers, and supervisory personnel.

GENERAL

1. Which company official is responsible for the transition plan and its implementation?

    Name _____

    Title _____

    Address _____

2. Which company official has primary responsibility for the self-evaluation?

    Name _____

    Title _____

    Address _____

    Telephone _____

3. Describe the steps that will be taken to ensure integration with and consistency between the transition plan and the self-evaluation.

4. Identify all the facilities the company rents, leases, or otherwise uses for any business, social, or related activities.

5. For each of those facilities identified, establish steps to be taken to ensure that such facilities are accessible, or that the use of such facilities will not result in the inaccessibility of any company activities.

6.   Identify any facilities that have been constructed or leased since September 2, 1969, with federal construction or least funds. In each case, determine whether or not such facilities have been constructed in accordance with ANSI or equally effective standards.

7.   For those facilities identified that were not constructed in accordance with ANSI standards, establish immediate steps that will be taken to ensure that necessary modifications are made.

8.   Identify steps that will be taken to inform employees of general accessibility standards so that they may report problem areas to the responsible company official. Also, identify steps that will be taken to adopt and implement procedures for informing interested persons (including those with sight and hearing impairment) of the existence and location of the company's accessible activities.

9.   All steps to be taken as a result of program accessibility requirements contained in Section 504 and in the company's transition plan should be incorporated into an organized process for ensuring adequate planning, data collection, scheduling to complete the required action, records maintenance, and monitoring activities.

COMPANY SELF-EVALUATION*

1.   Is the company covered by Section 503 of the Rehabilitation Act of 1973 or Section 402 of the Vietnam-Era Veterans Readjustment Assistance Act of 1974? (That is, does it have one or more federal contracts or subcontracts valued at $2,500 or $10,000 or more, respectively?)

Yes _____   No _____

If yes, identify steps that will be taken to ensure coordination and consistency in Section 503/402 and Section 504 compliance efforts.

*If the company employs, or has employed in the past, a sufficient number of handicapped persons to make statistical studies meaningful, it is recommended that such studies be conducted to measure possible discrimination in employment based on handicap. Employers subject to Section 503 and Section 504 requirements may find some of the following recommendations helpful in meeting their specific compliance responsibilities.

2.   Review the general processes whereby the company solicits, advertises, and processes applications for employment.

3.   Identify those aspects of the application process described above that discriminate (or have the potential to discriminate) on the basis of handicap. Study the selection and accessibility of recruitment sites and any communications to applicants that may not reach all handicapped persons. Identify all steps that will or should be taken to ensure equal opportunity for handicapped persons.

4.   Identify all aspects of the selection criteria used for employment decisions. For each, analyze the skill, achievement level, or other factor that the selection criterion purports to measure.

5.   For each selection criterion listed above (for example, a pre-employment test), identify steps that will be taken to ensure that it measures solely what it purports to measure and that impaired sensory, manual, or speaking skills (unless those skills are the ones the test purports to measure) are not being measured as well.

6.   Does the company make available to employees (and applicants for employment) tests that are designed for persons with impaired sensory, manual, or speaking skills?

                    Yes _____   No _____

If yes, identify the tests that are available, the procedure for notifying applicants that such tests are available, and the process through which they are provided. If no, identify steps that will be taken to make certain that such special tests are made available by the company and that applicants are notified regarding the availability of alternative testing.

7.   Identify steps that may be necessary to ensure that employees involved in the selection process are trained properly in the administration of tests designed for persons with impaired sensory, manual, and speaking skills.

8.   Identify those tests or criteria that screen out (or tend to screen out) handicapped applicants or employees.

9.   For each test or criterion identified above, determine whether HEW's Office for Civil Rights (OCR) has identified any

alternative tests or criteria that do not screen out as many handicapped persons as the test now being used by the company. Where alternative tests or criteria have been identified by OCR, determine the steps that will be taken to employ these alternatives in place of the tests or criteria currently used.

10.   For each test or criterion identified above for which OCR has *not* indicated any alternatives, either provide OCR with background information related to its validation as job-related, or determine steps that will be taken to modify the test or criterion or discontinue its use for classes of handicapped persons who are screened out.

11.   Identify steps that will be taken to ensure that no pre-employment physical examinations are conducted for applicants who have not received conditional offers of employment.

12.   Will the company be conducting, for all applicants, pre-employment physical examinations after conditional offers of employment are extended?

Yes _____   No _____

If yes, identify steps that will be taken to ensure that all applicants will receive such examinations prior to beginning employment, that the results of such exams will not be used to discriminate on the basis of handicap, and that the results of such exams will be collected and maintained on separate forms that will be accorded confidentiality as medical records.

13.   Is the company:

■ Taking remedial action at the request of HEW's OCR?
■ Taking voluntary action to overcome the effects of conditions that resulted in limited participation in programs by the handicapped?
■ Taking affirmative action under Section 503?

If the answer to all three questions is no, identify steps that will be taken to ensure that no applicants for employment are asked questions (during interviews or on application forms) regarding the nature or severity of their handicaps.

If the answer to any of the three questions above is yes, identify steps that will be taken to ensure that applicants are told that information is being requested on a voluntary basis, that failure to provide such information will not result in adverse treatment, that information will be kept confidential, and that information will be used solely in connection with remedial, voluntary, or affirmative action efforts.

14.   Determine the accessibility of the company's facilities (including the personnel office) that are used by employees and applicants. Identify modifications that are likely to be required in order to ensure equal employment opportunity through reasonable accommodation.

15.   Review the company's method of job classification and description. Identify any factors in this method that discriminate on the basis of handicap or otherwise classify, segregate, or limit persons because of a handicap. For each such factor, determine steps that should be taken to modify the method (or related policies or procedures) to ensure nondiscrimination in the future. Among other things, consider organizational structure, career lines of progression, and seniority rights.

16.   Will the company be analyzing all job descriptions at once to determine essential and nonessential functions for each, or will essential and nonessential functions be determined prior to posting or advertising an employment opening? If the former method is used, identify the general procedure to be followed during the analysis of job descriptions. If the later method is used, identify steps to be taken to ensure that essential and nonessential functions will be well defined before job openings are posted or advertised.

17.   Review the company's system of wage and salary administration. Identify any factors in this system, or any policies or procedures related to this system, that discriminate (or have the effect of discriminating) on the basis of handicap. For each, identify steps that will be taken to ensure nondiscrimination in the future. Consider actions related to rates of pay or compensation, or changes in rates of pay or compensation.

18.   On the basis of a review of all pertinent policies, procedures, and practices related to employment, identify any discrimination (or potential discrimination) that may exist in personnel actions such as hiring, upgrading, promotion, the award of tenure,

demotion, transfer, layoff, termination, the right of return from layoff, and rehiring. Determine steps that will be taken to ensure nondiscrimination in the future, if discrimination exists now.

19.   Identify any contractual relationships that the company has with regard to its employees, including agreements with employment or referral agencies, labor unions, providers or administrators of fringe benefits, or training and apprenticeship programs.

20.   On the basis of a review of the specific terms of collective-bargaining agreements and/or the company's experience in dealing with unions, identify the terms or practices that result (or could result) in discrimination because of handicap. Determine steps that need to be taken to renegotiate union contract terms or eliminate discriminatory practices to ensure nondiscrimination in the future.

21.   On the basis of a review of the specific terms of fringe benefit plans (including medical, hospital, accident, and life insurance and retirement policies or plans, whether they are administered by the company or by an outside firm), identify terms that discriminate against the handicapped. Determine steps that need to be taken to modify terms to ensure nondiscrimination in the future.

22.   Identify the terms of any other contractual relationships that are discriminatory or have the potential to be discriminatory. Determine steps that need to be taken to modify such terms to ensure nondiscrimination in the future.

23.   Identify the social, recreational, and other programs the company sponsors or makes available to its employees. Determine steps that may be required to ensure that such opportunities are made available to handicapped employees. Examine, for example, transportation or sports services that are provided to employees.

24.   List all programs of leave granted by the company, including leaves of absence, vacation, and sick leave. On the basis of a review of policies and procedures governing these programs, discuss for each the modifications that may be required to ensure nondiscrimination.

25.   Review all programs of apprenticeship, management training, and professional development the company offers its

employees. On the basis of a review of policies and procedures governing such programs, and procedures used for selecting and providing support to employees for such programs, identify steps that will be necessary to ensure future nondiscrimination for handicapped employees.

26.   Review all policies, procedures, and practices of company committees or similar panels, and identify any factors in the voting or selection processes and the activities of such groups (including the accessibility of their meeting sites) that discriminate on the basis of handicap. Describe steps that will be taken to ensure equal opportunities for handicapped managers, supervisors, and workers.

27.   Identify any parking facilities that the company makes available to its employees or applicants for employment. For each facility, determine whether or not parking accessibility has been achieved for handicapped persons and, if not, what steps will be taken to ensure an equal opportunity for handicapped persons to use such facilities. Include in this analysis any policies or procedures related to such facilities that discriminate (or have the potential to discriminate) against handicapped persons.

28.   The company must develop some standards for determining whether an accommodation to the known physical or mental limitations of an otherwise qualified handicapped applicant or employee is "reasonable" or imposes an "undue hardship." Identify the general standards that will be used for making these determinations. Also, on the basis of these standards, identify some examples of accommodations that would be reasonable and also some accommodations that would impose an undue hardship.

29.   Determine the general process whereby accommodations will be made for applicants who require them. For example, will there be a person to contact for all employees interviewing someone (or in the process of hiring someone) who may require an accommodation? Determine all organizational factors related to the process whereby accommodations will be made.

30.   Identify the steps that will be taken to ensure adequate documentation of any decisions regarding refusal to hire or promote due to undue hardship, since such a defense will have to be

clearly justified. Determine who has the authority to make decisions based on undue hardship. For example, will decisions regarding undue hardship be made centrally? If so, is there a person who is clearly authorized to make decisions on undue hardship?

31.   If the companies employs 15 or more persons, have grievance procedures been established that will allow employees to file complaints with the company on matters related to Section 504? (It should be noted that grievance procedures need not apply to the complaints of applicants for employment.)

Yes _____   No _____

If yes, identify procedures that will ensure that all employees (including those with sight or hearing impairments) will be informed periodically of such procedures. If no, identify steps that will be taken to establish such procedures and to communicate them periodically to all employees (including those with sight and hearing impairments).

32.   Determine steps that will be taken to notify all employees (including those with sight or hearing impairments) periodically of the company's obligation under Section 504, including specific prohibitions or requirements. Some sample notifications follow.

- There may be no discrimination on the basis of handicap in any employment decision or action, policy, procedure, or practice.
- Prior to posting or advertising any job, essential and nonessential functions of the job should be defined.
- Alternative tests are available for applicants or employees with impaired sensory and speaking skills, and will be used whenever employee testing is affected by such impaired skills.
- There can be no pre-employment medical examination required. Companies should prepare a statement regarding whether all or no applicants must receive a pre-employment physical examination between the period when a conditional offer is extended and the start of employment.
- There must be no discrimination on the basis of handicap in recruiting, advertising, or processing applications for employment. Steps, if any, that the company will be taking to ensure nondiscrimination should be identified (for example, assisting

job applicants in submitting forms and advertising for blind workers through national organizations for the handicapped).

- Tests and criteria that screen out handicapped persons must not be used. Specify a company official responsible for developing alternative tests and criteria.
- Pre-employment questions regarding the nature or severity of handicaps may not normally be asked unless the company is taking voluntary, remedial, or affirmative action to comply with Section 504.
- Pre-employment questions regarding the applicant's ability to perform the essential functions of a job effectively and safely may be asked.
- Reasonable accommodations will have to be made to the known physical and mental limitations of otherwise qualified handicapped persons. Companies should clarify the procedure for making decisions regarding accommodations.
- There may be no discrimination on the basis of handicap regardless of the provisions in contractual agreements with unions, employment or referral agencies, providers of fringe benefits, providers of training or apprenticeship programs, and similar organizations. This requirement could force some companies to undertake major modification of contractual agreements affecting workers.
- Recreational and social opportunities for employees must be provided to handicapped employees on an equal basis.
- Handicapped persons must have an equal opportunity to use parking facilities provided to employees.
- There may be no discrimination on the basis of handicap in determining vacations, sick leave, and leaves of absence.
- There may be no discrimination on the basis of handicap in opportunities for such company programs as management training, including travel to meetings and conferences.
- Handicapped applicants and employees must not be counseled toward more restrictive careers than nonhandicapped persons.

33. All steps taken as a result of employment requirements should be the subject of individual summary reports. This proce-

dure is recommended unless a procedure more suited to a company's administrative processes is devised for ensuring adequate planning, data collection, scheduling to complete the required action, records maintenance, and monitoring activities.

34.   Self-evaluation is an ongoing process that cannot be neglected or treated casually. Employers must ensure that evaluations that uncover problems are followed by positive steps to achieve compliance. The Summary Report Form which follows will aid employers in monitoring the success or failure of their evaluation efforts and determining the need for further corrective measures.

SELF-EVALUATION GUIDE—SUMMARY REPORT FORM

_____
(Date)

I. Preliminary Information

Nature of noncompliance identified: _____

_____

Action to be taken: _____

_____

Person responsible for compliance (include telephone number):

_____

Procedures to be followed: _____

_____

Data or information required: _____

_____

Schedule for completion (include individual steps):_____

_____

Projected impact on the company:_____
Relationship to "outside" organizations or person: _____

_____

Policy changes: _____
Staffing consideration: _____

_____

Space or facility needs: _____

_____

Communications needs: _____

Equipment, supply, or vehicle needs: _____

Cost factors: _____

Other considerations: _____

II. Compliance

(Brief comments on objectives)

_____

_____

_____

III.

Date action was completed: _____
Action that was taken: _____

Actual impact on the company: _____
Relationship to "outside" organizations or persons: _____

Policy changes: _____

Staffing considerations: _____

Space or facility needs: _____

Communications needs: _____

Equipment, supply, or vehicle needs: _____

Cost factors: _____

Other considerations: _____

IV.

Describe steps that will be taken to ensure that the policy, practice, or procedure developed as a result of this action will be followed in the future. Also, describe any steps that will be taken to monitor future compliance action. _____

_____

_____

_____

V.

Describe, where applicable, any additional voluntary steps that will be taken by the company to eliminate the effects of past discrimination. _____

_____

_____

_____

2
State Laws Affecting Employers

Whereas the federal laws and regulations discussed in Chapter 1 apply only to those employers doing contractual business with or receiving financial assistance from the federal government, most state laws barring discrimination against the handicapped regulate the activities of all employers within the state.

Federal law presents several obstacles to handicapped complainants and the activist organizations that support them. Neither the U.S. Constitution nor federal statutes apply directly to employers *not* doing business with the federal government. Furthermore, even when they do have jurisdiction, federal courts have been inconsistent when interpreting an individual's implicit or even explicit private right of action against an employer charged with discrimination. Until Congress amends the Civil Rights Act of 1964 (as many groups are seeking) to include the handicapped as a protected class, there will be limited remedies under federal law for the disabled complainant.

For these reasons, state laws and courts offer an increasingly inviting avenue for the handicapped individual seeking redress for alleged employer discrimination.

Some states, such as California, Wisconsin, and Minnesota, have rather stringent laws governing antidiscrimination in the private employment of handicapped persons. A number of state courts are upholding their statutes on the handicapped against challenges that rely on the apparently conflicting authority of other state and federal laws.

Although only 37 states plus the District of Columbia and New York City have laws prohibiting employment discrimination against the handicapped, all 50 states plus the District of Columbia have laws requiring that new and remodeled buildings be made accessible to the mobility-disabled. The chart in Appendix L illustrates the actions taken by various state legislatures to protect the employment rights of handicapped citizens. Because the various state laws differ in emphasis and intent, employers with multistate facilities are confronted with the task of complying with a number of statutes, some written in ambiguous terms. An examination of just a few of the more active state programs will reveal a distinct trend toward more stringent regulation of employers at the state level.

California

In California, the Department of Rehabilitation oversees programs dealing with the employment of the handicapped and the elimination of architectural barriers. The Mobility Barriers Section of the department is charged by state law with ensuring that all newly constructed or remodeled facilities, whether publicly or privately funded, are accessible to the physically handicapped. Through a program called the Community Access Network (CAN), volunteers supplement the efforts of the Mobility Barrier Section staff in the investigation and resolution of complaints.

In requiring that facilities be made accessible, the California law covers the same kinds of accommodations required under federal law, as discussed in Chapter 1 (for example, the modification of curbs, parking areas, and entrances). As a guide to building owners, including those operating publicly used facilities such as theaters and restaurants, California refers to the Uniform Building Code as adopted by the International Conference of Building Officials. Employers throughout the United States should consider alternative guidelines such as the Uniform Building Code in adapting their facilities to the handicapped, particularly in light of the possibility that no federal agency will adopt the revised ANSI standards when they are completed.

To enhance the opportunity for handicapped citizens to make their views known, California holds public hearings throughout the state under the auspices of the Office of the State Architect, Handicapped Compliance Unit. Also, the Department of Rehabilitation has set up a special Citizens Complaint Program to investigate what has been viewed by the state as a flood of charges by handicapped persons against businesses. Under this special citizen's program, a prototype complaint guide has been prepared showing handicapped persons how to file complaints or, if they prefer, initiate lawsuits.

In the area of employment, the California code protects the physically handicapped against discrimination. A physical handicap under state law includes an "impairment of sight, hearing, or speech or impairment of physical ability because of amputation or loss of function or coordination, or any other health impairment which requires special education or related services."

Wisconsin

An analysis of the Wisconsin Fair Employment Act provides a good example of the kinds of nondiscrimination laws that are emerging in states across the country.

The purpose of the Wisconsin law is "to encourage and foster to the fullest extent practicable the employment of all properly qualified persons regardless of their age, race, creed, color, handicap, sex, national origin, or ancestry." Legal experts in Wisconsin have pointed out that, in many instances, only the state law will provide the aggrieved handicapped individual with a remedy, since coverage is more comprehensive than under federal law. In a rather explicit warning to employers in Wisconsin, one section of the law states that the nondiscrimination provision shall be "liberally construed." The Wisconsin Supreme Court has voiced its agreement with this broad interpretation of the law.

Like federal law, the Wisconsin statute is civil in nature, with at least initial enforcement through the administrative process. The Department of Industry, Labor and Human Relations (DILHR) in Wisconsin administers the law in much the same way OFCCP enforces federal law.

The liberal intent of the Wisconsin law can be seen in the definition of covered employer. The law describes employer in *negative* fashion so as to *exclude* only social clubs and fraternal or religious associations not organized for private profit. Even domestic helpers are covered under the law, since they are not expressly excluded. Discrimination by labor unions is strictly prohibited. Employment agencies that discriminate cannot get their licenses renewed.

Wisconsin employers are *not* expected, however, to hire, retain, or promote unqualified handicapped persons. According to the law, an individual is excluded from coverage if "unable to efficiently perform, at the standards set by the employer, the duties required in that job." In addition, employers can exclude handicapped workers from life or disability insurance coverage or impose reasonable restrictions on such coverage. In this respect, the state law is less stringent than federal law.

As mentioned earlier, DILHR administers the Wisconsin law and takes an enforcement role as active as, if not more active than, OFCCP at the federal level. DILHR will assist individuals in the preparation of complaints, undertake complaint investigations, and negotiate settlements (where possible) through conciliation and persuasion. If settlements between the complainant and the employer cannot be reached amicably, then an appeal/hearing process will be instituted.

Remedies for complainants can include back pay for up to two years prior to the filing of the complaint. Complainants cannot recover actual damages or attorney fees, but employers can be fined up to $100 a day for noncompliance.

Liberal application of the Wisconsin law, as mentioned, is encouraged by the state courts. Individuals can sue simultaneously under federal and state law. Group intervention (for example, by activist organizations) on behalf of complainants is encouraged. Finally, class action suits are permitted.

One case testing the constitutionality of the Wisconsin law reached the state's Supreme Court and is worth examining. In *Chicago, Milwaukee, St. Paul and Pacific* v. *DILHR,* a young complainant was hired as a laborer in a diesel house. He performed his work to the satisfaction of the shop foreman and general supervisor. Two weeks later he was discharged without reason.

At a DILHR hearing (since the company did not agree with conciliation proposals), the company physician stated that he recommended termination because of the worker's prior history of asthma, a condition discussed during a 20-minute pre-employment examination. Finding no bona fide occupational qualifications against asthmatic workers, the state Supreme Court upheld DILHR and ordered the complainant reinstated at full seniority.

Minnesota

Section 363.11 of the Minnesota Human Rights Act instructs the state's Department of Human Rights to "construe liberally" the purposes of the act, one of which is to protect the rights of the disabled.

The Minnesota law covers practically every employer in the state with one or more workers. Exemptions are granted for some small family-owned and -operated businesses, religious and fraternal organizations, and for those employing domestic help. Businesses providing public accommodation, whether or not they are licensed, receive particular attention, as do companies in a contractual relationship with the state government.

"Disability" is broadly defined as a "mental or physical condition which constitutes a handicap." If a business refuses to hire a handicapped person and a complaint is filed, the burden falls on the employer to prove that the individual "poses a serious threat to the health or safety" of himself or others.

Employers in Wisconsin can require an applicant to undergo a physical examination to determine the person's ability to perform on the job. In addition, fringe benefits need not be paid during certain disabling periods.

Handicapped persons can file a complaint with the Department of Human Rights within six months of the date the alleged discrimination occurs. Hearing examiners are empowered to "make findings of fact and conclusions of law." In addition to issuing cease and desist orders against employers, a hearing examiner can order the payment of compensatory and punitive damages, reinstatement or upgrading, and back pay.

State contractors are given particular attention under Minnesota law, to the extent that employers must secure a certificate of compliance before doing business with the state. As under federal law, failure to comply with state law can result in cancellation of a state contract.

Both the Department of Human Rights and the employer have the right to appeal the decision of a hearing examiner in state district court and even up to the state Supreme Court. The court has the discretion to award reasonable attorney's fees to the prevailing party.

Other State Laws

Illinois has two laws protecting the handicapped. The Fair Employment Practices Act prohibits discrimination by private employers of 15 or more persons against an individual with a "physical or mental handicap unrelated to ability." The Illinois Equal Opportunities for the Handicapped Act is even more stringent, governing all private employers, providing for a private right of action for damages, and prohibiting retaliatory measures by employers.

Nebraska law contains perhaps the most comprehensive state definition of covered handicapped persons, stating that "disability shall mean any physical condition, infirmity, malformation, or disfigurement which is caused by bodily injury, birth defect, or illness, including epilepsy or seizure disorder, and which shall include, but not be limited to, any degree of paralysis, amputation, lack of physical coordination, blindness. . . ."

The District of Columbia law covers a blind person who is "totally blind, [or] has impaired vision of not more than 20/200 visual acuity." "Otherwise physically disabled" persons are covered as well if they have "a medically determinable physical impairment" which impedes mobility or inhibits the ability to work.

Ohio law defines a handicap as a "medically diagnosable, abnormal condition which is expected to continue for a considerable length of time . . . which can reasonably be expected to limit the person's functional ability. . . ." Work conditions are covered by the Ohio statute.

The Rhode Island law specifically covers all kinds of physical handicaps, including epilepsy, disfigurement, paralysis, amputation, blindness, deafness, and hearing and speech impediments. However, no reference is made to coverage of mental disabilities.

In New Jersey, the state law contains a definition of covered handicapped individuals similar to Nebraska's but does *not* extend coverage to the mentally disabled. Iowa law defines disability as "a substantial handicap . . . unrelated to one's ability to engage in a particular occupation."

In summary, state laws (particularly where the right of private action is allowed) offer the handicapped individual a variety of remedies not readily attainable through federal courts or federal administrative channels. The very fact that several states present such a varied, if not confusing, array of statutes protecting the rights of the handicapped underscores the problem employers face in trying to achieve compliance at all their locations.

State Court Cases—On the Increase

Handicapped complainants have been successful in a number of states in bringing court action against employers. The following summary of state court cases and administrative hearings indicates the kinds of discrimination complaints employers can face even if they are not federal contractors or recipients of federal grants.

Employers will note, in some cases, the application of federal court decisions to state laws protecting the handicapped.

Wisconsin

Bucyrus-Erie Company v. *DILHR* (Wis. Cir. Ct., 1977). An applicant passed the employer's welding test but was not hired because he failed to pass a physical examination. The employer's doctor stated that the applicant's back condition would "substantially increase the likelihood of his injuring his back during the normal course of his duties as a welder." DILHR found that the applicant could safely and efficiently perform the job of welder and concluded that the employer had not fulfilled the obligation to show that he could not. Since the burden is on the employer to prove that the potential worker cannot perform safely and efficiently, failure to do so leaves the opposing presumption intact.

Connecticut General Life Insurance Company v. *DILHR* (Wis. Cir. Ct., 1976). The court held that an employee's "drinking problem" constituted a handicap under the Wisconsin Fair Employment Act, finding that the state law should be liberally construed. The employer was ordered to cease and desist from discriminating against the employee because of his handicap and to reinstate him to his former position, with back pay.

Dairy Equipment Company v. *DILHR* (Wis. Cir. Ct., 1977). An employee was terminated because he had only one kidney. The circuit court held that a handicap may be a condition which creates a perceived sensitivity to injury in the future as well as a condition which may in the future cause difficulties in job performance. Thus the definition of handicap under the Wisconsin Fair Employment Act clearly includes the absence of one kidney. The court also held that the Safe Place Statute in Wisconsin did not relieve the employer of its obligation not to discriminate against qualified handicapped persons, since there had been no showing of reasonable probability that working conditions would be hazardous to the employee's health.

Fraser Shipyards, Inc. v. *DILHR* (Wis. Cir. Ct., 1976). The court held that Fraser's policy of refusing employment to diabetics as welders was unlawful discrimination under state law. The company failed to show that the individual claimants were a hazard. The court noted, in viewing the employer's overly generalized claim, that the company could have shown a specific health hazard.

Journal Company v. *DILHR* (Wis. Cir. Ct., 1976). The court upheld the DILHR's finding that an employer must provide disability insurance to a worker, even if the worker signs a waiver exempting the employer from covering his pre-existing medical conditions. Therefore, it was judged that the company violated the Wisconsin Fair Employment Act by discriminating against an employee with a preexisting condition (a deviated septum) on the basis of handicap.

J.C. Penney Company v. *DILHR* (Wis. Cir. Ct., 1976). According to DILHR, the company discharged a keypunch operator because of her handicap, rheumatoid arthritis, in violation of the Wisconsin Fair Employment Act. The court agreed that rheumatoid arthritis constitutes a handicap but ruled against DILHR for waiting months after discharge from employment to determine that the employee was able to perform the functions of the job.

Soo Line Rail Road Company v. *DILHR* (Wis. Cir. Ct., 1977). DILHR ruled that removal of a locomotive engineer from his job because of a heart condition constituted discrimination. The circuit court held that the DILHR's jurisdiction over the matter was not preempted by the Railway Labor Act; that exhaustion of contractual remedies (under a collective-bargaining agreement) was not a prerequisite to proceeding under the state statute but only for an action under the common law; and that Soo Line had failed to prove that the employee was unable to efficiently perform his duties as a locomotive engineer. However, the court remanded the matter to DILHR to redetermine the amount of back pay, holding that the original order was excessive.

Western Weighing and Inspection Bureau v. *DILHR* (Wis. Cir. Ct., 1977). An inspector was terminated after a physical examination revealed he had a congenital back condition known as spondylolisthesis. The circuit court upheld DILHR's finding, holding that the employee's back condition presented only a possible hazard to his health and had nothing to do with his present ability. The court held that the two-year delay between the filing of the complaint and the DILHR ruling was not so excessive as to deny due process. The court also held that the Railway Labor Act did not bar DILHR's jurisdiction under the Wisconsin Fair Employment Act.

Chrysler Outboard Corporation v. *DILHR* (Wis. Cir. Ct., 1976). The court agreed with DILHR that the employer had unlawfully discriminated against a job applicant with leukemia by denying him employment on the basis of his handicap. Chrysler did not contend that the applicant was unable to perform the duties required by the job. The court held that the risk of future absenteeism and higher insurance cost did not constitute legal basis for discriminating against the complainant.

Colorado

Casias v. *Industrial Commission* (Colo. App., 1976). The plaintiff appealed the denial of unemployment compensation benefits because of falsification of his employment application when he failed to disclose his condition of epilepsy. The employer's physical form stated that the employer had a policy not to hire epileptics. The court held that the applicant would be entitled to unemployment benefits unless the falsification of an employment application is found to be material to the applicant's job performance. The case was remanded to the State Industrial Commission for a factual determination.

Silverstein v. *Sisters of Charity of Leavenworth* (D. Colo., October 31, 1977). An epileptic sued two health care corporations because of their alleged refusal to employ her as respiratory therapist. She sought damages on three separate claims: breach of contract, unlawful discrimination against a physically disabled person, and 29 U.S.C. 794. The court held that no private cause of action existed under the state statute and that the state and federal statutes did not provide for exemplary damages. The court stated that the plaintiff may pursue declaratory or equitable relief under the state act. The case was remanded with directions to reinstate the declaratory judgment claim. On remand, the trial court found that the plaintiff failed to establish a breach of contract and that the hospital policy was not unlawful discrimination in violation of the

Colorado statute and 29 U.S.C. 794, but was a legitimate employment policy supported by substantial medical opinion.

Washington

Chicago, Milwaukee, St. Paul and Pacific Railroad Co. v. *Washington State Human Rights Commission* (Wash., 1976). The Supreme Court upheld the state law against claims that it was unconstitutionally vague. The Washington law provides that it is unlawful for any employer to refuse to hire any person because of such person's physical handicap.

Clark v. *Chicago, Milwaukee, St. Paul and Pacific Railroad Co.* (Wash. Super. Ct., 1975). An applicant for a brakeman's position was refused employment because of a past knee surgery. The court held that the railroad company's refusal to hire was based upon a bona fide occupational qualification, since it was necessary to consider the safety hazard to the applicant and any physical deterioration he might experience in the future. The court concluded that the job in question was very strenuous and would put considerable strain on the knee.

Holland v. *Boeing Company* (Wash. Super Ct., 1976). The court held that the defendant unlawfully discriminated against the plaintiff, who suffered from cerebral palsy, by transferring him to a job which he could not perform. In affirming the lower-court decision, the Washington Supreme Court held that it was an unfair practice for an employer to fail or refuse to make reasonable accommodations to the physical limitations of handicapped employees. The Supreme Court also upheld the award of reimbursement for vacation time expended during the trial and for attorney's fees, but remanded for determination of the appropriate amount. Attorney's fees of $22,473 were initially awarded under state law by the lower court.

Illinois

Magruder v. *Selling Areas Marketing, Inc.* (N.D. Ill., 1977). The court held that the discharge of the plaintiff was for good cause and was based on factors other than a physical or mental handicap. The court further held that the plaintiff failed to establish that he was, at material times, under a physical and mental handicap. Plaintiff's claim was brought under the Illinois Equal Opportunities for the Handicapped Act.

Oregon

Montgomery Ward & Company v. *Bureau of Labor* (Ore., 1977). The Bureau found that Montgomery Ward was guilty of discrimination when it failed to hire an applicant with a history of heart attack and continuing angina for a job as a heavy-household-appliance salesman. The state's Supreme Court held that the criterion for determining whether a refusal to employ constituted discrimination under the Oregon Handicapped Person's Civil Rights Act was not whether the employer had acted in good faith but whether the applicant was capable of fulfilling the job requirements.

Rhode Island

Providence Journal Co. v. *Mason* (R.I., 1976). The court held that a temporary disability resulting from "whiplash" was not covered by the Rhode Island Fair Employment Practices Act. The court stated that a "physical handicap" covered under the law must be a serious injury or impairment of more than a temporary nature.

Minnesota

State v. *Finch and Lakehead Services Co.* (HR-77-020 PE, Office of the Examiner, 1977). Shortly after the start of employment, an individual informed his supervisor that he was an epileptic. A month later, the supervisor asked the worker for a note indicating that the condition was under control. Meanwhile, the president of the firm noticed the worker's incapacity and ordered his replacement. Shortly thereafter, the president was told that the worker was an epileptic.

On the basis of the timing of the president's decision to fire the worker (that is, *before* receiving knowledge of the handicapping condition), the Minnesota Department of Human Rights ruled that Lakehead did *not* discriminate against the complainant.

City of Minneapolis v, *State of Minnesota* (File #746968, Hennepin County District, 1979). This case, among other things, reveals the inability of intrastate government bodies to agree on employment discrimination policies and illustrates the applicability of past anti-discrimination employment decisions at the federal level to state law.

The City of Minneapolis, applying its medical standards, fired one worker and refused to employ another individual because of pulmonary tuberculosis. However, private medical tests revealed that both individuals were noncontagious and safe for employment. The city's contention that its lung and chest standards were bona fide occupational qualifications was rejected as having no basis in fact. The court also rejected the supposition that substantially all persons who might have had tuberculosis would be unable to perform their work efficiently and without threat to others. The city was also unable to show the impracticability of ascertaining which individuals with a lung disability can be safely employed.

On appeal by the city to the state district court, the hearing examiner's findings were upheld. The city failed to meet the three-pronged "business necessity" test (discussed in Chapter 6 under "Activities in the Federal Courts") in the U.S. Supreme Court's decision in *Griggs* v. *Duke Power,* namely:

1. There must be a sufficiently compelling purpose for the policy.
2. The policy must effectively carry out that purpose.
3. There must be available no acceptable alternative practices which would better accomplish the business purpose advanced.

Thus employers can see vividly the broad impact of antidiscrimination statutes and court decisions that influence the interpretation of handicap legislation even at the state level.

State v. *Postier and Eggers* (File #418-60, Olmstead County District, 1980). A car dealership's service manager was dismissed because he was an alcoholic. The individual admitted his alcoholism during the job interview and revealed that he had gone through chemical dependency treatment.

The employer fired the service manager when it was reported that he had been drinking and had not showed up for work. However, it was later determined that an accident unrelated to his drinking had prevented the service manager from getting to work.

The hearing examiner stated that alcoholism is a handicap

similar to epilepsy or diabetes which, when controlled, constitutes a disability but not a disabling condition. Applying the "but for" clause in a 1976 U.S. Supreme Court case involving racial discrimination *(McDonald* v. *Sante Fe Trail)*, the hearing examiner held that the service manager would not have been discharged "but for" an incident involving his alcoholism.

Local Ordinances

As mentioned earlier, the District of Columbia and New York City are just two municipal governments which have passed laws prohibiting discrimination against the handicapped. The trend is decidedly in the direction of more stringent local legislation in this area.

Montgomery County in Maryland provides a good example of the kinds of emerging local antidiscrimination laws which are likely to proliferate. In Montgomery County, discrimination is prohibited against mentally or physically handicapped persons in housing, public accommodation, and employment. The definition of covered handicapping conditions parallels existing federal law.

In Montgomery County, discrimination complaints can be filed on a confidential basis with the Human Relations Commission by either an individual or an interested third party. If conciliation efforts fail, then a public hearing will be held. The commission has summons and subpoena powers and may seek injunctions against employers. Penalties can include cease and desist orders, consent agreements, mandatory affirmative action plans, back pay awards, reasonable attorney's fees, and monetary damage awards. Employers can appeal the commission's decisions to the county's Circuit Court.

3
Office of Federal Contract Compliance Programs

One of the major reasons the business community has good cause to take positive steps to comply with handicapped legislation is the emergence of the Office of Federal Contract Compliance Programs, the once sleepy agency authorized by Executive Order 11246 that has unquestioned authority to enforce Section 503 of the Rehabilitation Act and Section 402 of the Vietnam-Era Veterans Readjustment Assistance Act. OFCCP is now an integral part of the U.S. Department of Labor. Its authority extends only to federal contractors and subcontractors. HEW and 30 other federal agencies retain authority to enforce Section 504 against recipients of federal financial assistance. The distinction between OFCCP and HEW authority is discussed in detail in the first two sections of Chapter 1.

At one time, the confusion created by decentralization of agency enforcement could be used by some employers to defend their inability to comply with federal regulations giving handicapped individuals special rights. Formerly, a diversified contractor

103

with a food industry operation in one city might be visited by Department of Agriculture compliance officials while another of the company's divisions manufacturing machinery in another city might be subject to a Department of Defense audit. President Carter's reorganization and consolidation plan brought all federal contract enforcement for employment discrimination under the umbrella of a stronger, larger, and more dedicated OFCCP staff.

This chapter will examine the makeup of OFCCP, its operating procedures, its plans for the future, its compliance review techniques, and its investigatory methods.

If it wasn't enough of a warning to employers that OFCCP will be undertaking stronger enforcement action of its own volition, companies doing business with the federal government must keep in mind that the "new activists" will be prodding OFCCP to investigate discrimination complaints when the agency seems to fall short of its professed goals and its Congressional mandate.

The business community often finds out too late that a new government agency or community group can have a profound impact on its operation. The Occupational Safety and Health Act is just one example of a federal law whose enforcement was spurred on by activist groups. No businessman needs an introduction to Ralph Nader and his various activities on behalf of consumers. In recent years, the nation's largest corporations and even some major law firms have paid out millions of dollars to settle lawsuits charging general discrimination in employment simply because they weren't prepared for the challenge or didn't take the threat seriously.

Among those federal contractors and subcontractors who are aware of their requirements to act as equal opportunity employers, only few understand their obligations to two specific groups—the handicapped and veterans.

Instead of sympathizing with the business community's claim that it knows little or nothing about requirements to hire and accommodate the handicapped, OFCCP has announced even more stringent enforcement plans, operating under the theory that ignorance of the law is no excuse when discrimination appears to be rampant in the private sector.

As Secretary of Labor Ray Marshall put it, there is now only one name to remember for federal contract compliance: OFCCP. Marshall has indicated that on-site compliance reviews of randomly selected contractors (to be discussed later in this chapter) will be followed by an ambitious effort to conduct 17,000 additional reviews in fiscal year 1980. The primary goal of these reviews is to eliminate classwide, or "systemic," discrimination in employment and to investigate specific charges of noncompliance by employers with regard to handicapped workers and applicants for employment.

If Secretary Marshall's words weren't strong enough, the director of OFCCP has taken an even tougher stance against contractors and subcontractors failing to comply with the law. Citing jurisdiction over 300,000 prime contractors (and up to 3 million subcontractors) employing 31 million workers, the director has said that claims by employers that affirmative action allows incompetence is "the big lie." In addition to investigating complaints, according to the director, OFCCP will be looking for classwide or "systemic" discrimination, perhaps best exemplified by such personnel actions as screening out all epileptic job applicants even when epilepsy has no bearing on the requirements of the job being filled. Systemic discrimination need *not* be intentional to be illegal. Affirmative action by means of "screening in" handicapped persons is regarded favorably by OFCCP as the opposite of systemic discrimination. Another major effort at OFCCP, in addition to ending systemic discrimination, will be to get severely and not just mildly disabled persons into other than "dead-end" jobs.

OFCCP has the muscle to back up its rhetoric. It has grown quickly from 200 to more than 1,000 employees in its bid to achieve full bureaucratic status. In the fall of 1979, OFCCP announced that over 100 attorneys would be added to the Office of the Solicitor so that discrimination complaints can be processed more quickly. In addition, regional offices were given new authority to file administrative complaints under Section 503. This decentralization should increase the number of OFCCP complaints and settlements.

OFCCP is also opening 71 new offices in 63 cities, to be staffed by over 900 compliance officers. OFCCP's director points out that the consolidation of compliance authority in one federal agency will eliminate inconsistency and duplication—and will improve enforcement as well. No longer can the business owner rely on the confusion created by multiagency directives to sidestep compliance with legislation pertaining to the handicapped. As a reward for noncompliance, whether intentional or not, the businessman can look forward to harassment, stiff penalties, unfavorable publicity, and the possible loss of government contracts.

Having vowed to increase its random compliance reviews, OFCCP now has the staff to do so. These reviews will cover an across-the-board examination of policies and practices toward disabled workers and applicants as well as other classes such as minorities and women. In a rare revelation of its priorities, OFCCP has indicated that although it will seek fully compensatory remedies for victims of discrimination, it does not intend to seek damages for mental stress. Target companies (including those in transportation and communication) thought to be principal violators of the law will receive closer scrutiny than others.

A top priority of OFCCP, however, will be to respond to individual complaints, which will make every industry vulnerable. Pointing to back pay awards of more than $1 million from January 1977 to September 1979 to disabled veterans and handicapped workers, OFCCP has stated clearly that it hopes to increase the number of financial settlements in the future as an incentive for employers to eliminate discrimination. In 1977, the largest single award was for close to $20,000. OFCCP has been able to handle most complaints against employers through conciliation.

What all this rather modest activity in the past forebodes for the future of federal contractors and subcontractors is difficult to say, but it must be viewed in the context of ever increasing OFCCP compliance action, the growth of organizations serving the handicapped, a proliferation of federal, state, and local legislation, and, most important, the willingness of handicapped workers and applicants to force employers to give them equal employment opportunities. Very often, handicapped workers and applicants, no longer timid about enforcing their rights, are spurred on by the support of the OFCCP and special-interest groups.

Illegal Prohibitions and Employer "Excuses"

One problem area the OFCCP will be looking at is what has been termed "illegal prohibitions." OFCCP contends that employers quite often and rather arbitrarily compile long lists of disqualifying medical conditions or physical and mental problems, which are then used to automatically reject handicapped applicants.

Under the federal laws reviewed in Chapter 1, reasons for disqualification of a handicapped job applicant or for refusal to advance a handicapped employee must be shown to be related to the specific requirements of the job. OFCCP points out, for instance, that it is strictly prohibited to deny employment opportunities to all epileptics. An employer might, however, refuse to employ as a crane operator a specific epileptic individual subject to seizures.

Imposing arbitrary lifting requirements is another illegal practice at which OFCCP will be looking. If a job requires lifting only 30 pounds and the job requirement is listed as requiring 100 pounds lifting capability, then the employer can expect to be scrutinized by OFCCP and possibly cited if a handicapped worker or applicant suffers discrimination.

Application forms can also result, often inadvertently, in illegal discrimination against the handicapped. Employers are not prohibited from requesting data that are needed to determine an applicant's ability to perform the job. However, OFCCP has decided that it is strictly prohibited to ask an applicant to "list all health disabilities," since such a request is deemed an attempt to screen out handicapped individuals. On a related subject, pre-employment medical examinations should be given (according to OFCCP) only as long as the information is not used to screen out individuals who are otherwise eligible for the job with reasonable accommodation.

Many employers express fundamental trouble comprehending why OFCCP expects them to accommodate handicapped applicants and workers. Personnel staff at many companies insisted that they don't even understand the legal definition of the term "qualified handicapped individual" (see the first section of Chapter

1 for definition). Some employers are simply bewildered by the prospect of modifying the workplace or altering job responsibilities to meet the particular needs of a handicapped individual. The fact is, though, that these "adjustment" problems are inconsequential to OFCCP. Employers are expected to know and meet their legal requirements. One reason OFCCP expects reasonable accommodation is that financial incentives are available to offset the employer's costs for such efforts (see Chapter 5 for complete details). Whatever confusion or problems exist for employers, however, one single fact remains clear: OFCCP intends to carry out its statutory mandate.

OFCCP insists that standards of performance or excellence on the job need not be lowered to accommodate the handicapped. Thus an alcoholic who cannot meet attendance and job performance standards is not a qualified handicapped individual who should be considered for employment. But to screen out automatically all qualified handicapped individuals who are or may have been alcoholics may be to invite intervention by OFCCP. In short, employers must be diligent in applying any standard of employee selection, making sure that long-established precepts do not stand in the way of reasonable accommodation for the handicapped applicant or worker who is otherwise qualified for the job. Employers must examine carefully all personnel practices to ensure that illegal prohibitions aren't being engendered, even unintentionally.

The New Organization at OFCCP

In 1977, streamlining of compliance enforcement with regard to federal contractors and subcontractors began with a reduction of the number of federal agencies with contract compliance responsibility from 16 to 11. In October of 1978, responsibility for all enforcement was housed in OFCCP with a large-scale transfer of personnel and budgets from the other federal agencies.

Under the direction of its ten regional offices, OFCCP is opening area offices in 63 major cities chosen for their concentration of contractors and for their large number of "protected groups" such as the handicapped persons. For the first time, OFCCP will have offices beyond the continental United States in Alaska, Hawaii, and Puerto Rico. For a complete list of OFCCP's regional and area offices, see Appendix F.

OFCCP intends to undertake enforcement efforts regularly during its periodic review of contractors. In taking this unprecedented approach, OFCCP is purposely trying to give a boost to affirmative action programs for handicapped persons, disabled veterans, and Vietnam-era veterans. OFCCP has even developed a new training manual and handbook to help enforcement officers improve their compliance reviews. In addition, a new *Federal Contract Compliance Manual* was prepared (and made public) by OFCCP in October 1979 for use by investigators during compliance audits. This manual, which sets forth all significant OFCCP compliance procedures and rules, can provide employers with an excellent insight into the workings of OFCCP (See Appendix O for ordering information).

Training for investigators will include workshop sessions on how to handle employer attitudinal barriers, how to detect "screening out" provisions in job standards, and how to suggest reasonable and inexpensive accommodations to contractors (for example, a ramp for wheelchairs or amplifiers for workers with hearing impairments).

OFCCP is now set up with four divisions in its national office, as follows:

Division of Program Operations. This division reviews the effectiveness of program enforcement policies. It evaluates regulations and works with the Solicitor of Labor to develop new and modified regulations, as well as to develop and test new enforcement procedures.

Division of Program Policy. This division monitors regional operations and complaint trends and coordinates contractor audit scheduling. By "targeting," it can choose which contractors to audit. This division also directs the compliance reviews of nationwide companies and monitors what OFCCP considers federal contracts of national importance.

Division of Program Analysis. This division prepares the agency's budget and draws up recommendations for OFCCP's short-term and long-range goals. It also is responsible for designing and implementing a management information system (MIS) to improve OFCCP's overall compliance operation.

Division of Enforcement Coordination. This division serves as a point of review for all actions taken against employers, assuring that formal hearing processes and investigations are carried out properly. It also establishes standards for conciliation agreements and conducts reviews of other federal agencies to assure conformance with OFCCP requirements.

The Management Information System (MIS)

Calling it contract compliance "at the touch of a button," OFCCP has installed a computerized system that will compile data on the thousands of companies that do business with the federal government. The primary purpose of the MIS will be to document the hiring and promoting practices of companies with federal contracts and subcontracts.

The MIS can churn out a tremendous amount of data on employers and can even furnish an EEO profile of an individual company. Using its computers, OFCCP will be able to track compliance reviews from beginning to end and determine their status almost instantly. The computer can indicate in which regional OFCCP office an inquiry should be answered and can even tell OFCCP if an employer has a history or pattern of receiving similar complaints. If necessary, the computer can compare the most recent complaint received with a company's overall affirmative action history.

In OFCCP's opinion, the MIS will change the face of contract compliance and improve the management of its growing enforcement program.

What's Ahead with OFCCP?

Obviously, the reorganization and consolidation effected in 1978 gives OFCCP the opportunity to put new teeth into its enforcement efforts. Employers must not lose sight of the fact that

OFCCP has broad authority over the entire equal employment opportunity enforcement program of the federal government with regard to contractors and subcontractors. Protection of the handicapped and veterans is merely OFCCP's latest authority.

Let's assume that OFCCP is conducting a general compliance review of a government contractor. Under new OFCCP policy, the compliance officer is directed to audit the employer's specific plan for handicapped persons, disabled veterans, and Vietnam-era veterans even if a complaint hasn't been filed by someone in one of these three protected classes. And OFCCP has decided that if a complaint is being investigated, a close examination of a company's overall personnel practices might be in order.

Under its new mandate, OFCCP will have more than 1,000 fully trained employment opportunity specialists (EOS) in the field to carry out regular reviews, conduct random audits, and investigate complaints. Although OFCCP has been reluctant to identify specific industries where equal employment opportunity for the handicapped is lacking (although the transportation and communication industries were targeted initially), it has promised to take a close look at the overall equal employment opportunity programs of companies in the construction, banking, insurance, and coal mining industries. The underlying assumption in this specialized approach to compliance is that once OFCCP gets a feel for enforcement of handicap legislation, it will start to identify additional target industries for closer attention.

In a rare glimpse given of bureaucratic philosophy, OFCCP has announced that it will be looking at what are called the "five shalls" to ensure adherence by contractors and subcontractors to handicapped requirements:

1. Each contract shall contain an affirmative action clause.

2. All applicants and employees who believe they would benefit from declaring their handicap shall have the opportunity to identify their disability.

3. Personnel procedures shall be reviewed periodically by contractors to determine that the procedures allow for careful consideration of the applicant's qualifications for the job or training activity.

4. Physical or mental criteria for a particular job shall be reviewed periodically to determine that they accurately reflect the characteristics an individual needs in order to perform the job.

5. Communications within the company shall ensure that all employees, particularly supervisory personnel, are aware of the company's policies of nondiscrimination against handicapped persons in order to ensure that all personnel conform to the policy.

The five "shalls" are discussed in more detail in the model affirmative action plan at the end of Chapter 7, in a manner which will permit their full development as company policy. Their importance to employers is reflected in the procedures to be followed by OFCCP in conducting Directed Compliance Reviews.

Directed Compliance Reviews (DCRs)

A DCR is a random audit of a federal contractor or subcontractor in one of the ten regions of the U.S. Department of Labor. A DCR is *not* scheduled because an employer has been charged with discrimination or because the employer is in a target industry. The DCR is used by OFCCP to identify compliance problems of a common nature and to help the agency improve the quality and effectiveness of its overall enforcement program.

DCRs are necessary, according to Secretary of Labor Marshall, because of the tremendous human suffering faced by the unemployed handicapped person. Pointing out that there are several million handicapped people in the United States, the director of OFCCP has stated publicly that his office can't wait for complaints to be filed. In other words, OFCCP is dedicated to seeking out potential cases of discrimination even where there is no indication that they exist. It is this commitment that permeates the entire structure of OFCCP, suffusing the staff with a determination to accelerate and toughen enforcement activity through DCRs and other means. As we have seen, OFCCP now has the staff and the organization—even the computer—to carry out these reviews effectively.

OFCCP believes that discrimination is so strongly institutionalized that only a flexible enforcement "game plan" that includes DCRs can help eradicate employment barriers to the handicapped. In defining what it considers institutionalized discrimination, OFCCP more than hints at the kinds of personnel practices it will be looking at closely. For one thing, OFCCP has expressed a deep concern about systemic and advancement violations. The agency will also be evaluating job descriptions and employment requirements which it considers unfair and unnecessary. For example, OFCCP cites the following "negative" personnel policy of one employer as a model *not* to be duplicated by federal contractors and subcontractors.

DISQUALIFYING CONDITIONS

No person shall be employed or permitted to remain in employment in a job classification who has an established medical history or clinical diagnosis of any of the following:

- Cardiovascular symptom [16 disqualifying conditions were listed, including the use of a pacemaker].
- Respiratory system [4 disqualifying conditions were listed].
- Vision [6 disqualifying conditions were listed, including the use of contact lenses].
- Hearing [3 disqualifying conditions were listed, including the use of a hearing aid].
- Bones and joints [3 disqualifying conditions were listed].
- Diseases of the blood [3 disqualifying conditions were listed].
- Gastrointestinal and genitourinary conditions [15 disqualifications were listed].
- Brain and nervous disorders [8 disqualifying conditions were listed, including epilepsy].
- General medical conditions not otherwise listed [4 disqualifying conditions were listed, including diabetes and skin disease].

In this single example of an employer's improper personnel selection standards, OFCCP detected 62 job disqualifications which it would view as discriminatory.

Another common, institutionalized practice OFCCP will be looking at during a compliance audit is group classifications of disqualifying physical and mental conditions, such as:

Group A—employable without restriction.
Group B—employable with restriction.
Group C—physical or mental limitation.
Group D—unfit for employment.

In conducting a Directed Compliance Review, OFCCP officials will apply the rule of the "five shalls" already discussed. Each region of OFCCP has already conducted 30 on-site reviews of randomly selected contractors in the Standard Metropolitan Statistical Area (SMSA) which the regional office governs. Dun & Bradstreet printouts were used to identify contractors in each region. Prior to these reviews, compliance officers, using the network of Department of Labor information sources as well as its own field staff, gathered data on selected contractors with regard to employment and training practices.

The results of the initial 300 DCRs should be nothing less than alarming to employers, *over 90 percent* of whom claimed, according to the OFCCP, that they didn't even know there was a requirement to hire the handicapped. OFCCP will not release the names of contractors who were audited, but preliminary statistics reveal that these employers violated consistently the major requirements of the handicap legislation. Results from nine out of ten of the Labor Department's regions indicated that the following specific deficiencies were detected at audited employers:

- 69 percent hadn't listed all job vacancies with the state employment services, as required by Section 402 of the veterans law.
- 57.3 percent failed to invite handicapped individuals to identify themselves.
- 53.3 percent hadn't reviewed their personnel processes (for example, job descriptions).
- 53 percent had not properly disseminated information about their affirmative action plan either inside or outside their companies.
- 51.1 percent didn't have an affirmative action clause in their appropriate subcontracts, purchase orders, and so on.
- 50 percent hadn't reviewed physical and mental job requirements.
- 46.3 percent hadn't reviewed their employment practices.

- 44 percent didn't have an outreach program for recruiting disabled people.
- 28.6 percent hadn't displayed the federal nondiscrimination poster (see Appendix A for a copy).
- 25 percent didn't have an adequate affirmative action plan.
- 24 percent didn't even have an affirmative action plan.
- 17 percent made no reasonable accommodation to disabilities.

The director of OFCCP has called these preliminary findings discouraging and, like Secretary of Labor Marshall, has promised more vigorous enforcement of the handicap and veterans laws. Presumably, this pledge will be carried out, at least in part, by means of additional DCR-type audits of employers.

With these examples of what OFCCP views as blatant discrimination in mind, let us examine the procedures to be followed and the actions that might be taken by OFCCP during a typical Directed Compliance Review, keeping in mind that the audit in all probability will *not* be prompted by a discrimination complaint. In establishing methodology for future audits of contractors, the initial DCR findings discussed above will undoubtedly influence what compliance officials will be examining during any kind of discrimination complaint audit.

Procedurally, the DCR audit involves five main components: preparation and planning; on-site review; off-site analysis; conciliation; and enforcement. OFCCP will be using a number of forms and questionnaires during the DCR. Since these forms may be helpful to the employer in achieving compliance and in understanding "OFCCP philosophy," they have been included in Appendix I to this chapter.

Preparation and Planning

OFCCP advised its auditors in the field to conduct initial DCRs with smaller contractors so as to gain experience in the area of compliance review procedures. Auditors have been directed to cooperate with local compliance agencies (for example, the state employment service) in scheduling DCRs so as not to place undue burden on contractors.

Before the audit can be scheduled, OFCCP must notify a

company by certified mail, return receipt requested, that it will be reviewed. This notification is used in part to establish the beginning of the 15-day period within which the contractor should submit its affirmative action plan to the regional office of OFCCP for review prior to the audit.

The certified letter is also used to request that the contractor make available the following information during the initial audit:

- Any contract signed with a federal agency after September 1973 or, in the case of a large number of contracts, a representative number of contracts in excess of $50,000.*
- Collective-bargaining agreements.
- Management organization chart.
- Uncompleted employment application form.
- Applicant flow data on known or self-identified handicapped applicants.
- General medical guidelines and the instrument for recording medical information.
- Physical and mental job qualification requirements for specific occupations.
- Types of accommodations made for handicapped workers and disabled veterans.
- The process by which applicants and employees who believe themselves to be covered by Section 503 or Section 402 are invited to identify themselves.
- The procedure used to review personnel processes to enable handicapped employees, Vietnam-era veterans, and disabled veterans to receive proper consideration for employment and advancement in employment (plus a schedule of reviews actually conducted).
- Pertinent personnel and employment data for either the last 12 months or the last 100 personnel actions.

If the employer doesn't submit a copy of his affirmative action plan and other requested data within the 15-day period designated, the auditor will probably call and schedule a visit within five days,

*Only employers with 50 or more workers and with contracts over $50,000 in value need to develop *written* affirmative action plans.

asking that the plan and the supportive data be made available at that time.

If an employer does submit his affirmative action plan to OFCCP for review prior to the on-site visit, he can be sure that the plan will be studied carefully before and during the DCR to ensure that:

■ The chief executive of the company has issued a firm statement of personal commitment, legal obligations, and the importance of affirmative action as a business goal.

■ Managers and supervisors, as well as all employees and union officials, have been fully informed of the commitment to affirmative action by top management.

■ Appropriate contacts with the media and public and private employment recruitment sources have been made.

■ All subcontractors, vendors, and suppliers have been notified in writing of the company's affirmative action program, with a request for supportive action.

■ A top-management official with ready access to the company's chief executive has been appointed as the manager of the company's affirmative action program.

■ A system to monitor and evaluate the progress of each aspect of the affirmative action plan has been established and given the same priority as other business objectives.

■ A written explanation is available which describes deficiencies uncovered in the affirmative action plan as a result of the auditing and reporting system designed to uncover such problems.

■ A discussion on action-oriented programs developed and affirmative action taken is included in the plan along with objectives established to offset existing deficiencies.

■ The following actions have been taken, where necessary: job-related mental and physical job qualifications have been studied and revised; personnel processes have been reviewed to ensure proper consideration of the qualifications of applicants; the employment process has been made accessible to handicapped individuals; specific accommodations have been made to handicapped workers; outreach programs have been developed and implemented; and job-listing and quarterly-reporting require-

ments affecting veterans have been met (for example, in cooperation with the state employment service).

After reviewing the affirmative action plan and other supportive data, but prior to the on-site review, the auditor will draw up a
summary of deficiencies to be discussed with the employer. The
auditor will also verify the contractor's mandatory job-listing and
quarterly-reporting requirements by contacting the local office of
the state employment service. Auditors will use a form entitled
"Mandatory Job Listing Data Collection," which is shown in Appendix I to this chapter. In short, the auditor will be well prepared
to conduct a Directed Compliance Review when he arrives at an
employer's facilities.

On-Site Review

When he arrives at an employer's facilities, the auditor will brief
the company's representative on the general requirements of Sections 503 and 402 of the handicap and veterans laws, respectively.
He will then discuss the overall corporate organization in terms of
which facilities might be affected by the DCR (for example, headquarters, subsidiaries, number of plants). The company will be
asked about subcontractors with which it does business to determine if the affirmative action requirement has been satisfied. To
verify inclusion of the affirmative action clause in subcontracts and
other agreements, the auditor will review a sample contract and
possibly a sample purchase order.

After this preliminary review, the auditor will want to tour the
company's facilities with an eye toward accommodations made for
handicapped employees. As the tour progresses, the auditor will
request material supportive of any affirmative action claims made.
If material is not made available voluntarily, the auditor will
undoubtedly make note of this reluctance to cooperate and report
it to his immediate supervisor. For instance, if access to medical
records or reproduction of personnel documents is requested and
disallowed, the auditor will take careful notes so as to identify the
documents in question in case a subpoena is issued for their release
in the future. Employers should expect their staff to be virtually
inundated with questions touching on all phases of compliance and

affirmative action, and should be ready to deal with the type of investigation discussed below.

Employers and their staffs will be asked to verify information on covered contracts and subcontracts; contract modifications; contract extensions; posting of notices; relationship with the local office of the state employment service; number and kinds of potentially handicapped workers who were invited to identify themselves; jobs for which mental and physical requirements were reviewed and changed; and complaints that have been processed and resolved during the employer's internal review procedure. Nothing less than careful preparation will allow an employer's staff to handle this kind of far-reaching and detailed inquiry.

Next, the auditor will attempt to make some sort of initial on-site analysis of the contractor's performance. He will try to identify problems with the affirmative action plan so as to enable the OFCCP to conduct a more factually oriented review later on in discussions with other company personnel. The initial on-site evaluation of the affirmative action program will cover the broad areas previously discussed in the "Preparation and Planning" section.

Employers should expect the auditor to make every effort to conduct extensive interviews with a number of workers prior to his departure. Employers are allowed to limit the number of such interviews on the basis of business necessity and possible interference with employer–employee relations. Obviously, the auditor will be selecting interviewees who can help most with the review of the employer's affirmative action program. The auditor must follow certain guidelines during these interviews but can be expected to pose probing, far-ranging questions to personnel managers, affirmative action managers, medical staff, supervisors, and even salaried workers such as laborers. In conducting interviews, OFCCP staff have been advised to use the questionnaires shown in Appendix I to this chapter.

At the end of the initial on-site review (it is quite possible that additional visits will have to be scheduled), the auditor will probably make an oral summary of the more obvious deficiencies uncovered. These findings are not to be construed by the contractor as official notification of noncompliance. Only the assistant regional administrator of the Department of Labor can issue official notification of noncompliance to a contractor.

Off-Site Analysis

After leaving a contractor's facilities, the auditor will evaluate information gathered during his visit with an eye toward whether personnel practices and procedures and overall company attitudes operate to discriminate against qualified handicapped applicants or workers. Specific contractor deficiencies uncovered during the on-site review must be spelled out and documented by the OFCCP investigator, with recommendations prepared for correcting problems. Again, this information is passed on by the auditor to the assistant regional administrator, who, in consultation with the Office of the Solicitor at the Department of Labor, decides if the contractor is not in compliance.

When the off-site analysis is completed, a letter will be prepared for mailing to the contractor. Variations of the letter, known as "Notification of Results of Compliance Review," will be prepared based on compliance or noncompliance. If noncompliance is alleged, then specific recommendations for corrective action must accompany the findings. The letter must include the following information:

Coverage. The legal jurisdiction over the contractor must be stated.

Findings. The investigator's findings and conclusions must be set out, with specific violations indicated.

Conclusions. If it has been concluded officially that the contractor is in violation of the law, then an invitation must be made to participate in conciliations.

Signature. The letter must be dated and signed by the assistant regional administrator of the Labor Department, but only after it is reviewed for legal sufficiency by the Office of the Solicitor.

Conciliation

OFCCP officials have stated frequently that every effort will be made to secure compliance through conciliation and persuasion within a reasonable time of the violation. If a contractor or subcontractor is found to be out of compliance, he must make a specific commitment in writing to take corrective action to meet the requirements of the law before the company's OFCCP record can be expunged. The employer's written commitment must indicate the precise action to be taken and the dates for completion. If the commitment is approved by the OFCCP, then the contractor can be considered to be in compliance provided that the commitment is kept. The written commitment is acceptable to OFCCP if it comes from a responsible corporate official. For a sample conciliation agreement, see Appendix I to this chapter.

At the time specified in the written commitment for achieving compliance, the auditor will revisit the contractor to determine whether or not the commitment has been fulfilled. If it has been, then the contractor will be notified in writing.

Enforcement

If conciliation cannot be achieved, then the auditor's file plus any other materials developed in the regional office will be referred to the Office of the Solicitor in the Department of Labor, undoubtedly with the recommendation that an administrative complaint be issued against the contractor.

The Future of DCRs

Looking at the results of OFCCP's initial DCRs, it can be expected that the agency will continue and even increase its random compliance audits of contractors and subcontractors. DCRs, when viewed together with regular investigations by OFCCP, pose a formidable obstacle to contractors trying to dodge the question of handicapped people's employment rights.

How Does OFCCP Investigate a Complaint?

The Directed Compliance Review program has given employers some hints as to OFCCP's approach to uncovering contractor and subcontractor discrimination against handicapped applicants and workers even if no one has complained. What action does OFCCP take when a complaint is actually filed? Since substantial compliance activity will result from complaints, it is necessary that employers understand OFCCP's standard operating procedures (SOPs) in such situations. Employers must keep in mind that the SOPs are the "bible" to OFCCP's equal employment opportunity specialists. All essential SOPs are included in OFCCP's *Federal Contract Compliance Manual* now available to the public (see Appendix O for ordering information).

Standard Operating Procedures

Responsibility for establishing policy for the enforcement of Section 503 of the Rehabilitation Act and Section 402 of the Vietnam-Era Veterans Readjustment Assistance Act rests with OFCCP's Veterans and Handicapped Workers Operations Branch.* Complaint investigations are conducted by employment opportunity specialists (EOSs) in the regional office of OFCCP nearest to the employer allegedly in violation of the law. In the discussion of Directed Compliance Reviews, the EOS was referred to as an auditor, but the former term gives a better indication of the function and qualification of these OFCCP staff members.

If a complaint is filed, it is officially acknowledged by OFCCP in a letter to the complainant. Once coverage is established over both the complainant and the employer, the complaint becomes a case and a case file is developed.

If the complainant is an employee, then the complaint is channeled by OFCCP through the contractor's "internal review procedure." If the complaint can't be resolved satisfactorily within 60 days or if the contractor doesn't have an internal review procedure, the OFCCP regional office will initiate an investigation. One way for an alert employer to avoid the time-consuming and potentially expensive OFCCP investigatory process is to make sure he has an effective internal review procedure, as discussed in the model affirmative action plan in Chapter 7. There is simply no substitute for preventive action when it comes to avoiding costly discrimination charges, regardless of whether or not the charges are well founded.

*A few years ago, OFCCP's national and regional offices were staffed by 100 persons. By the end of 1979, national, regional, and area offices employed over 1,000 administrative, support, and compliance staff persons.

If a complaint is filed by an applicant rather than an employee, the internal review procedure doesn't apply and an investigation is initiated immediately.

In certain circumstances, OFCCP will not even bother to conduct an investigation. For example, if it can't be verified that the employer is a federal contractor or subcontractor, if a complainant is judged as not handicapped, if there is an inordinate delay in filing a complaint (usually more than 180 days after the alleged violation, unless waived by the Assistant Secretary of Labor), if the complainant provides incomplete information and doesn't supplement it within a reasonable time, or if the complainant withdraws his complaint, then OFCCP will most likely not even develop a case file.

If OFCCP decides to proceed with an investigation, both the complainant and the contractor will be notified. Normally, an on-site visit—including a plant tour, a review of pertinent records, and an examination of the company's affirmative action plan—will be undertaken in the manner described earlier during a DCR audit. Witnesses on both sides will also be interviewed.

At any time during the investigation, the two parties can agree to proceed with conciliation efforts. If the complainant agrees to the remedies proposed by the contractor, then OFCCP will seek to negotiate a written agreement and close the case.

If initial conciliation efforts don't succeed, OFCCP will complete its investigation and issue a "Notice of the Results of Investigation" to both parties. If a violation is found, another invitation to conciliate will be made. If the complaint can't be resolved through these informal means, the contractor will be afforded the opportunity for a formal hearing, at which time he should be prepared with a thorough defense of his position.

Contents of a Complaint

The law requires that a complaint by a handicapped worker or applicant (or veteran) contain certain information with which employers should be familiar. The following elements are necessary:

■ Name, address, and telephone number of the complainant.

- Name and address of the contractor or subcontractor who committed the alleged violation.
- A brief description of the act or acts considered to be a violation.
- A signed statement that the individual is handicapped, has a history of a handicap, or was regarded by the contractor as having an impairment, plus any documentation of impairment.
- Other pertinent information available which will assist in the investigation and resolution of the complaint, including the name, if known, of any federal agency with which the employer has contracted.
- For veterans, a copy of separation form DD-214 and, where applicable, a certificate of the percentage of disability issued by the Veterans Administration, updated within a year prior to the date the complaint is filed.

The allegation must be in writing, but it does *not* have to contain a detailed description of what violation occurred, nor is it necessary that the precise law or laws allegedly violated be identified. OFCCP will, in other words, respond to a general request for redress directed to any component of the Department of Labor or to any federal agency that might have prior enforcement responsibility.

To assist handicapped individuals and veterans in filing complaints, OFCCP has developed a complaint form (Form CC-3), which is included in Appendix II to this chapter. However, failure to use this form will not invalidate the complaint.

Procedurally, complaints by handicapped workers are supposed to be filed with the nearest OFCCP office, whereas veterans' complaints should be filed with the Veterans Employment Service through the veterans employment representative at the local state employment service office. However, veterans may also file directly with OFCCP.

Initial Processing of a Complaint

If coverage of the employer and the complainant is established, the first page of the complaint is stamped with the date it is received by OFCCP to establish the official record of filing. Each envelope is secured to the documents it contains so that the postmark can be retained as part of the official record in the event a challenge is made to the period of jurisdiction. If incomplete information is furnished by a complainant, OFCCP will immediately request the additional information in writing, allowing 60 days for a response. If the information is not provided within this period, the complaint will be dismissed unless the investigator determines that the delay is beyond the control of the complainant. As a further aid to handicapped persons, OFCCP has prepared two forms, "Missing Information" and "Follow-Up Request for Information from Complainant," to keep the complaint process alive. These forms are also included in Appendix II to this chapter.

All communications made as part of the investigation will be logged on an OFCCP contact sheet, again as a means of verifying essential information gathered during the processing of the complaint. When deemed necessary, OFCCP will conduct face-to-face interviews with the complainant, the contractor, and witnesses.

OFCCP has considerably improved its investigatory methods for determining if an employer is a federal contractor. First, OFCCP can turn to a special Dun & Bradstreet listing of federal contractors maintained in the regional offices and updated regularly. In addition, each assistant regional administrator of the Department of Labor maintains printouts of federal contractors in his region. If still stymied, OFCCP will turn to the procurement officers of federal agencies with which the employer is thought to be doing business. Finally, OFCCP will ask employers to identify whether or not they are federal contractors or subcontractors.

Procedures for Initiating Investigations

Before scheduling an investigation of an employer, OFCCP will ascertain whether or not the complainant must use the internal review procedure mentioned earlier. The investigator will ask the employer by certified letter, return receipt requested, to identify an internal review procedure within ten days.

Establishing a Case

Once jurisdiction has been established for both the complainant and the employer, the complaint is considered to be an official case by OFCCP. In setting up the case file, OFCCP is assiduous in its attention to detail. The file is divided into six parts by integral tabbed dividers. Documents are arranged chronologically, with the most recent item entered on top.

OFCCP places items it gathers during its investigation in the case file as follows:

Section A includes the initial complaint, the postmarked envelope, and OFCCP's official complaint form (CC-3), if available.

Section B includes all correspondence, such as letters to and from the contractor, the complainant, the union, and congresspersons.

Section C includes investigative materials, such as statements from witnesses, supporting records and documents, case diary notes, and results of the affirmative action plan review.

Section D includes medical reports and doctors' statements.

Section E includes any legal documents, such as notification of results of investigation, conciliation agreement, debarments, injunctions, or termination of the contract.

Section F includes miscellaneous materials.

Closing a Case Before an Investigation

The decision not to pursue a complaint must be approved by the assistant regional administrator of the Department of Labor. OFCCP can close a case for a variety of reasons, as we have already seen. For their own protection, employers should seek a letter from OFCCP verifying that the case has been closed and that further investigation will not be conducted.

OFCCP Investigative Resources

Many employers have no idea of the broad scope of OFCCP's investigative resources. Before initiating an on-site investigation, OFCCP staffers make every effort to ascertain a contractor's "EEO posture"—that is, how the employer has faced up to general equal employment opportunity obligations in the past.

OFCCP investigators have been instructed to talk with diverse community groups and build up a virtual dossier on federal contractors. OFCCP advises consultation with the American Coalition of Citizens with Disabilities, the National Federation of the Blind, and the Disabled American Veterans, among other handicapped groups. For general information on contractors, investigators have been urged by OFCCP to gather "rich anecdotal evidence" from community leaders, residents, affected class members, contractor officials, and, of course, complainants.

For sources within the government, OFCCP investigators are directed to the Labor Department's Wage and Hour Division, the Equal Employment Opportunity Commission, the state employment service system, and state and local fair employment agencies. OFCCP's philosophy in encouraging this pervasive investigative approach is to use past violations of *general* equal employment opportunity regulations (for example, equal pay requirements) to support charges of *specific* handicap violations.

The Investigation Process

At the start of every investigation, OFCCP will contact the complainant and the contractor to outline procedures to be followed. Then interviews will be held with witnesses for both parties. One of the pivotal events in the investigation will be the investigator's initial visit to the employer's facilities.

The history of equal employment opportunity investigations has revealed the absolute necessity for employers to be prepared for a close scrutiny of their personnel practices and their affirmative action plans. The sad lesson of inadequate documentation used by an ill-informed management and personnel staff to defend a company's ill-conceived affirmative action efforts is too well known to be ignored.

In preparing for the hypothetical OFCCP complaint investigation, a company has to decide well in advance precisely what kinds of documents it will release and what kinds it will protect. In light of both Freedom of Information Act decisions and OFCCP policies, the general plea of confidentiality is a difficult one for employers to make successfully. What protective measures should employers consider? Highly sensitive information—for example, executive salary records and top-personnel-management discussions —should not be comingled with files dealing with affirmative action. Employers should also consider coding of salary data.

Before the OFCCP investigator arrives, employers should have a strategy developed for handling complex negotiations and requests for information. Top management should sit down with managers and top personnel staffers to review areas of responsibility, affirmative action accomplishments, and major compliance problems. Where problems exist, some sort of negotiation strategy should be contemplated. By viewing the investigator as another professional doing his job, employers can avoid the frequent tendency to challenge inconsequential findings or—far worse—turn the investigation process into an adversary relationship. An effort to approach the investigator with respect and cooperation can go a long way toward making the investigation less painful than it might otherwise end up.

In conducting a plant tour, the investigator will observe the work area where the complainant worked (or would have worked, in the case of an applicant), inspect for physical accessibility to the premises, look for the required federal poster, and observe any special equipment, devices, or accommodations for handicapped workers. Inquiries will also be made as to the contractor's capability for making such accommodations.

Personnel and medical records pertinent to the complaint, as well as personnel processes, will be studied by the investigator. OFCCP feels that these kinds of information are highly relevant in determining the validity of a complaint, since they offer either evidence of an employer's efforts to comply with the law or expose the employer's disregard for the needs of the handicapped worker. If an employer refuses access to personnel and/or medical records, OFCCP will send a written request for them, citing statutory authority. Anticipating employer reluctance to release these documents, OFCCP has designed a "Letter to Contractor Regarding Access to Records," which is included in Appendix II to this chapter.

During the initial on-site visit, the investigator will want to take a close look at the following:

The affirmative action plan.

Copies of contracts or subcontracts.

Contract award numbers.

Dates of awards.

Contract amounts.

Contractual services to be performed.

Contract expiration date.

Company policy statement on affirmative action.

As we have already seen in the discussion of Directed Compliance Reviews, OFCCP puts tremendous emphasis on the existence, quality, and responsiveness of an employer's affirmative action plan. To ascertain the adequacy of the plan, particularly in light of the complaint investigation in process, OFCCP has designed the "Questionnaire for Persons Doing an AAP Review," which is also included in Appendix II to this chapter. Employers should review this questionnaire carefully in conjunction with the model affirmative action plan in Chapter 7.

OFCCP gives its investigators very careful instructions for interviewing witnesses for both parties. When an interview is completed, the investigator is instructed to review, sign, and date the statements made. Witnesses are asked to do the same. Interviews are to be conducted in question-and-answer form—and in private. Interviewees are asked whether they are aware of any documentary evidence that would either support what they have said or discredit what someone else has said.

In interviewing a contractor's witness, the investigator is cautioned to expect hostility, since it is assumed that the witness will view the OFCCP as biased in favor of the complainant. To emphasize their impartiality, investigators are told to "take detailed notes and project a neutral attitude" in discussions with the contractor's witnesses. Investigators have been instructed to use a form entitled "Interview of Contractor's Personnel Staff" in processing a complaint. This form, which is included in Appendix II to this chapter, illustrates the probing nature of OFCCP's employer inquiries.

When interviewing employees of the contractor, particularly those who seem to favor the contractor's position, the investigator is instructed to gather information about the nature and scope of the business. In effect, OFCCP hopes to establish a general impression of the employer, whether negative or positive, on the question of affirmative action and equal employment opportunity. To support any such impressions, investigators are also urged to secure specific documents such as personnel manuals, collective-bargaining agreements, and records on basic employment practices for study after the initial interview. When necessary, as with medical and personnel records, OFCCP will demand items withheld during the investigation by sending contractors a written letter, citing a statutory right to the items.

Executives and managers can be represented by legal counsel during their own interviews. But OFCCP makes clear that this right does not extend to hourly paid employees who are not part of management. If a contractor insists that an attorney be present during employee interviews, investigators have been instructed to reschedule these interviews away from the contractor's premises.

OFCCP strongly emphasizes the need for its investigators to back up interviews with solid, irrefutable documentation. Note taking is stressed. In fact, instructions are given on how to label, cross-reference, and even "shorthand" notes to improve efficiency and accuracy. To increase the value of interviews as evidence, investigators are urged to sign their names at the bottom of statements and, wherever possible, to electronically tape the interview after securing the interviewee's permission. Employers can expect investigators to use a form entitled "Initial Interview Format" during this process of gathering evidence from all parties involved in the complaint process. Since the form gives valuable insights into the attitude of OFCCP toward employers, it is included in Appendix II to this chapter.

In OFCCP's view, medical disputes must be handled carefully by its investigators to avoid the appearance of partiality. As discussed earlier in this chapter, OFCCP will scrutinize outmoded and unreasonable job qualifications—and disqualifications—particularly since contractors are obligated to modify job requirements to accommodate otherwise qualified handicapped individuals. When a third medical opinion is necessitated by disagreement between the complainant and the contractor or because of conflicting testimony, then the assistant regional administrator will authorize and attest to the completion of the doctor's services. The third-party doctor's services must focus only on the job qualifications of the specific position for which the complainant applied. Previous medical opinions are *not* to be included with the background information, since they may bias the third-party medical opinion.

Personnel Records and Forms

The entire personnel process is of significant concern to OFCCP. An inaccessible personnel office, for instance, is an immediate red flag for OFCCP when it is investigating a discrimination complaint. Once inside the personnel office, OFCCP will scrutinize carefully the following personnel records and forms:

Recruitment. OFCCP will examine recruiter activity logs, job orders placed with private employment agencies, records of job interviews, and records of job offers.

Hiring. OFCCP will examine applicant logs, completed job requisition forms, completed interview scoring sheets, records of employment tests, and investigative reports.

Promotion. OFCCP will examine company policies, manuals, job descriptions, seniority rosters, union agreements, supervisory evaluations, personnel files, promotion or transfer request forms, bid records, and grievance records.

Training. OFCCP will examine request forms, designation forms, roster of employees attending courses, and instructor appraisals.

Terminations/layoffs/recalls. OFCCP will examine company policies, seniority rosters, records of grievance hearings, completed exit interview forms, and layoff and recall records.

During its examination of personnel records and forms—in fact, in looking at the contractor's entire affirmative action effort—OFCCP will look at employment patterns for at least the prior three to four years.

The Application Form

Another obvious red flag to OFCCP, besides an inaccessible personnel office, is a discriminatory application form. For many employers, nothing short of rewriting application forms and re-vamping related interviewing techniques will bring them into compliance.

Federal regulations prohibit questions unrelated to the job on application forms. Often phraseology itself can be crucial. For example, a question about an applicant's possible epilepsy would be unacceptable, whereas a question about an applicant's ability to perform a job safely would be acceptable. OFCCP's goal here is to eliminate false assumptions about a handicapped individual's ability to perform a specific job.

Broad or vague questions on an application form are a clear signal to OFCCP that the employer has not made a valid affirmative action effort. Employers will want to expunge such items as "Do you have any health problems?" or "List all hospitalization in the past five years." Employers should add positive statements to the application form, such as "This Company is an affirmative action employer," "Job candidates are invited to declare themselves as handicapped individuals but are not required to do so," and "Any information voluntarily provided about disabilities will be kept confidential."

The two application forms shown in Figures 3-1 and 3-2—the first one blank and the second one completed by a handicapped individual—indicate clearly the type of problems a typical employer can face.

On the blank application (Figure 3-1), we see that the employer is asking a number of discriminatory questions about physical and mental handicaps, alcoholism, and unfavorable military service. Furthermore, this form contains no specific declarations about the employer's required affirmative action toward the handicapped.

On the completed application form (Figure 3-2), the employer has clearly invited a challenge of discrimination if the handicapped individual isn't offered employment. Questions were asked about "physical defects" that had no bearing on the ability to perform in the secretarial position for which the individual applied. Even though the application form indicated that the company was an equal opportunity employer, no specific invitation was made to handicapped individuals to avail themselves of the company's mandatory affirmative action program.

Figure 3-1. Employment application form.

PACKARD

AN EQUAL OPPORTUNITY EMPLOYER

The Packard Company observes all federal and state regulations related to discrimination in employment. Please read the entire form before you begin filling it out. Answers should be typed, printed, or carefully written in ink so that they are clear and readable. Please answer all questions, indicating "None" where applicable. Resumes will not be accepted in lieu of any information required on this form. This application must be completed in its entirety before any offer of employment may be considered.

PERSONAL

Last name	First	Middle	Other last name(s) by which you have been known

Temporary street address	City	State	Zip Code	Telephone number Area No.

Permanent street address	City	State	Zip Code	Telephone number Area No.

Social Security no.	Are you under 18? ☐ Yes ☐ No	Are you 65 or older? ☐ Yes ☐ No	Citizen of U.S.A.? ☐ Yes ☐ No	How, or by whom, were you referred to this company?

Have you previously been employed by this company? ☐ Yes ☐ No | Location | From (Mo./Yr.) | To (Mo./Yr.)

List below the names of any individuals employed by PACKARD who know you.

Name | Where employed

Name | Where employed

Describe any physical handicap, chronic disease, surgery, or serious illness (including hospitalization for drug addiction or alcohol).

If you have ever been hospitalized for a mental illness, can you submit a psychiatrist's certificate that you are mentally competent?
☐ Yes   ☐ No   ☐ Not applicable

Do you now occasionally or regularly use "controlled substances" (drugs) such as heroin or other opium derivatives, LSD, or cocaine; or amphetamines and barbiturates, except as prescribed by a licensed physician?   ☐ Yes   ☐ No

Have you ever received worker's compensation for any industrial injury? ☐ Yes ☐ No | Nature of injury

When (Mo./Yr.) | Number weeks absent | Employer at time of injury

Have you ever been denied security clearance? ☐ Yes ☐ No	Do you hold or have you held in the last 12 months a security clearance? ☐ Yes ☐ No	Level	Granting agency	Company where cleared

Position Desired	Minimum salary req'd (per)	Shift desired	Date available

TRAINING AND EDUCATION

If you did not graduate from high school, circle highest grade completed: 1   2   3   4   5   6   7   8   9   10   11   12

High school attended	City	State	From (Mo./Yr.)	To (Mo./Yr.)	Diploma received? ☐ Yes ☐ No

U.S. Military Service School (Name)	Location	Course	From (Mo./Yr.)	To (Mo./Yr.)

Apprentice, Business or Technical Schools (Name)	Location	Course	Certificate or Diploma Received? ☐Yes ☐No	From (Mo./Yr.)	To (Mo./Yr.)

List Licenses Held: (Professional Engineer, Electrician, etc.)

Have you attended college?   ☐Yes   ☐No   If "yes" complete the section below

College or University	Dates From	Dates To	Field of Specialization	Grade Point Average	Grade Max Possible	Degree Conferred Title	Degree Conferred Date
Name							
Location							
Name							
Location							
Name							
Location							
Scholarships			Class Standing	% of Self-Financing		Total Units (If no degree)	

Thesis Subject	Thesis Supervisor

Scholastic Honors	Honor Societies	Extra Curricular Activities

List publications, inventions or scientific awards received:

List professional organizations to which you belong (not those denoting race, religion, national origin, color, ancestry):

1. _____   2. _____   3. _____

Indicate principal hobbies

U.S. MILITARY

Past	Branch of service	From (Mo./Yr.)	To (Mo./Yr.)	Separation ☐Discharged ☐Retired	Type of discharge	Highest rank
Present	Check appropriate box if you are a member of ☐National Guard ☐ Ready Reserve ☐ Standby Reserve	Branch of Service	Rank	Unit	Address	

WORK EXPERIENCE

Beginning with the most recent, list all employment, including part time and self-employment, for the past 10 years. Also list significant experience more than 10 years ago. Report all activities for last 10 years, using space on last page to account for periods of unemployment, military service, schools, etc.

Employer	Address	From (Mo./Yr.)	To (Mo./Yr.)

Name of Supervisor	Title	Telephone No.	Ext.	Starting Base Pay (per)

Starting Position	Current or Last Position	Current Base Pay (per)

Description of Duties	Other Compensation (bonus, O.T.)
	Reason for wishing to leave
	May we contact this employer? ☐Yes ☐No

USE THIS SPACE TO ENTER INFORMATION ON ANY ITEM REQUIRING FURTHER EXPLANATION

If you have a sealed record on file with the commissioner of probation with respect to certain offenses, you may disregard such offenses in answering these questions.

1. Have you ever been convicted of a felony? ☐ Yes ☐ No

2. Have you been convicted within the five years immediately preceding the date of this application of a misdemeanor? (If the conviction was the *first* for any of the following offenses, you should answer "No": drunkenness, simple assault, speeding, minor traffic violations, affray, or disturbance of the peace.) ☐ Yes ☐ No

3. If the answer to question 2 is "No", disregard this question. If the answer is "Yes", have you been convicted of any other misdemeanor at any time? ☐ Yes ☐ No

4. Have you ever been convicted by a general court-martial? ☐ Yes ☐ No

PLEASE READ THE FOLLOWING STATEMENT CAREFULLY BEFORE SIGNING

As a condition of employment you must successfully meet company medical requirements and submit to a physical examination to determine your fitness for the work to be performed. You may also be asked to furnish proof of citizenship and meet government security requirements as may be necessary. The following documents will be required at time of hire: birth certificate, social security card, and discharge certificate or separation papers if you served in the armed forces.

I authorize the company to investigate my background and to obtain information concerning my ability and desirability as an employee.

I certify that the statements made by me herein and other information given by me pursuant to my becoming an employee of this company are true, complete and correct and are made in good faith, and I understand that any misstatement or omission may be the basis for immediate dismissal.

| Date | Applicant's Signature |

Comments

PLEASE DO NOT WRITE BELOW THIS LINE

| Employment Interviewer | Date |

PERSONAL DATA TO BE COMPLETED AFTER HIRE

Notify in case of emergency	Address	Telephone Area No.
Date of Birth	Sex	Marital Status	No. Dependents (Exclude yourself)	Height	Weight

HIRING INFORMATION

Employee Number	Department	Job Code	Job Title
Payroll	Base Pay	Hire, Rehire or Reinstate	Date of Action	Date Start Work
Type of Badge	Level of Security Required	Signature of Person Hiring	Reporting to

CHECK LIST

☐ Benefits	☐ Birth Certificate	☐ Conflict of Interest	☐ Educational Certificate	☐ Employee Handbook	☐ Income Tax Information	Medical Code
☐ Non-Resident Alien	☐ Patient Agreement	☐ Physical Exam	☐ Social Security Card	☐ United Way Solicitation	☐ U.S. Bonds	
☐ Veterans Service Papers Checked		☐ Affirmative Action Program		☐ _____		

Figure 3-2. Employment application form completed by a handicapped person.

THE MIGHTY CORPORATION

AN EQUAL OPPORTUNITY EMPLOYER

LEGAL NAME _SMEREK_ (Last)   _RUTH_ (First)   _A._ (Middle)

PRESENT ADDRESS _32 HERBERT PLACE JERSEY CITY, NJ_ (No. Street) (City) (State & Zip)   TEL. NO. _JC6-5201_

PERMANENT ADDRESS _Same as above_ (No. Street) (City) (State & Zip)   TEL. NO. _____

IN CASE OF ACCIDENT NOTIFY _CLYDE SMEREK_   TEL. NO. _Same_

ADDRESS _Same_ (No. Street) (City) (State & Zip)   RELATIONSHIP _Husband_

SOCIAL SECURITY NUMBER _123   45   6789_

ARE YOU SEEKING   PERMANENT EMPLOYMENT _YES_   TEMPORARY _____   PART TIME _____

POSITION APPLIED FOR _Secretary_   SALARY EXPECTED _$160./wk_

LOCATION PREFERRED _____   HOW SOON CAN YOU REPORT _Immediately._

ARE YOU WILLING TO WORK NIGHTS, WEEKENDS, HOLIDAYS? _Occasionally_   YES _____. NO _____

ARE YOU WILLING TO DO SHIFT WORK? _____   YES _____ NO _X_

ARE YOU WILLING TO TRANSFER TO ANOTHER CITY? _____   YES _____ NO _X_

HAVE YOU EVER FILED APPLICATION WITH MIGHTY BEFORE? _NO_ WHEN _____ WHERE _____

HAVE YOU EVER   BEEN EMPLOYED BY MIGHTY? _No_   WHEN _____ WHERE _____

MALE _____ FEMALE _X_ DATE OF BIRTH _9/24/28_ U.S. CITIZEN _Yes_

SINGLE _____ MARRIED _X_ DIVORCED _____   SEPARATED _____ · WIDOWED _____

NUMBER OF CHILDREN _none_ AGES OF CHILDREN _____ OTHER DEPENDENTS _____

NAME OF SPOUSE _CLYDE SMEREK_   OCCUPATION _Salesman_

DO YOU HAVE A VALID DRIVERS LICENSE? _No_ DO YOU OWN A CAR OR HAVE ACCESS TO ONE? _NO_

DO YOU OWN YOUR HOME? _NO_   DO YOU RENT? _YES_   LIVE WITH PARENTS? _NO_

DO YOU HAVE ANY LOANS OR DEBTS PAST DUE? _NO_ EXPLAIN _____

HAVE YOU EVER BEEN CONVICTED OF VIOLATING ANY LAW (Other than traffic violations)? _NO_

NAME OF PERSONAL ACQUAINTANCES IN OUR EMPLOY _none_

NAME AND RELATIONSHIP OF RELATIVES IN OUR EMPLOY _none_

HEIGHT _5'5"_ WEIGHT _130_   COLOR EYES _Blue_   COLOR HAIR _Brown_

ANY DEFECTS IN HEARING _No_ SPEECH _No_ EYESIGHT _No_ VISUAL ACUITY _____

DO YOU HAVE ANY OTHER PHYSICAL DEFECTS? _YES_   EXPLAIN _Artificial leg —_
The result of a car accident one year ago.

TIME LOST LAST TWO YEARS BECAUSE OF ILLNESS _4 mos._ NATURE OF ILLNESS _Lost leg_

PREVIOUS EMPLOYMENT RECORD

FROM MONTH/YR.	TO MONTH/YR.	EMPLOYER (GIVE FULL NAME OF COMPANY)	
3/66	2/79	YBQ Shipping Corp.	Executive Secretary
		SUPERVISOR'S NAME Mr. Peckhardt	
2/60	3/66	Atlas Industrial, Inc.	Executive Secretary
		SUPERVISOR'S NAME Mr. Nebel	
		SUPERVISOR'S NAME	
		SUPERVISOR'S NAME	

EDUCATION

	NAME & ADDRESS, CITY & STATE	FROM	TO	DID YOU GRADUATE	MAJOR COURSE
Grammar School	PS #23 Jersey City, N.J.	1933	1942	Yes	
High School	Dickenson High Jersey City, N.J.	1942	1946	YES	Business
College					
Business, Technical or Other Schools	Katherine Gibbs New York, N.J.	1946	1947	Yes	Exec. Sec'y

List Your Leisure Activities in School and at the Present   Reading, Sewing, Cooking

CHARACTER REFERENCES

List Three Personal References (Other Than Relatives or Former Employers) Who Have Known You for at Least Five Years.

NAME	ADDRESS (Street, City, State & Zip)	OCCUPATION	YEARS KNOWN
LYDIA LEWIS	83 Cottage Street, Jersey City	Housewife	22
JEROME KAPLAN	1100 Kennedy Blvd. Jersey City	Lawyer	17
GENE CROFTS	79 Freedom Ave. Jersey City	Salesman	20

QUALIFICATIONS

DO YOU TYPE? YES   WORDS PER MINUTE: _____ ELECTRIC 65   MANUAL _____
DO YOU TAKE SHORTHAND? YES   SHORTHAND SPEED 80 TELETYPE YES   SPEED 60
DICTAPHONE   YES   ADDING MACHINE YES
OTHER OFFICE MACHINES   Copier, word processor, mag cards

BRIEFLY STATE WHY YOU ARE APPLYING FOR EMPLOYMENT WITH MIGHTY
I am interested in a job change and the advertisement I saw in the
Jersey Journal seemed very interesting. The job description, the company,
and the company benefits all appeal to me.

U.S. ARMED FORCES RECORD N/A	SELECTIVE SERVICE RECORD
(Circle) Air Force, Army, Navy, Marines, Co. Guard	Order No._____ Classification_____
Type of Discharge _____ Ser. No. _____	Local Board No. _____
Induction Date _____ Discharge Date _____	Date of Classification _____
Rank _____	Address of Local Board _____

In short, both employers have invited closer scrutiny of their operations by OFCCP simply because they failed to revamp one of the more obvious areas of discrimination—the application form.

Conciliation

If the contractor wishes to discuss the settlement of a complaint, the investigator may initiate conciliation sessions. In some cases, OFCCP feels that it will be appropriate to enter into a settlement without formal completion of the investigation and issuance of the notification letter. However, if the early resolution of the complaint favors the contractor, even though the complainant may concur, OFCCP has instructed its investigators to proceed with the investigation.

If one party agrees to conciliation, or if a party refuses to participate, there is no prejudice to either party in any future resolution of the dispute. By the same token, participation in conciliation sessions is not to be construed by OFCCP as any evidence of a violation of federal law. If initial conciliation efforts fail and a "Notification of Results of Investigation" is drawn up, both parties will again be invited to enter into conciliation discussions. If this latest conciliation attempt fails, then the contractor will be afforded a formal administrative hearing before OFCCP.

A conciliation agreement must be in writing to be valid, and it may include one or more of the following remedies:

- Hiring or full reinstatement to the position in question, including all benefits such as seniority, medical vacation, and sick time.
- Award of lost or back wages (OFCCP will monitor this aspect).
- Award of full retirement benefits and/or seniority.
- Expunction of record.
- Revision of a job description or its physical standards.
- Implementation of reasonable accommodations.
- Revision of the contractor's policies and procedures.
- Adoption of an affirmative action plan.
- Posting of prescribed notices.
- Revision of employment practices, including, but not limited to, hiring, upgrading, transfer, rates of pay or other forms of

compensation, and selection for training, including apprenticeship and on-the-job training.

During conciliation negotiations, OFCCP will attempt to remedy past discrimination without regard to artificial barriers that employers might try to erect. For instance, OFCCP will invoke the "rightful place" principle when an employer contends that a collective-bargaining agreement or a seniority system precludes affirmative action or nondiscrimination. Application of this principle ensures that a handicapped applicant or employee will not be deprived of a job or a promotion he would have secured if it had not been for the discriminatory practice. In short, the employer could be required to alter immediately the personnel practices or policies that discriminate against the affected class member.

One way OFCCP envisions the application of the "rightful place" principle is in the area of training. An employer might be directed to provide training, even on an accelerated basis, to a handicapped person, with the job left open until the person completes training. In this way the potentially irreversible effects of discrimination would be avoided.

In the compensation area, OFCCP may be looking to negotiate conciliation agreements that include back pay and "front pay." For willful violations of the law, back pay awards are allowed for up to three years. When violations are not willful, the maximum recovery pay period is two years. Back pay can include interest computed at the prevailing legal rate.

Employers should note that a willful violation doesn't necessarily mean that there was *intent* to discriminate but merely that the contractor should have known that his actions were violations of the law. The old adage, ignorance of the law is no excuse, clearly applies to the handicap statutes.

If OFCCP rules that the individual discriminated against must wait to gain or regain his "rightful place" at work, then "front pay" can be awarded as well. In such a case, front pay will compensate the handicapped individual for the economic loss suffered as of the date of the conciliation agreement, up to the time employment commences.

To encourage conciliation agreements, OFCCP has designed a

"Sample letter of Settlement," to which is appended a series of "Model Settlement Clauses" defining various kinds of settlements. This letter with the appending settlement clauses is included in Appendix II to this chapter.

If the conciliation agreement is approved by the contractor and then by the Office of the Solicitor, the investigator will send the agreement to the complainant for review and signature. If acceptable to the complainant, the agreement is signed by the OFCCP's assistant regional administrator. OFCCP expects federal contractors to achieve 95 percent of their compliance goals, particularly when there has been a failure in meeting the terms of a prior conciliation agreement.

Pursuing a Formal Hearing

For the contractor who desires to challenge the findings of the OFCCP investigator, there are administrative and legal remedies which can be pursued, but not without considerable time and expense. If a contractor is determined to fight a discrimination complaint to the end, he can look forward either to the formal administrative hearing process of the Labor Department or to federal court action. DOL's hearing process is quite similar to the HEW process discussed in Chapter 6 but is considered less formal.

Appendix I
Questionnaires and Forms for OFCCP Directed Compliance Reviews

U. S. DEPARTMENT OF LABOR
Employment Standards Administration
Office of Federal Contract Compliance Programs

MANDATORY JOB LISTING DATA COLLECTION

PERIOD (1 year)

From: _____

To: _____

Data must be for identical period when completing parts 2, 3, and 4

2. ES MANDATORY JOB LISTING EVALUATION

Name of Employment Service Contacts

Address: _____

Zip Code _____

Telephone: _____   Area Code _____

Date: _____

1. SUITABLE JOBS DATA	No. LISTED OPENINGS	Referrals			Placements				Hires	
		VE	DV	TOT	VE	DV	TOTAL			
Officials and Managers										
Professionals										
Technicians										
Sales Workers										
Office and Clerical										
Craft Workers (Skilled)										
Operatives (Semi-skilled)										
Laborers (Unskilled)										
Service Workers										
TOTAL										

4. QUARTERLY REPORTS (1 year) Filed at ES Office at:

	H I R E S	
	VE	DV	TOTAL
1st Quarter			
2nd Quarter			
3rd Quarter			
4th Quarter			

3. ON-SITE MANDATORY JOB LISTING EVALUATION

Name of Contractor: _____

Name of Contractor's Representative: _____

Address: _____

Zip Code _____

Telephone: _____   Area Code _____

Date: _____

EMPLOYMENT OPPORTUNITIES	NUMBER OPENINGS LISTED	HIRES		
		VE	DV	TOTAL
Total	a/			

a/ This figure should reflect total opportunities contractor had to hire and list, and may well be higher than number of actual hires and listings.

EOS Signature _____   Date _____

Form CC-9T

PERSONNEL MANAGER/AAP DIRECTOR

1. Name_____

    Address_____

    Telephone No. _____

2. Exact Job Title _____

3. How long have you been employed by contractor? _____

4. What are your job duties?_____

    _____

    _____

5. What is contractor's hiring process?_____

    _____

    _____

    Describe the process which occurs when a person is:

    not hired _____

    terminated_____

    not transferred_____

    demoted_____

    not promoted_____

    Who is the final decision maker in the above process?

    _____

6. Is a pre-employment medical exam required? Yes___ No___

    If yes, when?_____

7. Describe the physician/contractor relationship. (i.e., is the doctor on the Company payroll?) Who determines medical qualifications for the job, the doctor or personnel?_____

   _____

8. After the medical examination, what happens if the person failed the exam?_____

9. Do you have a written job description?   Yes___ No____
   Evidence _____

   _____

10. Do the job descriptions include physical/mental requirements?
    Yes___ No___   Evidence _____
    Prior to interviewing new applicants, does the interviewer have at his disposal the physical/mental requirements for particular job vacancies? _____

11. When do you review the physical/mental requirements? ___

    _____

12. What information do you transmit to the examining physician regarding the potential applicant?_____

    _____

13. What is your policy on medical inquiries of individuals?

    _____

    a) Have you made such inquiries and under what circumstances?

    _____

    b) Give specifics to preceding a) _____

    _____

14. How many known qualified handicapped persons have been employed from _____ to _____?
(Name, Job Title, Date of Employment, Salary) _____

_____

_____

15. How many qualified handicapped persons have you advanced between _____ and _____?
(Name, Job Title, Date of Advancement)_____

_____

16. What personnel staff were selected and trained to ensure nondiscrimination and affirmative action for handicapped? (Memo of such entry in personnel file of persons so trained?

_____

_____

Describe training _____

_____

17. Have you made reasonable accommodations for handicapped employees? (Names, dates, job titles, accommodations)

_____

_____

_____

18. How many handicapped persons are represented in Company activities? _____ Evidence _____

_____

_____

19. Does the Union Contract contain nondiscrimination clauses?

    Evidence_____

    _____

20. Have you notified, in writing, all subcontractors, vendors
    and suppliers requesting action of AAP and requested action
    on their part? (Evidence, interviews and contact person/
    or individual responsible)_____

    _____

    _____

RECRUITMENT

21. Describe your policy on recruitment to ensure affirmative
    action for qualified handicapped persons_____

    _____

    _____

    Copy of recruitment policies.

22. What evidence do you have that applicants are aware of your
    commitment to AAP?_____

    _____

    _____

23. What recruiting and training sources have been informed of
    AAP and with which you have established working relationships?
    Be specific: give names and verify via telephone at
    time of review if possible._____

    _____

    _____

    _____

24. With what rehabilitation agencies and facilities have you established contacts and from whom do you seek technical assistance and advice?_____

_____

25. Are your personnel officers provided with job descriptions to assist in recruiting handicapped persons?_____

_____

26. In what Company activities do the handicapped participate? Evidence, interview a handicapped person_____

_____

_____

27. With which rehabilitation facilities and schools do you participate in work-study programs and on-the-job training? Specific names, document - _____

_____

_____

INTERNAL COMMUNICATIONS

28. How do you communicate your AAP and individual responsibilities to employees?_____

_____

a) Do you have special meetings with employees?_____

_____

b) How often?_____

c) What documents do you have to support the preceding?

_____

29. How do you re-inform employees of commitment to affirmative
    action? Evidence_____

    _____

    How do you invite applicants/employees to identify
    themselves? Evidence _____

    _____

    Do you have an internal review process for handling complaints
    under §503, as amended,/§402?   Yes___   No____
    Describe_____

    _____

30. Is AAP included in Company policy manual, posted on
    bulletin boards, publicized in Company newspapers,
    magazines, etc.? Evidence _____

    _____

    _____

    Is there notice posted indicating time and location for
    employees and applicants to review AAP? Yes___ No___
    Evidence_____

    _____

31. Are both handicapped employees and non-handicapped employees
    pictured in public information activities, such as advertising?
    Evidence _____

_____   _____

EMPLOYMENT OPPORTUNITY SPECIALIST   DATE

MEDICAL REPRESENTATIVE

1. Name_____

   Address_____

   Telephone No._____

2. Exact Job Title_____

3. How long have you been employed by contractor?_____

4. What are your job duties?_____

   _____

   _____

   _____

5. What is your role in the hiring process?_____

   _____

6. Do you see all applicants once they are selected for a

   job? Yes___ No___

   At what point in the personnel process are applicants

   referred to you?_____

7. Does the contractor have medical standards?_____

   _____

8. What information is transmitted to you from Personnel prior

   to your seeing an applicant?_____

   _____

9. Have you assisted Personnel/Labor Relations in reviewing

   physical and mental job requirements?_____

   _____

10. Do you review applicant's medical history prior to
     the examination?   Yes____ No____
     a. Are any applicants rejected on the basis of this
         information? Specify_____

         _____

         _____

11. Have you been consulted by EEO/Personnel in the development
     of the Company's affirmative action plan? Yes____ No____

12. Do you have any questions/comments?_____

     _____

     _____

     _____

     _____

EMPLOYMENT OPPORTUNITY SPECIALIST   DATE

SUPERVISORS

1. Name_____

    Address_____

    Telephone No._____

2. Exact Job Title_____
    _____

3. How long have you been employed by contractor?_____
    _____

4. What are your job duties?_____
    _____
    _____

5. Are employees evaluated on job performance? Yes___ No___

    How?_____
    _____
    _____

    a) How often?_____

    b) By whom?_____

6. How are transfers made by the Company?_____
    _____
    _____

7. How long is the trial period for employees?_____
    _____

Is the length of the trial period standard for all
employees?_____

Is the length of trial period extended?_____

Why?_____

8. Are there written job descriptions?   Yes___ No___

9. Do job descriptions include physical/mental requirements?

Yes ___ No ___   _____

What are these requirements?_____

_____

_____

10. Are you involved in selection process?_____

_____

_____

11. What criteria do you use in the selection process? _____

_____

_____

12. What is the process of terminating a person?_____

_____

_____

_____

13. Has management informed you of their commitment to
affirmative action for the handicapped?_____

_____

_____

14. Does management have an affirmative action plan for the handicapped?   Yes_____   No_____

15. Do you have any questions/comments?_____

_____

_____

_____

_____

EMPLOYMENT OPPORTUNITY SPECIALIST   DATE

LABORER

1. Name_____

    Address_____

    Telephone No. _____

2. Exact Job Title_____
    _____

3. How long have you been employed by contractor?_____
    _____

4. What are your job duties?_____
    _____
    _____

    Are you rotated on the job? Yes___   No___

    To what areas?_____
    _____

5. How were you selected?_____
    _____

6. Was a physical examination required for employment? _____
    _____

7. What would happen if you were injured on the job?_____
    _____

    Describe the job areas _____
    _____
    _____
    _____

8. While on probation, were you graded on job performance?

    _____

    How were you graded, based on what?_____

    _____

9. Are there production standards?   Yes___   No___

    How was your production measured?_____

    _____

10. Are you evaluated on job performance?_____

    a) How often?_____

    b) By whom?_____

    How are promotions made?_____

    _____

11. How were you selected by the Company? Describe the hiring

    process_____

    _____

    _____

12. Have you been informed by Company officials of affirmative

    action for handicapped?   Yes___   No___

13. Have you seen handicapped posters?   Yes___   No___

14. Were you interviewed by more than one person in the

    selection process?_____

15. How much of your job includes strenuous movement?_____

    _____

16. Were you aware of the invitation to identify yourself as a

    handicapped person?_____

    a) Did the contractor take affirmative action in making

    accommodations?_____

    _____   _____
    EMPLOYMENT OPPORTUNITY SPECIALIST   DATE

CONCILIATION AGREEMENT

PART I: GENERAL PROVISIONS

A. This Agreement is made pursuant to Section 503 of the
    Rehabilitation Act of 1973, as amended, and Section 402
    of the Vietnam Era Veterans' Readjustment Assistance Act
    of 1974, and Title 41, Code of Federal Regulations (CFR)
    Parts 60-741/60-250.

B. This Agreement is entered into by the Office of Federal
    Contract Compliance Programs, United States Department of
    Labor, hereinafter referred to as OFCCP, and _____
    __(name of contractor)__.

C. Pursuant to 41 CFR 60-741.25/41 CFR 60-250.25, a comprehensive
    review of the _____(name of facility)_____ of
    __(name of contractor)_____ was conducted on ___(date)_____.
    Information obtained by the OFCCP in the course of the review
    indicates that ____(name of contractor)___ has failed to comply
    with the requirements of the Acts and the regulations by
    (list alleged violations).

D. This Agreement does not constitute an admission of any
    violation of Sections 503 and 402 of the respective Acts.
    The provisions of this Agreement shall become a part of
    __(company's name)_____ Affirmative Action Program for 19__.

Subject to the performance by _(contractor's name)_ of all promises and representations contained herein and in its Affirmative Action Program for 19__, all questions raised in paragraph C of failure to comply with the Acts and regulations shall be deemed resolved. However, it is understood that making the commitments contained herein does not preclude future determinations of noncompliance based upon a finding that the commitments are not sufficient to achieve compliance.

E.   ___(Contractor's name)___ agrees that the OFCCP may review compliance with this Agreement. As part of such review, OFCCP may require written reports, may inspect the premises, examine witnesses, and examine and copy documents deemed by OFCCP to be relevant to the execution of this Agreement.

F.   Nothing herein is intended to relieve ___(contractor)___ from compliance with the requirements of the Acts, and the regulations.

G.   ___(Contractor)___ agrees that there will be no retaliation of any kind against any beneficiary of this Agreement, or against any person who has given testimony or assistance in this compliance review, or who files a charge or participates in any manner in any proceeding under the Acts.

H. If, at any time, the OFCCP obtains information which
    indicates that the ____(contractor)____ has violated any
    portion of this Agreement, the contractor shall be notified
    promptly of that fact in writing, including a statement of
    that information. After providing such information, OFCCP
    shall have the right to proceed immediately to an adminis-
    trative enforcement hearing pursuant to 41 CFR 60-741.29/
    41 CFR 60-250.29. Violation of this Agreement may subject
    the _____(contractor)_____ to sanctions set forth in
    41 CFR 60-741.28/41 CFR 60-250.28 and/or other appropriate
    relief.

PART II: SPECIFIC PROVISIONS

____(Contractor's name)____, its agents, assigns and successors
in interests hereby agree:

PART III: REPORTING

____(Contractor's name)____ agrees to report on its progress
toward fulfilling the provisions of this Agreement as follows:

_____   _____
ESA Assistant Regional Administrator   Date
  for OFCCP

_____   _____
          Contractor, Title   Date

Appendix II
OFCCP Forms for Complaints and Interviews

U. S. DEPARTMENT OF LABOR Employment Standards Administration Office of Federal Contract Compliance Programs	COMPLAINT OF VIOLATION OF AFFIRMATIVE ACTION OBLIGATIONS BY FEDERAL CONTRACTORS (Veterans/Handicapped Workers)

IMPORTANT NOTE: Please read thoroughly all instructions as well as the Privacy Act statements before completing this form. This form is to be used only by those alleging violations of Section 503 of the Rehabilitation Act of 1973, as amended, and/or Section 402 of the Vietnam Era Veterans' Readjustment Assistance Act of 1974, amending 38 U.S.C. 2012. You are covered by one of the above Acts if you are a handicapped person, have a history of a physical or mental handicap, or are regarded as handicapped by the employer, or if you are a disabled veteran or a veteran discharged within the last four years.

1. Complainant's Name	2. Check (✓) the Act(s) under which you are filing: _____ Handicapped Worker _____ Veteran
3. Address (Street, City, State, Zip Code)	4. Telephone Number (Include area code)

5. If you are being represented (e.g. by an attorney, union, organization), provide the following information concerning your representative:

a. Name and address	b. Telephone Number (Include area code)

6. What is the name of the company that, you allege, violated the affirmative action clause?

a. Name and address	b. Telephone Number (Include area code)

7. (TO BE ANSWERED ONLY BY THOSE EMPLOYEES CURRENTLY WORKING WITH THE COMPANY NAMED IN ITEM 6.)
Does the company have an internal review or grievance procedure?

_____ Yes   _____ No   _____ Don't know

8. If you are a veteran, Check (✓) if you:

_____   a. Are entitled to disability compensation under laws administered by the Veteran's Administration for a disability rated at 30% or more. (If you check this item, send your Veteran's Administration Form VAL-5, or its equivalent with this form.)

_____   b. Were discharged or released from active duty for a disability incurred or aggravated in line of duty. (If you check this item, send the medical information resulting in your discharge or release, or a summary sufficient to establish the reason for discharge or release with this form.) (This information is available from your Master Military Record at the National Personnel Record Center (OSA), 9800 Page Blvd., St. Louis, Mo. 63132.)

_____   c. Served on active duty for a period of more than 180 days, any part of which occurred between August 5, 1964 and May 7, 1975, and were discharged or released therefrom with other than a Dishonorable Discharge; and were discharged or released within the 48 months preceding the date(s) that you are alleging violation. (If you check this item, send your Department of Defense Form, DD-214 with this form.)

Form CC-3
Sept. 1976

9. If you are filing this complaint under Section 503 of the Rehabilitation Act of 1973, describe your physical or mental handicap or history of such handicap. If you are not presently handicapped, please state the physical or mental condition which gives rise to this complaint:

_____

_____

_____

_____

10. What is the exact or approximate date(s) of the alleged violation(s)? (Month, day, year)	11. Check (✓) the most apparent violation:
	___ Failure or refusal to hire ___ Promotion
	___ Layoff or recall· ___ Discharge
	___ Employee benefits ___ Other (Specify)

12. Describe as clearly as possible your complaint of the alleged violation(s). Include relevant information to dates, places, names and titles of persons involved as well as your job skills or training. (You may continue on another sheet of paper if additional space is required, but remember to write your name at the top of the paper and attach to this form.)

_____

_____

_____

_____

_____

_____

_____

_____

THE PRIVACY ACT OF 1973 requires that the Department of Labor provide the following statements to each individual from whom it requests information. (1) The authority for collecting this information is Section 503 of the Rehabilitation Act of 1973, as amended, and/or Section 402 of the Vietnam Era Veterans' Readjustment Assistance Act of 1974, amending 38 U.S.C. 2012. The submission of this information is voluntary. (2) This information is used to process complaints under the above Acts. (3) The information collected may be used in the course of settlement negotiations with the respon-' dent contractor or subcontractor, and/or in the course of presenting evidence in a public hearing, including possible disclosure to opposing counsel, or be disclosed to the Office of Management and Budget in connection with the review of private relief legislation. (4) Failure·to provide the information will restrict the action which the U.S. Department of Labor can take on your behalf.

13. I certify that the information given above is true and correct to the best of my knowledge or belief. (A willful false statement is punishable by law: U.S. Code, Title 18, Section 1001). I hereby authorize the release of any medical information needed for the investigation.

_____   _____
            Signature   Date

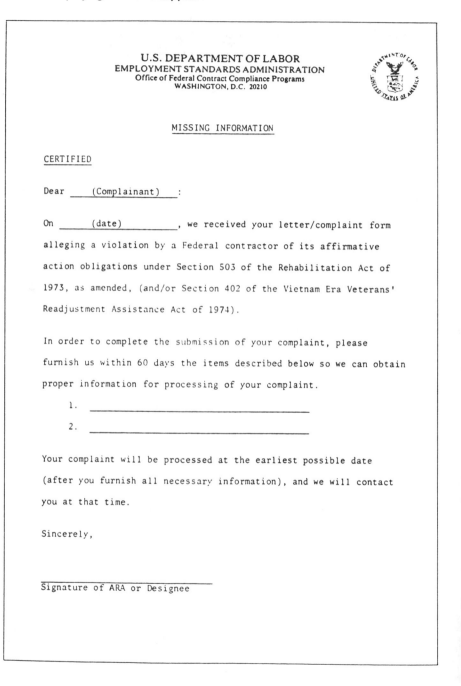

U.S. DEPARTMENT OF LABOR
EMPLOYMENT STANDARDS ADMINISTRATION
Office of Federal Contract Compliance Programs
WASHINGTON, D.C. 20210

MISSING INFORMATION

CERTIFIED

Dear _____ (Complainant) _____ :

On _____ (date) _____ , we received your letter/complaint form alleging a violation by a Federal contractor of its affirmative action obligations under Section 503 of the Rehabilitation Act of 1973, as amended, (and/or Section 402 of the Vietnam Era Veterans' Readjustment Assistance Act of 1974).

In order to complete the submission of your complaint, please furnish us within 60 days the items described below so we can obtain proper information for processing of your complaint.

1. _____

2. _____

Your complaint will be processed at the earliest possible date (after you furnish all necessary information), and we will contact you at that time.

Sincerely,

_____
Signature of ARA or Designee

U.S. DEPARTMENT OF LABOR
EMPLOYMENT STANDARDS ADMINISTRATION
Office of Federal Contract Compliance Programs
WASHINGTON, D.C. 20210

FOLLOW-UP REQUEST FOR INFORMATION FROM COMPLAINANT

CERTIFIED

Dear _____ (Complainant) _____ :

The following information previously requested from you on

_____ (date) _____ is needed to continue the processing of

your complaint against _____ (contractor) _____ :

    1. _____

    2. _____ Information needed _____

If you wish this office to puruse your complaint, it is necessary

for you to promptly submit this information.

Unless this information is submitted within ten (10) days, your

complaint file will be closed pursuant to part 60-741.26(d) of

Section 503 / part 60-250.26(d) of Section 402.

Sincerely,

_____
Signature of ARA or designee

U.S. DEPARTMENT OF LABOR
EMPLOYMENT STANDARDS ADMINISTRATION
Office of Federal Contract Compliance Programs
WASHINGTON, D.C. 20210

INITIAL INTERVIEW FORMAT

The following interview format is to serve as a guide for developing a minimum data base for processing a complaint. This format is to be used as a tool for interviewing complainant, contractor's or complainant's witness.

1. Name _____

2. Address _____

    _____

3. Social Security Number _____   4. Birthdate _____

5. Telephone Number: Work _____   Home _____

    The best time for you to be reached by telephone is _____

6. Contractor complaining against:

    Name _____   Telephone _____

    Address _____

    City _____   State _____   Zip _____

Questions 7 and 13 are for current or former employees only.

7. How many employees in contractor's work force? _____

    How many employees on your shift/department? _____

8. How were you discriminated against? _____

    _____

    _____

    _____

    _____

9. Date of alleged discrimination _____

10. What is your handicapping condition? _____

    _____

    What handicap does the contractor claim you have? _____

    _____

11. Are you currently under treatment for the condition? _____

12. Are there any persons that you feel could provide evidence in your
    support?

    | | | TELEPHONE | |
NAME & ADDRESS, IF KNOWN	TITLE	HOME	WORK

13. If you (complainant) were employed at the time of the discrimination,
    answer these questions:

    A. Date hired _____

    B. Date of discrimination _____

    C. Job title and duties at time of discrimination _____

        _____

        _____

    D. Are you currently employed? _____

    E. Name of immediate supervisor _____

    F. Name of other supervisors/management staff _____

        _____

        _____

G. Who makes decisions as to promotions/demotions/terminations?

_____

_____

H. Have you filed a grievance or has there been an internal review of your complaint? _____

I. Why do you think you were terminated/laid-off/denied promotion?

_____

_____

_____

_____

J. What were the reasons given to you for termination/demotion/denied promotion? _____

_____

_____

_____

K. Were others terminated/demoted/denied promotion? Yes _____ No _____

Name	Address	Phone	Position
_____	_____	_____	_____
_____	_____	_____	_____
_____	_____	_____	_____
_____	_____	_____	_____

L. Were you evaluated on job performance? Yes_____ No _____

By whom? _____

How often?_____

M. Are other handicapped persons/disabled veterans/Vietnam era
veterans employed by the contractor? YES _____ NO _____.

14. If complainant was an applicant for employment and was not hired,
ask the following questions:

A. For what type of job did you apply? _____

B. Why weren't you hired? _____

C. Who told you that you were not going to be hired? _____

D. What reasons did this person give for your being rejected for
employment? _____

_____

E. Were you advised by the employer that they are an affirmative
action employer? _____

F. Did you observe the poster entitled "Equal Employment Opportunity
is the Law"? _____

15. Do you have a complaint filed elsewhere on this matter? _____

Where? _____ When did you file? _____

16. Since you were discriminated against, what have you done to resolve
the complaint? _____

17. Were you given a physical exam? _____ By whom? _____

18. Were you given an opportunity to demonstrate ability to do the job?

_____ How were you treated? _____

Did you suggest accommodations? _____

What was the company's reaction? _____

_____

_____

19. What is your work experience? (jobs held; times)

Job	Dates	Duties
_____	_____	_____
_____	_____	_____
_____	_____	_____

20. What kind of training do you have? _____

21. Were you in the military service? YES _____   NO _____

    Type of work you did in the military? _____

22. What specifically would you like this office to do for you?

    _____

    _____

23. Do you have any questions/comments? _____

    _____

    _____

    _____

_____   _____
(Signature of Complainant)   (Date)

_____   _____
(Signature of Investigator)   (Date)

U.S. DEPARTMENT OF LABOR
EMPLOYMENT STANDARDS ADMINISTRATION
Office of Federal Contract Compliance Programs
WASHINGTON, D.C. 20210

INTERVIEW OF CONTRACTOR'S PERSONNEL STAFF

The following interview format is to serve as a guide for developing
a minimum data base for processing a complaint. This format is to
be used as a tool for interviewing the contractor's personnel staff.

1. NAME _____

    ADDRESS _____

    _____ TELEPHONE _____

2. How long have you been employed by the contractor? _____

3. What is your job title? _____

    a) Educational background _____

    b) Are you aware of your employer's obligations under the
       Handicapped Workers Program and Veterans Program? _____

4. What definition of handicapped person/disabled veteran/Vietnam

    era veteran do you use in your personnel practice?_____

    _____

5. Who, if anyone, from the company has attended a meeting or

    discussed affirmative action as related to the handicapped

    with you?_____

6. Was the list of company's vacant positions available to you

    prior to the interview of ___(complainant)___ ? _____

7. Did you know the physical requirements for job vacancies prior to interviewing job applicants? _____

8. Does the job application contain information about the applicant's physical/mental condition/veteran status? _____

—————————————————————————————   ————————————————
Signature of Investigator   (Date)

U.S. DEPARTMENT OF LABOR
EMPLOYMENT STANDARDS ADMINISTRATION
Office of Federal Contract Compliance Programs
WASHINGTON, D.C. 20210

QUESTIONNAIRE FOR PERSON DOING AAP REVIEW

1. If required, is there a written Affirmative Action Plan? _____

2. What is the name of executive for AAP? _____

3. Is personnel office accessible to handicapped applicants and
    employees? _____

4. Are there ramps or equipment which have been modified? _____

5. Is a notice posted in a conspicious place entitled "Equal
    Opportunity is the Law"? _____

Prior to asking the questions, request that the AAP policy be

specifically shown to you.

_____   _____
Signature of Investigator   Date

U.S. DEPARTMENT OF LABOR
EMPLOYMENT STANDARDS ADMINISTRATION
Office of Federal Contract Compliance Programs
WASHINGTON, D.C. 20210

NAME _____   TELEPHONE _____

ADDRESS _____

I. GENERAL RESPONSIBILITIES OF CONTRACTOR

1. How many known qualified handicapped persons/veterans have

    been employed from _____ to _____?

    (Name, job title, date of employment, salary and handicap)

    _____

    _____

    _____

2. How many known qualified handicapped persons/veterans have

    you advanced in employment between _____

    to _____?

    (Name, job title, date of advancement, and handicap)

    _____

    _____

    _____

3. What personnel staff were selected and are they aware of the

    requirements of the Handicapped Workers Program/Veterans

    Program? _____

    _____

NAME _____   TELEPHONE _____

ADDRESS _____

4. Have you notified subcontractors, vendors and suppliers of
   their affirmative action requirements?_____

5. How are known handicapped persons/veterans represented in
   company activities? _____
   Evidence _____
   _____
   _____

6. Does the union contract contain non-discrimination clauses?
   _____
   Evidence _____
   _____
   _____

_____   _____
Signature of Interviewer   Date

NAME _____   TELEPHONE _____

ADDRESS _____

II.   EXECUTIVE MANAGEMENT OF AFFIRMATIVE ACTION POLICY

    7.   Who is the executive manager of affirmative action

       activities? _____

       Does the manager have final decision making authority?.

       _____

    8.   What support and support services are provided to the

       Executive Manager for affirmative action? (Document and

       name persons). _____

       _____

       _____

       _____

    9.   Has the manager communicated scope and methods of AAP

       internally?_____

       a) How?_____

       _____

       b) How often?_____

       c) To whom?

    10. Has the manager communicated scope and methods of AAP

       outside of the company? _____

       a) How? _____

       _____

NAME _____   ADDRESS _____   TELEPHONE _____

b) How often?_____

_____

c) To Whom? _____

_____

11. Has the manager designed and implemented AAP audit and reporting system

for evaluations and corrective action? _____

_____

a) What kind of a system was designed? _____

_____

b) When was the system implemented? _____

_____

c) What corrective action has been taken as a result of the system?

Document _____

_____

_____

_____

12. Is the manager liaison between contractor and enforcement agencies?

Evidence _____

_____

_____

_____

13. Is the manager liaison between contractor and handicapped/veteran

organization? _____

_____

14. Does the manager or manager's staff:

a) Offer career counseling for all handicapped employees/veterans?

_____

NAME _____   TELEPHONE _____

ADDRESS _____

III. RECRUITMENT

15. What is your policy on recruitment to ensure affirmative
     action for qualified handicapped persons/veterans? _____

     _____

     _____

     _____

16. How do you inform applicants of your commitment to AAP?

     _____

     _____

17. What recruiting and training sources have been informed of
     AAP and with whom have you established working relationships?
     Be specific, give names and verify, if possible. _____

     _____

     _____

     _____

     _____

18. With what rehabilitation agencies or Veterans Administration
     facilities have you established contacts, and from whom
     do you seek technical assistance and advice? _____

     _____

     _____

NAME _____   TELEPHONE _____

ADDRESS _____

19. Are your personnel officers provided with job descriptions
    to assist in recruiting handicapped persons/veterans?

    _____

20. In what company activities do the handicapped employees
    and/or veteran employees participate? For evidence, inter-
    view a handicapped person/veteran _____

    _____

21. With what rehabilitation/Veterans Administration facilities
    and schools do you participate in work-study programs and
    on-the-job training? Specify names; document _____

    _____

    _____

    _____

IV. INTERNAL COMMUNICATIONS

22. How do you communicate your AAP and individual responsibilities
    to employees? _____

    _____

Name of Interviewee

Signature of Interviewer   _____
                                                    Date

NAME _____   TELEPHONE _____

ADDRESS _____

V.   ACCOMMODATIONS

   23.   Have you made reasonable accommodations for handicapped

         employees/veteran employees?_____

         _____

         a) Names, dates, job titles, accommodations _____

         _____

         _____

   24.   What is your policy on medical inquiries of individuals?

         _____

         _____

         a) Have you made such inquiries and under what circumstances?
             Give specifics of such instances.

             _____

             _____

         b) Do you have any across-the-board rules such as no

             diabetics, no persons with history of cancer, etc.?

             _____

         c) Have any handicapped/veteran applicants or employees

             requested additional accommodations which you have not

             implemented?_____

             What are they?_____

NAME _____   TELEPHONE _____

ADDRESS _____

VI. PUBLICATIONS

    25. Is AAP included in company policy manual, posted on

         bulletin boards, publicized in company newspapers,

         magazines, etc? Evidence _____

         _____

    26. Are both handicapped employees and non-handicapped

         employees pictured in public information activities,

         such as advertising? Evidence _____

         _____

         _____

Date documents requested are to be submitted to OFCCP office:

_____

Signature of Interviewer   Date

NAME _____   TELEPHONE _____

ADDRESS _____

    1. Evidence of counseling program - how is it communicated

        to handicapped persons/veterans that such a program exists?

        _____

        _____

    2. Who has received such counseling between _____

        to_____

b) Evaluate training programs, hiring and promotion patterns to

    ensure that affirmative action is on-going.

    Evidence _____

    _____

c) Evaluate each subsidiary as to their compliance to affirmative

    action _____

    _____

    1. How many locations are there? _____

    2. Does each location have an AAP? _____

        Evidence

    _____

d) Inform supervisors that their work is evaluated on the basis of

    other AAP efforts and results. Evidence _____

    _____

Signature of Interviewer   _____
                                                  Date

U.S. DEPARTMENT OF LABOR
EMPLOYMENT STANDARDS ADMINISTRATION
Office of Federal Contract Compliance Programs
WASHINGTON, D.C. 20210

SAMPLE LETTER OF SETTLEMENT

The following is a sample settlement letter which may be used as a prenotification settlement agreement, or a settlement agreement after successful conciliation. Appropriate clauses are to be selected and included to cover the specific situation.

CERTIFIED

Dear _____(Contractor)_____ :

This is to confirm that on _____(date)_____ , _____(contractor)_____ and [EOS (Handicapped/Veteran)] , Employment Opportunity Specialist (Handicapped/Veteran), United States Department of Labor agreed to settle the complaint of __(complainant)__ against _____(contractor)_____ alleging a violation of the Affirmative Action clause in your Federal contract required by Section 503 of the Rehabilitation Act of 1973, as amended / Section 402 of the Vietnam Era Veterans' Readjustment Assistance Act of 1974. The terms and conditions of agreement are as follows:

1. Lost Back Wages: Contractor agrees to reimburse the complainant, _____(name)_____ , in the amount of $_____ , less legal deductions. This amount is the pay complainant would have earned if he/she had been employed by the contractor on _____(date)_____ through _____(date)_____ . Complainant was offered and accepted employment with the contractor to commence

on _____(date)_____, but the offer was withdrawn prior to commencement of employment because of _____

_____

2. Expungement of Unsatisfactory Entries from Personnel Records:
    The contractor agrees to remove from its personnel records and
    files any notations, remarks or other indications indicating that
    the complainant was rejected from employment for medical reasons.

    The contractor further agrees that in furnishing verbal or written
    references concerning the complainant, as may be requested by the
    complainant or by prospective future employers, the contractor will
    exclude all reference to his rejection and the events and judgments
    connected with it.

In further consideration of said payment, _____(contractor)_____ agrees
as follows:

1. The aforementioned payment of the sum of $_____ is the entire
    and only consideration for this settlement agreement.

2. This settlement is the result of a compromise and shall never at
    any time, for any purpose, be considered an admission of liability
    or responsibility on the part of the parties herein.

For and in consideration of the aforesaid payment, the U.S. Department
of Labor hereby accepts this Agreement for the purpose of making a full
adjustment and settlement of any and all claims arising out of the filing

of a complaint by ___(complainant)_____

Sincerely,

_____
Signature of ARA or Designee

I have read the provisions set forth above and they completely and
accurately reflect our agreement to resolve this complaint. As to the
rights under the Rehabilitation Act of 1973, as amended, under 29 USC 701
(et seq) / Vietnam Era Veterans' Readjustment Assistance Act of 1974
under Title 38 USC.

_____   _____
Signature of Contractor   Date

_____
Title

___(Complainaint)_____ has read this agreement and fully understands
it and has voluntarily accepted it.

_____   _____
Signature of Complainant   Date

_____   _____
Signature of ARA or Designee   Date

cc: National Office/VHWPOD

Complainant Disability Code _____

MODEL CLAUSES

(A) Failure or Refusal to Hire Clauses

1. Immediate Employment of Complainant. Contractor agrees to offer immediate employment to the complainant in the position of ___(job title)___ at a pay rate of $_____. This offer will be in writing by certified letter, return receipt requested. Within ten (10) days after receipt of this offer, the complainant shall accept it or notify contractor that the contractor's offer of employment is declined.

2. Back Pay. Contractor agrees to reimburse the complainant in the amount of $_____. This amount is the pay complainant would have earned, minus interim earnings, if the complainant had been employed by the contractor during the period between the date of rejection and the expiration of the ten day period provided to enable complainant to accept contractor's offer of employment, minus legal and payroll deductions.

3. Fringe Benefits and Retroactive Seniority. Contractor agrees to make those contributions and adjustments that would have been made to complainant's group life insurance plan, company savings plan, retirement or pension plan, other fringe benefits that would have accrued if the complainant had been hired at the time when the complainant was rejected, and will adjust complainant's

seniority to that which would have occurred if hired at the time of rejection.

4. <u>Affirmative Performance Report</u>. Contractor agrees that on _____ (date) _____, it will provide to __(name of investigator)__ a report on its offer of employment to the complainant, the manner in which back pay was made, and the restoration of seniority and fringe benefits. The report will include as attachments photocopies of the contractor's letter offering employment to the complainant, the certified mail return receipt signed by the complainant, and other relevant documents.

(B) <u>Failure to Promote Clauses</u>

1. <u>Promote Complainant</u>. Contractor agrees to promote immediately the complainant to the position of _____ (job title) _____ at a pay rate of $_____ or to a position comparable in pay, duties and benefits which is acceptable to the complainant.

2. <u>Back Pay</u>. Contractor agrees to reimburse the complainant in the amount of $_____. This amount is the difference between the pay earned by the complainant and the pay which the complainant should have earned if he (or she) had been promoted on __(date)__, minus payroll and legal deductions.

3. <u>Fringe Benefits and Retroactive Seniority</u>. Contractor agrees to make those contributions and adjustments which would have been

made to complainant's group life insurance, company savings
plan, retirement or pension plan and other fringe benefits and
will adjust complainant's seniority to that which would have
accrued if the complainant had been promoted on ___(date)___.

4. Affirmative Performance Report. Contractor agrees that
by ___(date)___, it will provide to _(name of investigator)_
a report describing which positions were offered and which
position the complainant accepted, the back pay granted, and
describing the manner in which the adjustment of seniority and
fringe benefit was made. The report shall include as attachments
copies of the normal documentation associated with these transactions.

(C) Discharge Case Clauses

1. Reinstatement of Complainant. Contractor agrees to reinstate
immediately the complainant as an employee in good standing
without loss of seniority.

2. Back Pay. Contractor will reimburse in the amount of $_____.
This is the amount complainant would have earned, minus interim
earnings, but for the contractor's dismissal during the period
between the date of discharge and the date of reinstatement,
minus legal deductions.

3. Fringe Benefits and Retroactive Seniority. Contractor agrees to make those contributions and adjustments that would normally have been made to the complainant's group life insurance plan, company savings plan, retirement or pension plan and other fringe benefits, and will restore to the complainant seniority rights and to that which would have accrued had the complainant not been dismissed.

4. Expungement of Unsatisfactory Entries from Personnel Records. The contractor agrees to remove from its records and files any notations, remarks, or other indications indicating that the service performed by the complainant prior to the determination, and in connection with the determination, were other than, or anything less than, satisfactory.   The contractor further agrees that, in furnishing verbal or written references concerning the complainant, as may be requested by the complainant or by prospective future employers, the contractor will exclude all reference to this discharge and the events and judgments connected with it.

U.S. DEPARTMENT OF LABOR
EMPLOYMENT STANDARDS ADMINISTRATION
Office of Federal Contract Compliance Programs
WASHINGTON, D.C. 20210

LETTER TO CONTRACTOR REGARDING ACCESS TO RECORDS

In those instances when access to records is denied by the contractor, the following letter is to be used to inform the contractor of the provisions of the regulations.

Re:

Dear _____ (Contractor) _____:

In response to your letter in which you refuse access to the requested medical/personnel information, I would like to call your attention to part 60-741.53 of the provisions of the regulations governing Section 503 of the Rehabilitation Act of 1973, as amended,/ part 60-250.53 of the provisions of the regulations governing Section 402 of the Vietnam Era Veterans' Readjustment Assistance Act of 1974, "access to records of employment," which states:

> ". . .Each prime contractor and subcontractor shall permit access during normal business hours, books, records and accounts pertinent to compliance with the Act, and all rules and regulations promulgated pursuant thereto for the purpose of complaint investigations of performance under the affirmative action clause of the contract or subcontract. Information obtained in this manner shall be used only in connection with the administration of the Act."

You may be assured that this information furnished will be treated confidentially.

Sincerely,

_____
Signature of ARA or Designee

Part Two
Compliance

4
Accessibility and Mainstreaming

As federal contractors or subcontractors, subject to Section 503 and Section 402 requirements of the two federal laws discussed in Chapter 1, or as recipients of federal financial assistance subject to Section 504 requirements, employers are required to make their facilities accessible to the handicapped. By "mainstreaming" the handicapped individual, the employer is fulfilling his obligation to integrate the handicapped person into the workforce and the workplace. Providing separate or segregated facilities which may or may not be equal is discouraged. However, the mainstreaming requirements of the above laws do not mean that the entire workplace must be accessible, but only those areas used by handicapped employees.

Because of close scrutiny by OFCCP and activist organizations, the subtle as well as the more blatant or obvious forms of discrimination against handicapped persons must be dealt with by employers, whether or not the discrimination is unintentional. A few years ago, a new bank building received an award for barrier-free design. Everyone seemed pleased, including the architect, with the impressive structure. Then someone noticed that there was no curb cut leading from the bank's parking lot to the sidewalk, thereby preventing wheelchair-bound individuals from using the bank's facilities. This oversight emphasizes the need for employers to look at the entire access system of their facilities and not just the individual elements. One way to achieve this "panoramic" viewpoint is to carefully "walk through" the entire sequence of activities of a particular handicapped worker or applicant during a typical day. There is no shortcut to achieving the reasonable-accommodation requirements of the law; hasty decisions to modify facilities, even though well intentioned, could have a long-term deleterious effect.

Generally speaking, the American National Standards Institute (ANSI) guidelines for making facilities accessible should be followed. However, the ANSI standards are undergoing revision, and there is considerable discussion on the application of alternative guidelines that are more creative and flexible, as discussed later in this chapter. For example, employers should take a careful look at state building codes as an alternative to ANSI guidelines. Copies of state codes can normally be secured through governors' committees on the handicapped (see Appendix H for listing).

While professionals are debating the finer points of the law, most experts in the field agree that an employer can take fairly clear-cut steps if he wants to comply with federal regulations specifying the establishment of a "barrier-free" work environment with "reasonable accommodation" to the handicapped. Employers have been shocked by stories of the phenomenal expenses they will face in making facilities accessible. At the same time, activist organizations representing the handicapped have claimed that accessibility expenses will be nominal. The General Accounting Office estimates that, in new building construction, accessibility features may cost as little as .1 percent of total construction expense. The experience of one large corporation is relevant, since the cost of making its new $30 million headquarters building accessible was only $10,500. Another large corporation was told by its engineers that modification of its headquarters would cost $160,000 if accessibility according to federal standards was to be achieved. Outside consultants, however, showed the corporation how the alterations could be made for less than $8,000. In the final analysis, though, the desire to pay for accommodations or the urge to resist another federal government regulation will have no bearing on the obligation to do so.

In actuality, specific worker accommodations can be made by the employer only on an individual basis, whereas general accessibility, such as installing curb cuts or parking spaces for the handicapped, can be achieved for all classes of handicapped persons. For example, someone with a leg brace might be allowed to park in an area close to the building normally designated as executive parking, or someone visually impaired might be assigned to the day rather than the night shift.

Key Definitions

Practical considerations must be taken into account when an employer sets about making his facilities accessible to handicapped workers and applicants. The following definitions will help employers in their accessibility planning.

Accessible refers to those facilities which may be entered or used by individuals despite handicapping conditions; employers must respond to the needs of workers with sight or hearing disabilities as well as those with manual or mobility impairments.

Barrier-free refers to the complete removal, elimination, or avoidance of those elements in the workplace that are obstacles to the handicapped worker's full and free use of the environment.

Readily accessible refers to providing access for handicapped workers that is substantially equivalent in terms of ease and convenience of use to that afforded the able-bodied employee.

Reasonable accommodation refers to the adaptation of the work environment, schedules, or requirements so as to accommodate the known physical or mental limitations of a handicapped applicant or employee. Accommodations could include job restructuring, part-time or modified work schedules, acquisition or modification of equipment or devices, and the providing of readers and interpreters.

Usable refers to those parts of the environment that can be used or operated by individuals with physical or sensory limitations.

Whom Does an Employer Need to Accommodate?

The employer's central concern will be with accommodating the needs of four basic types of handicapped persons or disabled veterans: (1) wheelchair-bound people, (2) people on crutches, (3) blind people, and (4) people with a hearing impairment. Many employers have simply not been exposed to the wide range of impairments which qualify a person legally as a handicapped employee or applicant. The following definitions should prove helpful.

Temporary impairments encompass fractures, pregnancy, and convalescence from disease, trauma, or surgery (including recovering from injuries resulting from carrying or moving large or heavy loads).

Activity impairments encompass heart, lung, or neurological diseases, forms of arthritis or rheumatism, and extremes of size and weight due to dwarfism and obesity.

Semiambulatory mobility impairments encompass difficulties in walking, climbing, bending, or similar activities (that is, impairments necessitating crutches, canes, walkers, braces, artificial limbs, or orthopedic shoes).

Nonambulatory mobility impairments encompass confinement to a wheelchair either all or part of the time.

Manual impairments encompass either partial or total loss of manual dexterity in one or both hands.

Visual impairments encompass color blindness, loss of sight in one eye, cataracts, ophthalmologic diseases, or total loss of vision.

Hearing impairments encompass partial loss of hearing or total deafness.

Aging impairments encompass any of the disabling conditions identified above.

Codes and Ordinances

Building codes and regulations can be promulgated by a number of government bodies. As discussed in Chapter 5, even the Internal Renevue Service has established construction or renovation guidelines which employers accommodating the handicapped must adhere to if they wish to qualify for tax credits. Codes either prescribe the kinds of materials and construction permitted or set forth specific standards of performance (for example, load limits and fire resistance).

Local building codes are normally tied to a series of adjunct codes for such things as electrical and plumbing requirements. Whereas large cities often adopt their own codes, smaller communities have been known to follow their state's code. The variety of approaches which can be taken by local governments makes it necessary for an employer to be well versed in the local regulations when facilities are constructed, leased, or renovated.

The City of Chicago promulgated its own building code, with enforcement authority held by the Commissioner of Buildings. Amendments to the Chicago code have emphasized the need to make *existing* structures barrier-free. For example, if a building in Chicago exceeding 15,000 square feet in size undergoes renovation, the structure must be made totally barrier-free *if* the cost of the renovation is more than 50 percent of the building's original cost. Additional amendments to the Chicago code are expected to strengthen the accessibility rights of handicapped citizens.

At the state level, increasingly stringent requirements are being placed on the private sector to make facilities barrier-free. In Massachusetts, an architectural barriers board with the authority to write and enforce its own regulations for new buildings was created in 1974. If an addition to a building exceeds 20 percent of the floor area of the initial building, the *entire* structure must be made barrier-free. Once the board sets forth regulations, they automatically become a part of the Massachusetts state code.

The authority of the Massachusetts board supersedes all less stringent codes in the state. The board can even enforce its regulations by instituting court action. Regulations apply to "privately financed buildings that are open to and used by the public." This definition is broad enough to cover commercial buildings of more than two stories where more than 40 persons are employed, buildings with an assembly capacity of more than 150 persons, hotels and motels, and other commonly frequented facilities for the general public.

Clearly, employers must be keenly aware of a variety of local, state, and federal codes when the option to construct or renovate a facility is entertained.

Adapting the Building

Next to revamping personnel practices and recruitment policies, adapting facilities to the handicapped employee or applicant is the most important requirement for employers under federal law. When designing and constructing new facilities, it is essential to begin with a complete awareness of the needs of the handicapped.

The phrase "mainstreaming" is often used in discussions about accessibility; it refers to bringing the handicapped person into the major work and traffic flow of the facilities. Employers should avoid the tendency to make special accommodations for the handicapped person, since accessibility modifications should allow handicapped persons to work next to and use the same facilities as other workers.

As mentioned earlier, and much to the surprise of some employers, independent studies have shown that adapting facilities to the handicapped need not necessarily be an expensive proposition. For example, Mainstream, Inc., of Washington, D.C., completed a study of 45 diverse facilities, which indicated that the cost of accessibility through the removal of architectural barriers could average 5¢ per square foot. Mainstream compared this cost with the annual cost of cleaning and polishing floors—13¢ per square foot. The American Mutual Insurance Alliance Fund has found that barrier-free buildings can be insured at lower rates. It has even been estimated that businesses can reduce workers' compensation benefits because barrier-free facilities produce fewer slip-and-fall accidents.

Even if the myths about the tremendous expense faced in achieving accessibility can be stripped away, it is only prudent for employers to establish priorities in adapting facilities to the handicapped. Generally speaking, the following are considered essential to minimum accessibility:

Building access through a primary public entrance, including parking and other site accommodations.

Primary use access to such facilities as offices and meeting rooms, including vertical access in multilevel buildings.

Convenience and support access to such facilities as toilet rooms, water fountains, and public telephones.

For the cost-conscious employer, meeting the accessibility requirements will be considered in terms of creative space management rather than (as some believe it must) expensive modifications to the entire facility.

In determining the kinds of accommodations to be made, employers should consider the following:

Purposes for which the facilities are used.

Labor force turnover.

Climate.

Location of the population served.

Attitude of management toward accommodation.

Future growth and expansion plans.

Availability of alternative facilities.

Although several federal agencies have referred to the American National Standards Institute (ANSI) guidelines (ANSI 117.1) on accessibility design criteria, and although the ANSI guidelines are even cited in some compliance regulations, there is considerable debate among experts over the wholesale adoption of these guidelines by employers. For one thing, the ANSI guidelines are thought to be antiquated. For another, they have proved at times to be wasteful and expensive, particularly if followed verbatim.

If employers contemplate the use of ANSI guidelines, they should do so with considerable caution. Alternative building codes can be used to develop equally viable accessibility plans. An architect trained in the area of accessibility, along with other experts, should be consulted in developing a thorough and responsive accessibility plan, particularly when stringent state and local building-code demands must be balanced with federal requirements. Handicapped individuals and their organizations can also be of assistance in identifying barriers and suggesting ways for their removal.

Establishing Priorities

Unquestionably, employers must establish priorities in every phase of their affirmative action program for the handicapped. The accessibility effort is no exception. Some adjustments, such as to personnel offices, should be made immediately, since they affect the hiring process—a key area of concern in the overall compliance picture. In the view of many, inaccessibility to a personnel office is prima facie evidence of discrimination, since the handicapped job seeker cannot even fill out an application form. In terms of long-range planning (for example, when considering the modification of the physical plant for growth or remodeling purposes), employers should be particularly alert to the accessibility requirements; if they're not, barriers to the handicapped may very well be erected inadvertently, and those barriers will have to be removed later at considerable expense.

Before any employer can determine what accommodations to make, a basic understanding of the needs of handicapped applicants and workers is paramount. Although wheelchair-bound individuals are only one category of disabled, the Office of Federal Contract Compliance Programs (OFCCP) points out the particular restrictions these persons face at the normal workplace. If an employer intends to make parking spaces, entrances, doors, corridors, and other areas accessible, as discussed shortly, then the dimensions of a typical adult-size wheelchair shown in Figure 4-1 should be taken into account.

What actual expenses have employers faced in making their facilities partially or wholly accessible to the handicapped? One of Mainstream, Inc.'s surveys conducted at a clothing manufacturing plant provides a good example. The facility was approximately 290,000 square feet. Five hundred people were employed. According to Mainstream, almost all the architectural barriers discovered were in the rear half of the plant and in the parking areas.

The plant had four identical production lines with jobs in the

Figure 4-1. A typical adult-size wheelchair.

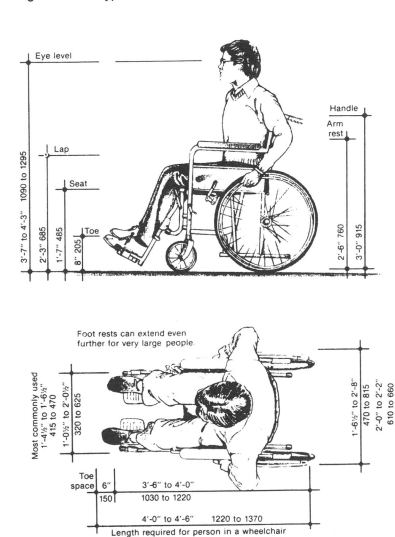

Reprinted from *Office of Federal Contract Compliance Veterans and Handicapped Workers Training Workbook,* Washington, D.C.: U.S. Department of Labor, Employment Standards Administration, May 1979.

back of the plant paralleling those in the front. Therefore, it was determined that accessibility along with equal employment opportunity requirements could be achieved in the front of the plant by assigning employees with disabilities to this area. Recommendations made to ensure that the front half of the plant would be totally accessible resulted in espenses of approximately $4,000 according to Mainstream. Broken down by item, these expenses included:

$ 490   for accessible parking

$2,020   to modify bathrooms

$ 20   to adjust door closers

$ 20   to lower a pay telephone

$ 30   to lower a drinking fountain in the cafeteria

In addition, the preparation of a life safety plan and the installation of a tactile warning system (that is, doors to hazardous areas were identified and then locked to prevent inadvertent entry by visually impaired workers) were estimated to cost nothing. Additional recommendations were made to ensure long-range accessibility. However, the Mainstream recommendations described above resulted in a cost to the employer of just 1½ cents per square foot.

Below are some specific guidelines for employers to follow in creating an accessible system for handicapped employees and applicants. The items discussed are generally accepted as those to which an employer should give immediate priority.

Parking. Employers should try to provide parking spaces for the handicapped with a minimum width of 12 feet and as close as possible to accessible building entrances. There should be a level aisle area next to the parking space approximately four feet wide, giving the handicapped person with a wheelchair, for instance, room to get into or out of the vehicle. To prevent the aisle from being blocked, it should be marked clearly "for handicapped use only."

Two normal parking spaces can be combined to create one handicapped space with an aisle. Three consecutive spaces can be

Figure 4-2. A typical parking space for the handicapped with curb cuts to walkway.

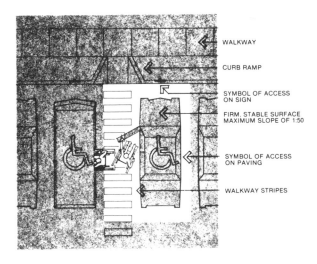

WALKWAY

CURB RAMP

SYMBOL OF ACCESS
ON SIGN

FIRM, STABLE SURFACE
MAXIMUM SLOPE OF 1:50

SYMBOL OF ACCESS
ON PAVING

WALKWAY STRIPES

Reprinted from *Job Ready*, prepared by the Easter Seal Society of Washington for the State Division of Vocational Rehabilitation. Reproduced by permission of the Easter Seal Society of Washington.

utilized to create two handicapped spaces with a common aisle in the middle. Spaces should be marked with the symbol of access (shown later in Figure 4-9).

Curb cuts. Once out of his vehicle, the handicapped person needs convenient access to the walkway and building. Therefore, curbs in the route of travel will need curb cuts at least 4 feet wide or curb ramps that are marked so as to prevent obstruction. In designing curb cuts, employers should make sure that they don't interfere with normal traffic or drainage. The American Association of Architectural Standards has estimated the cost of a curb cut at approximately $150. See Figure 4-2 for a typical parking space with curb cuts accessible to the walkway.

Walkways. To avoid creating undue hazards for the handicapped person, smooth and level walks with a nonslip surface are essential. To prevent wheelchair tires and crutch or walker tips from being trapped, joints or gratings in walks should be no more than one-half inch in size. On walks with slopes, handrails which extend beyond the ends of the slopes should be provided on each side. Consideration should be given to removing benches, trash containers, or other objects that might impede the movement of the handicapped person.

Ramps. Since many handicapped people have obvious difficulties with stairs, employers will want to consider the installation of ramps in making facilities accessible to the handicapped. Whereas straight-run ramps are most convenient to the handicapped person, space limitations may be a deterrent. In this case, switchback or L-shape ramps can be installed (see Figure 4-3). With the latter two ramps, level rest areas should be provided at each turn, preferably at intervals of not more than 30 feet.

Every effort should be made to minimize the slope of ramps (preferably not to exceed 1:12). Handrails should be provided on one or both sides at least 32 inches above the ramp surface and extending 12 inches beyond the top and bottom of the ramp. A level landing area at entrance doors should be provided with all ramps to permit a person in a wheelchair to maneuver without slipping back on the slope of the ramp.

As an alternative to installing ramps, employers may want to consider:

Regrading the approach area to make the ground area level with the entrance.
Wheelchair lifts.
Converting a window to an entrance.
Creating a new door.

Entrances. In general, employers should have one primary entrance which is accessible and connects with a route of travel that leads to all accessible space in the building. Special attention should be given to the removal of obstacles such as stairs and escalators that might block the proposed access route. Where possible,

Figure 4-3. Switchback and L-shaped ramps.

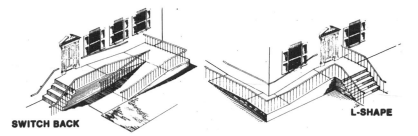

SWITCH BACK   L-SHAPE

Reprinted from Ronald L. Mace, Accessibility Modifications, Raleigh, N.C.: Special Office for the Handicapped. Department of Insurance, 1976. Reproduced by permission.

nonslip surfaces should be provided. Preferably, building entrances will be at ground level to allow for free passage of wheelchairs.

Doors. Doors should, quite obviously, be easy for the handicapped person to open and close—with one hand. Minimum width for a door is 32 inches when open, with double doors 32 inches wide for each side.

For manually operated doors, lever or push-type handles are most convenient. However, power doors are most accessible. Employers should try to avoid using revolving doors or turnstiles, particularly as the sole means of access to the building or work area.

Exterior door closers should not require more than eight and one-half pounds of pressure to open, while interior door closers should require no more than five pounds of pressure.

With an outswinging door, the approach should provide approximately 24 inches of clear space on the latch side to allow the person in a wheelchair to pull up beside the door and swing it open without having to back up. See Figure 4-4 for adequate door access.

Minor door adjustments can be made to aid the handicapped person and keep costs to a minimum. For instance, employers can:

■ Widen a door by removing the stop, altering the door jamb, or installing offset (hospital-type) hinges.

Figure 4-4. Door access for a wheelchair-bound person.

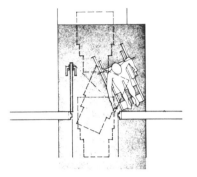

Reprinted from *Job Ready.*

- Adjust door closer pressure.
- Remove the closer or replace it with a light-pressure model.
- Add an auxiliary handle on the inside to assist the handicapped person in closing the door after departure.
- Paint the door or frame with a contrasting color to facilitate identification by the visually impaired.
- Lock doors leading to hazardous areas.

Floors. All floors should be level with a smooth, slip-resistant surface. Avoid thick carpets and mats. If floors are to be carpeted, employers should choose a firm, hard-surface carpet with tight weave and low pile. The carpet and the mat must be fastened down securely. Where the level of the floor changes, installation of a ramp or wheelchair lift may be necessary. Tactile floor signals and warning systems may be appropriate where there are serious hazards.

Thresholds. Thresholds should be no higher than one-half inch and have beveled (sloping) edges—if they cannot be removed. Thresholds with abrupt edges (for example, those leading into toilet rooms with ceramic tile floors) should either be replaced with sloped thresholds or removed entirely. See the accompanying figure (reproduced from *Accessibility Modifications)* for adapting existing thresholds.

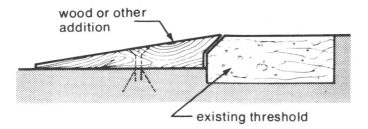

wood or other addition

existing threshold

Corridors. Corridors and hallways should be at least 36 inches wide. A width of 60 inches is needed to allow a wheelchair to turn around or to permit two wheelchairs to pass simultaneously.

Objects hanging lower than 80 inches from walls or ceilings into the corridor space should be removed, as they present hazards to those with visual impairments.

If hallways cannot be widened, employers should consider improving accessibility by removing obstacles such as drinking fountains, vending machines, and trash cans.

Elevators. Elevators are needed by handicapped persons for access between floors. Controls and emergency call equipment should be no higher than 48 inches from the floor.

To indicate arrival and direction of the elevator, visible and audible signals should be provided. Tactile markings with standard alphabet as well as arabic numerals should be placed next to call and floor buttons. Some employers will want to consider the addition of braille markings. Tactile floor markings should be affixed on each doorjamb at each floor. Handrails at a height of 32 inches should be provided on three sides of the elevator.

In modifying elevators, employers may also want to consider:

- Placing additional controls at a lower level if existing controls cannot be moved.
- Applying tactile markings to existing elevator control panels.
- Constructing an elevator shaft outside and abutting an exterior wall.
- Constructing a free-standing elevator connected to the building by bridges.

Stairs. To reduce tripping hazards for persons using crutches or similar walking aids, stairs should have a nonskid surface with uniform riser heights and tread widths. Exterior stairs should be lit for nighttime use. Risers should be closed and tread nosings should be gently sloped. If possible, circular or oval handrails one and three-quarters to two inches thick should be placed where they can be grasped easily on both sides of the stairways, with 12-inch extensions at the top as well as the bottom. See the accompanying figure for suggested handrails. (Reproduced from *Job Ready.*)

As illustrated below, square nosings on existing stairs can be modified by taking fillers to the face of the risers. (Reproduced from *Accessibility Modifications.*)

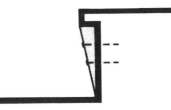

Toilet rooms. At least one wide stall in each toilet room should be completely accessible to the handicapped person. Turning-space clearance of 42 inches should be provided where privacy screens are installed. Within the toilet room, a 60-square-inch area should be provided to permit a wheelchair user to turn and exit facing forward.

Mirrors, dispensers, and other equipment in the toilet room

Figure 4-5. Alternative toilet-stall modifications.

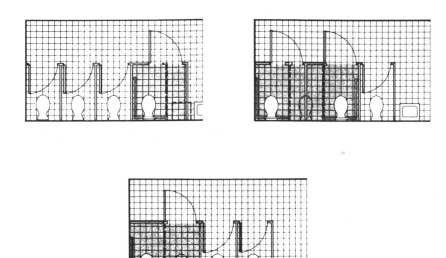

Reprinted from Job Ready.

should be installed so that their lower edges are not in excess of 40 inches from the floor. There should be at least one lavatory which permits wheelchair clearance beneath the apron. Where possible, lever handles should be installed on water faucets.

People who are insensitive to heat because they have lost feelings in their legs or other appendages can easily burn themselves without knowing it. Therefore, water supply and waste pipes should be insulated, particularly when the water temperature may exceed 110 degrees Fahrenheit.

Toilet stalls should have outswinging doors with a minimum clearance of 32 inches. Maneuverability is important within the stall and should allow for side as well as front transfer. Bars should be hung adjacent to and behind the toilet to facilitate the frontal as well as the side approach. Figure 4-5 shows how existing stalls can be altered to accommodate the wheelchair user.

Figure 4-6. Private toilet rooms.

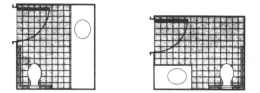

Reprinted from *Job Ready*.

Single toilet rooms should have a 60-square-inch clear floor area to ensure wheelchair maneuverability, as illustrated in Figure 4-6.

Drinking fountains. Fountains should be low enough (30 inches is recommended) for use by people in wheelchairs. Fountains shouldn't be placed in narrow alcoves. If the unit is recessed in an alcove, then the control and spout should project a minimum of 2 inches beyond the adjacent walls. The controls and the spout of the fountain should be placed at the front, and water should spout parallel with the front face of the fountain. Controls should be either hand or hand/foot. To avoid hazards to blind workers, employers should locate fountains so that they do *not* project into the corridor. If fountains are too high, employers should consider installing a paper cup dispenser at a point no higher than 40 inches. A typical fountain installed with the handicapped worker in mind is shown in Figure 4-7.

Public telephones. A row of telephones should include at least one mounted unit with dial and handset accessible to a person in a wheelchair. For workers with hearing disabilities, employers may want to consider equipping at least one telephone with volume control. Figure 4-8 shows how telephones can be adapted for the handicapped person.

Dispensing machines. These machines should have switches and controls that can be operated by employees with limited manual dexterity and strength. They should be placed within easy reach of wheelchair users.

Lighting. There are no specific standards regarding lighting, but employers should be concerned about reducing glare and reflec-

Figure 4-7. Drinking fountain suitable for the handicapped.

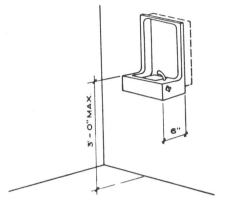

tions. Matte surfaces can help in this effort. For workers with low vision, employers should increase lighting in hallways and work areas. One guide to establishing proper light levels is the *Handbook of the Illuminating Engineering Society.*

Fire alarms and emergency devices. These units should be mounted so as to be within easy reach of workers in wheelchairs.

Alarm signals. Units (for example, flashing lights) should be

Figure 4-8. Public telephones (plan and elevation views).

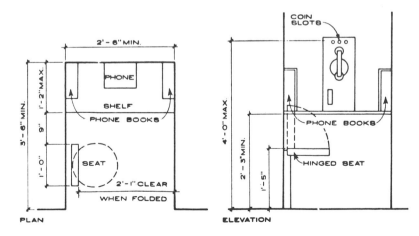

Figure 4-9. International symbol of accessibility for the handicapped.

visible as well as audible to aid workers with sight and hearing impairments. The flashing frequency of visual alarm systems should be less than 5 Hz cycles per second.

Signs. Maximum-visibility signs should be located to identify accessible routes and facilities. Letters should be large with a sharp contrast between the letters and the background of the signs. Raised letters should be used as a convenience to the blind worker. In addition, illuminated large letters placed on contrasting backgrounds are an aid to the partially sighted worker. Signs must convey essential directional information and operating instructions.

As a guide to employees, employers should also make liberal use of the international symbol of access seen in Figure 4-9. The symbol should be displayed prominently to identify accessible buildings at their entrances as well as accessible facilities inside, such as elevators, restrooms, water fountains, public telephones, recreation areas, and rest areas. An added suggestion is to include the symbol of access in any company advertising that includes a picture of the facilities.

Work stations. The work area is critical to the successful integration of the handicapped worker if the concept of "mainstreaming" is to become a reality. In some cases, experts agree that "standardization of adaptation" can be achieved for each type of mobility

Figure 4-10(a). Plan view showing clear floorspace requirement of the work station.

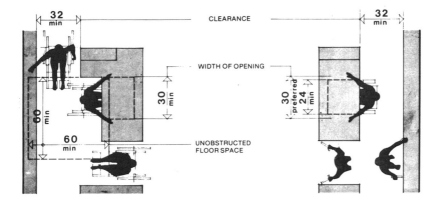

Figure 4-10(b). Elevation view showing height limitations of the work station.

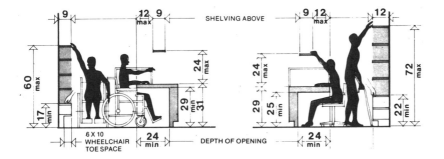

impairment. As already seen, however, special handicapping conditions requiring special adaptations need to be dealt with by employers.

After a handicapped worker has been hired, the employer should consult with him as to special needs and the adaptations he would find suitable. In fact, Sections 503, 504, and 402 regulations require such consultation. In Figure 4-10 there are pictured some common adaptations of the work station, covering areas such as shelving height, minimum desk height, wheelchair toe space, and unobstructed floor space.

Operating hardware. Most conventional hardware can be adapted inexpensively (or replaced) to serve workers with limited manual dexterity or with coordination, strength, or stamina problems. Lever-type hardware on doors, lavatories, and switches enhances their use by the handicapped worker.

Windows. Employers should try to minimize overillumination and glare, especially in work areas. Large areas of glass should be identified for the visually impaired with decals or some other kind of symbol.

Long-cane touch techniques. Some people with severe visual impairments use a long cane as a mobility aid. By swinging the cane from side to side at or near the floor level in an area extending approximately six inches outside both shoulders, the user detects hazards. To assist the movement of these individuals and to reduce hazards, employers should attempt to keep aisles clear and limit the intrusion of overhanging objects in the walking areas.

In this chapter we have examined just some of the accommodations employers can make for the handicapped worker. It must be remembered that the federal government expects employers to use imaginative and resourceful techniques in their adaptation efforts. By making a few routine adjustments in the workplace, the employer has *not* fulfilled his statutory obligation to make reasonable accommodation to the specific needs of qualified handicapped workers and applicants. Employers requiring special assistance in this area should consider seeking help from some of the organizations listed in Appendix B.

Since it is important to be diligent in scrutinizing and updating the entire affirmative action program, employers should designate some company official actively involved in the program to take periodic walking tours to assess the quality and effectiveness of adaptations. Then, management can determine the need for further modifications. In Appendix N, employers will find a convenient "walk-around" checklist to assist them in this effort, reprinted by permission of the National Easter Seal Society for Crippled Children and Adults.

Adapting the Tools and the Job to the Handicapped Worker

Adapting the facilities, as discussed in the preceding sections, is no more important than adapting the job, where feasible, to the particular handicap of the worker. These adaptations can qualify for the tax credit just as facilities accommodations can, if federal guidelines are followed properly. The science of biomechanics, also known as organomics or human factors engineering, has illustrated that greater loss control can be achieved by adapting the work environment to the worker rather than by assuming that the worker must adjust to the environment. In addition, federal and state funds (in addition to the tax credits) are often available to private companies willing to modify equipment and tools to accommodate the requirements of handicapped workers.

Adjustments in the work schedule, and not just specific job or tool adaptations, can be considered reasonable accommodations as well and should be used if they do not cause undue hardship to the employer. For example, a worker using leg braces may find it difficult to use public transportation during rush hours; in that case, a flexible work schedule would be a reasonable accommodation. At the same time, an employer would not be expected to make such an accommodation for a worker who occupied a strategic point on the assembly line and whose temporary absence would disrupt production. In this example, it would probably be more prudent to transfer the worker to another assignment. By making reasonable, commonsense accommodations such as schedule adjustments, an employer can quickly establish his intent to comply with the law.

Other types of accommodations which employers might want to consider, where appropriate, include:

- Replacing revolving doors with double air doors.
- Offering a day-shift assignment to a visually handicapped worker who has difficulty seeing in the dark.
- Allowing an alcoholic worker time to participate in a rehabilitation program.
- Giving a worker time off for kidney dialysis treatment.

- Teaching supervisors who work with epileptic workers how to handle an epileptic seizure.*
- Providing extra desk or shelf space for a blind secretary to store a voluminous braille dictionary.
- Offering sign language courses to supervisors who work with deaf employees.*

In all instances, the employer must not fall into the lax attitude of categorizing job assignments in a traditional, nonessential manner when they have no actual bearing on productivity. When it comes to assigning jobs to handicapped workers, supervisors not only must be reasonable, they must also be creative with the encouragement and support of top management.

At the Rehabilitation Research and Training Center of George Washington University (GWU) in Washington, D.C., studies on job accommodation have been going on for years with excellent results. GWU's research projects, concentrating on severly disabled individuals (the precise enforcement focus of HEW and OFCCP), have included job placement and follow-up studies. In one instance, a person with cerebral palsy with uncontrollable hand movements was placed as a homebound computer programmer. After a year, he was still on the job.

GWU project personnel were able to place in jobs those severely handicapped persons which even the state vocational rehabilitation agency had given up on. GWU found, as others have, that the cost of environmental and equipment modifications at the job site was nominal, particularly in comparison with employer expectations.

Equipment and Workplace Modifications

Following are some examples of equipment and workplace modifications, a few quite creative and others quite simple, made for handicapped employees.

Made-for-the-blind calculator. This device works like any other calculator except that it also talks in a loud, clear voice, allowing the operator to hear the input and output.

---

*These two accommodations could be excellent additions to an affirmative action plan, where applicable.

Computerized tape recorder. This machine, also known as a speech compressor, makes possible speed reading by ear; with it, a 60-minute speech can be heard in less than 24 minutes.

Desk. A regular desk can simply be propped up securely to accommodate a worker in a wheelchair.

Speaker phone. This device can be dialed with a pencil gripped by a holder, for use by quadriplegics.

Cassette dictation machine. This machine is equipped with a voice-actuated microphone and highly sensitive magnetically activated switches, which can be operated by a quadriplegic with a magnetic-tipped stick held in the teeth; the unit also enables paraplegics to transcribe dictation by using a hand control attached to a typewriter instead of the familiar foot pedal.

Electronic environments. These systems are designed to integrate different office functions. For example, the Veterans Administration has developed a system to allow a severely disabled person to use the telephone and operate various office machines on a virtually independent basis.

Vocational prosthesis. This concept refers to adding pieces to or modifying existing parts of vocational tools to make a job accessible to a handicapped person. For example, the micrographics industry has been adapting viewers with larger knobs and a lever to make gripping of the scan buttons easier. This may involve attaching longer levers on top of shorter ones to provide leverage for tape recorder play or designing editing error sheets that require less expenditure of energy.

Telebraille. This device enables deaf-blind persons to converse with each other. It is totally self-contained and portable. Using the standard telephone, braille characters are formed at a special audio frequency.

Typewriters. Various adaptations have been made to standard manufacturer models, using accessible controls and automatic carriage returns. Voice-keyed electric and electronically operated typewriters can also be purchased, as well as one-handed typewriters with specially designed keyboards.

Telephones. In addition to the speaker phone already mentioned, the telephone company offers a number of adaptive devices for deaf, blind, and otherwise handicapped users, including card dialers and head sets. The telephone company will send out a staff member to evaluate problems and suggest appropriate equipment. Special equipment for the handicapped is rented to employers at an additional monthly charge.

Type slate. A pegboard is designed whereby calculations are made by position.

Cube slate. Calculations are made from the cubes, with braille numbers on all six faces.

Page turners. These devices operate automatically and are available from select manufacturers.

Microminiature TV systems. These systems are built into an attaché case and include a travel reader for use in the office, home, or elsewhere. They operate either with batteries or through an electrical outlet.

Miniature binoculars. These units are slightly larger than a cigarette packet and enable the user to see a distance of 1,000 feet.

Synthesized vision eyeglasses. These glasses permit almost full vision to a person blind in or missing one eye, or to persons with half-vision or "tunnel" vision.

Optical-to-tactile conversion machine. This machine, known as an Optacon, allows a blind person to read books, computer programs, or calculator outputs. A tiny electric-eye camera scans a page of print and sends a signal which eventually forms identical raised letters and numbers which can be felt by the blind user. An Optacon costs approximately $3,000.

Electronic speech aids. These units change the frequency content and quality of a voice, with or without amplification, thereby improving its clarity and volume.

In-the-ear electronic speech clarifier. This device improves the speech and hearing of the cerebral palsied.

Cross-vision glasses. This unit improves sight to the blind side for persons who have had cataract surgery or for persons with monocular problems.

Braille writer. A typewriter is adapted with six keys used to "punch out" combinations of raised dots on cardboard. The combinations form numbers as well as the braille alphabet.

Braille recorder. This unit makes possible reading and writing in braille from and onto tape cassettes; calculations can be performed with input and output in braille.

Kurzweil reading machine. This computerized device converts all types of printed material into synthetic spoken English speech at approximately 150 words per minute. Users can read a variety of printed materials once they learn to understand the synthetic voice.

Miscellaneous adaptations. Regular office equipment and the work area are being modified by wheelchair accessories; environmental control units; intercoms and signaling and security systems; ramps; and posture or support systems.

Employers seriously intent on complying with the reasonable-accommodation requirement of the law must make a concerted effort to do so. Neither the Department of Labor's OFCCP nor HEW's Office for Civil Rights will sympathize with the argument that it is difficult or impossible to accommodate most handicapped applicants and workers. In addition to the state vocational rehabilitation agencies listed in Appendix G, employers should consult with some of the organizations listed in Appendix B in their efforts to adapt the work environment to the particular needs of handicapped individuals.

Occupational Adjustments

Clearly, manufacturers have taken giant strides in designing and producing equipment to improve the work performance of handicapped workers, thereby placing additional burdens on employers to fulfill their statutory obligations without claiming the inability to adapt either jobs or the work environment.

Many companies find it difficult to perceive the employment of handicapped persons in a wide range of occupations. For one reason, past efforts to employ the handicapped have often been gratuitous, and little if any pressure has been placed on businesses to expand opportunities beyond entry-level or dead-end jobs. For some employers, affiliation with a sheltered workshop has been their only involvement in programs to assist the handicapped. As we have seen, federal laws have made this approach obsolete for companies doing business with the federal government. Some companies, including one in the data processing industry, have taken the initiative by setting up demonstration projects for the disabled to show other employers and the government how reasonable accommodation can be achieved.

Unquestionably, the federal government and activist organizations are making every effort possible to ensure that handicapped persons receive job opportunities at all levels of employment. Still, many employers believe that the handicapped are capable of performing only limited tasks, which is one reason why the OFCCP is looking for what it considers "systemic discrimination" by contractors and subcontractors.

For many employers, only a wholesale realignment of employment practices will ensure compliance with handicap legislation. Once top management is committed to such a major undertaking, imaginative use of company and community resources will be necessary. A number of large employers have made this commitment, and the approach to affirmative action of at least a few is worth examining.

The critical first step of one *Fortune* 500 company, after securing top-management support, was to establish in-house coordination with key departments such as medical, employment, personnel, insurance, and employee benefits. Then, meaningful working relationships had to be established with outside resources such as the Veterans Administration, the American Heart Association, The National Association of the Blind, and local vocational rehabilitation agencies.

For its existing workers, the above-mentioned company set up an in-house rehabilitation program which includes a referral procedure, an interview with a counselor, review by the company's Rehabilitation Committee, job review to determine necessary restructuring, supervisor follow-up, and ongoing monitoring by a counselor. This company also purchased a special van for transporting wheelchair-bound workers. To further effective intracompany communications, courses in sign language are conducted for supervisors and workers. By the company's own estimates, $300,000 in worker compensation claims was saved in 18 months of the voluntary program to accommodate handicapped workers.

Another large employer gave three disabled workers the best parking places at its facilities. The company redesigned one of its bathrooms by installing an easy-to-open entrance door, removing the door to one stall, and adding handrails. Complementing the company's economical efforts, the state vocational rehabilitation agency provided several thousand dollars for a stairway elevator at the home of one of the disabled workers. The elevator carries the individual, still in his wheelchair, from his living room to a sunken garage.

The Handicapped at Work

Many handicapped activists are reluctant to even give examples of handicapped "success stories" for fear that the examples themselves will appear restrictive. The prevailing attitude today, among activists and in the government, is that there is no job a handicapped person can't handle. Employers should keep in mind that the following examples are given to stimulate ideas of the kinds of jobs which can be adapted, where reasonable, for handicapped workers and applicants. One inspiration for the handicapped might be the fact that the former head of the president's Committee on Employment of the Handicapped was a veteran who lost both hands. In addition, the director of HEW's Office for Civil Rights was a blind lawyer, and the current head of the Veterans Administration is a triple amputee. Employers should keep in mind that the law requires them to consult with handicapped workers to gain their ideas on how job assignments and the work environment can be modified to accommodate them.

Portfolio manager. A blind person is a financial manager for a major U.S. corporation. During a typical day, he handles between $25 million and $150 million. He gets securities information in braille on specially adapted equipment and checks figures on a programmable calculator that can print results in braille. He gets to work each day in New York City with the aid of a guide dog. Funds for the braille equipment came from a state vocational rehabilitation agency.

Telephone repairman. A blind man has been a repairman for

more than 25 years. His sighted colleagues refer to him as amazing as they watch him diagnose problems with complex pieces of switching equipment. When a troubleshooter is needed, he is called in first.

Dishwasher. A mildly retarded man works as a dishwasher in a restaurant. The food production supervisor calls him one of the company's better employees who also gets along well with other workers. The dishwasher received training and counseling under a special program for the handicapped set up by his state government.

Editor. An individual almost totally paralyzed from the neck down served as the editor of a community newspaper. He worked at a special U-shaped desk built onto his electric wheelchair. The desk unit was equipped with special editing stand and speaker telephone. After receiving his master's degree, the individual moved on to a job as a social worker.

Helicopter pilot. As a result of an accident, a pilot's voice was reduced to a whisper so that he couldn't use a two-way radio. Engineers redesigned the radio and built in a special speech aid. Another speech aid complementing the radio was fitted to the pilot. He now has his pilot's license back and is flying dangerous exploration missions in Canada.

Clerk. A person with severe cerebral palsy was given a job contingent on his ability to take messages by telephone, to type short notes and letters, to use the duplicating machine, and to perform other office duties. The clerk started with a special electric wheelchair, and added a one-hand writing aid and special self-feeding tools. The individual was trained to operate office machines and has been employed full-time ever since, eventually receiving job tenure.

Actuary. Blind from birth, this individual works for the Social Security Administration, handling complex statistical studies. He finished college and did graduate work in actuarial science. He uses a variety of braille instruments to perform his job.

Design draftsman. A paraplegic injured in Vietnam is now training to be a chemical engineer while working as a draftsman for a major U.S. manufacturer. He has been described by his coworkers as completely self-sufficient.

Machinist. An individual who is totally blind and lost his right hand, part of his thigh, and his sense of smell works as a machinist and, in his spare time, designs his own custom-built work tools.

Consumer counselor. A blind person works at a state agency, using a multiline telephone equipped with a shoulder rest so as to free his hands to use a braille writer for recording information. A braille Rolodex file, a light probe, and a brailled copy of the state government directory were adapted for his particular use. This individual's success on the job resulted in the placement of another individual as a general information specialist.

In its comprehensive study of its own program for handicapped workers, E. I. du Pont de Nemours & Company found excellent or average records in performance, attendance, safety—in fact, in all the critical areas related to productive employment. Particularly enlightening is the fact that du Pont's handicapped workers performed in a wide range of occupations, including craftsmen, professional managers, technicians, machine operators, clerical workers, service personnel, and laborers.

Employers already obligated to consult with handicapped individuals and organizations in recruiting personnel and developing affirmative action plans would also be prudent to seek advice about reasonable work-site accommodations and job adaptations. Employers should also consult the various other organizations and government agencies for the handicapped listed throughout the appendixes to this book.

5
Financial Incentives and the Liability Myth

While requiring employers to take positive steps in hiring, training, and advancing qualified handicapped persons, disabled veterans, and veterans of the Vietnam era, the federal government has provided some financial incentives to do so. These incentives include tax credits and training subsidies under a variety of federally administered programs.

Targeted Job Tax Credit (TJTC)

Under the Revenue Act of 1978, TJTC replaces what was known as the new jobs credit* and allows employers to claim a tax credit in 1979 and 1980 on qualified wages of new hires who are members of targeted groups. Vocational rehabilitation referrals and economically disadvantaged Vietnam-era veterans can qualify for TJTC, as described shortly.

*Even though the new jobs credit expired at the end of 1978, credits that could not be claimed in earlier years can be carried over to the seven succeeding tax years.

For an employer to take the credit, the targeted group member must have been hired *after* September 26, 1978, *unless* the individual is a vocational rehabilitation referral for whom a previous job tax credit was taken in a tax year beginning in 1977 or 1978. Even if a qualified worker is hired as far back as September 27, 1978, however, TJTC can *not* be claimed for wages earned prior to January 1, 1979.

For an employer to claim the credit, the new worker must be certified as a member of a targeted group by a designated local agency. Among agencies that can issue certification are the local offices of the State Employment Service (SES) and the Veterans Administration.

Employers taking affirmative action to hire and advance handicapped individuals and veterans can use TJTC to help document their compliance efforts. In the process, payroll costs can be reduced significantly.

To secure certification, a vocational rehabilitation referral for a job must (1) have a physical or mental disability that either is a substantial handicap or results in a substantial handicap to employment; and (2) be referred to the employer upon completing or while receiving rehabilitative services under an approved rehabilitative plan.

To secure certification, an economically disadvantaged Vietnam-era veteran referral for a job must:

1. Have served on active duty in the military for more than 180 days, at least one day of which was between August 5, 1964, and May 7, 1975, *or* have been discharged or released from active duty because of a service-connected disability which occurred sometime during the above-mentioned dates.
2. *Not* have served on more than a 90-day period of active duty for any day during the pre-employment period. (Note: the federal government normally considers the pre-employment period as the 60 days prior to the date of hire.)
3. Be a member of an economically disadvantaged family.
4. Be under 35 years of age on the date of hire.

TJTC can be computed only on qualified wages, which the IRS

considers as targeted group member wages an employer pays or incurs in 1979 or 1980. To figure the credit, employers use the same wages (including those not paid in money) that are subject to Federal Unemployment Taxes (FUTA), without the FUTA limitation.

Qualified first-year wages are wages certified employees earn during the first one-year period at a company. The first year begins on the day the certified worker commences employment but no earlier than January 1, 1979. As stated earlier, certified workers hired as far back as September 26, 1978, can be claimed for TJTC purposes as of January 1, 1979. Special rules may apply to vocational rehabilitation referrals for whom previous job credits were claimed. These first-year wages are subject to two limitations: a $6,000 limitation, which also applies to qualified second-year wages; and a 30 percent FUTA wage limitation. The amount of credit claimed for any certified worker *cannot* exceed 50 percent of the qualified first-year wages earned by the individual.

Employers face certain tax liability limitations when using TJTC. For instance, on tax years beginning in 1978 and ending in 1979, the amount of TJTC claimed cannot exceed 100 percent of the employer's federal income tax liability. For tax years beginning in 1979, the credit cannot exceed 90 percent of an employer's federal income tax liability. If the credit is more than a company's tax liability, however, the excessive portion may be carried back three years and carried forward seven years.

The Tax Reform Act of 1976

This act provides an additional tax benefit for employers hiring the handicapped. Originally issued as temporary standards, the following regulations were published as permanent on July 24, 1979.

As an amendment to the Internal Revenue Code, the Tax Reform Act (under Section 190 of the code) permits deductions for qualified architectural and transportation barrier removal expenses from the taxable years beginning after December 31, 1976, to those beginning no later than December 31, 1982. These deductions may be applied to expenditures paid or incurred during the taxable year which would normally be chargeable to an employer's capital account.

The maximum deduction for any taxable year is $25,000; it applies to a corporation as well as to an affiliated group of corporations filing a consolidated return. The $25,000 deduction is available to a partnership and also to each partner. Expenditures for a taxable year in excess of the $25,000 limit are to be treated as capital expenditures.

The term "qualified barrier removal expense" means any expenditure for the purpose of making any company facilities or transportation vehicles owned, leased, or otherwise used in connection with business more accessible or usable to handicapped individuals. The term "facility" means all or any portions of buildings, structures, equipment, roads, walks, parking lots, or similar real or personal property. Vehicles in a company fleet (for example, a van with modifications) would qualify for the credit.

Typical kinds of accommodations which employers can make and which might qualify for the credit are discussed in detail later in this chapter and in Chapter 4.

To qualify for the deduction, an employer must satisfy the IRS that the removal of the barrier makes the facility conform to the regulations and that the qualified expenses include only expenses specifically attributable to the removal of an "existing" architectural or transportation barrier. The key word is "existing," since expenses cannot include any part of an expense in connection with the construction or comprehensive renovation of a facility or the normal replacement of depreciable property. Also, the barrier removed for the handicapped must be "substantial," without creating barriers for others in the process.

The election to deduct qualified barrier removal expenses is made by claiming them as a separately identified item on the income tax return, which must itself be filed no later than the time prescribed by law. Once made, an election is irrevocable and applies to all qualified expenditures paid or incurred during the taxable year up to the $25,000 limitation. If such expenses exceed the limitation, the employer elects which expenditures comprise those deducted.

To justify barrier removal expenses, records and documentation must be kept by employers for a period of three years. Records should include architectural plans and blueprints, contracts, and any building permits.

Although typical kinds of barrier removals and accommodations are discussed in detail in Chapter 4, IRS guidelines and definitions are summarized here, since they have a direct bearing on an employer's claim of allowable deductions. Employers who have questions about their authority to deduct specific barrier removal expenses should consult with the IRS prior to undertaking the renovation. One example of a qualified expense, according to the IRS, is the construction of a ramp to remove the barrier posed by steps for wheelchair users.

After consulting with the federal Architectural and Transportation Barrier Compliance Board, the IRS adopted the American National Standards Institute (ANSI) guidelines for making facilities accessible to and usable by the physically handicapped (see Appendix O for information on how to secure these ANSI standards). Since the IRS (or any other federal agency) may decide not to adopt the revised ANSI standards when they are published, employers must be alert to the development of alternative standards that affect the definition of deductible barrier removal expenses.

IRS Guidelines for Barrier Removal

Unlike the Department of Labor and the Department of Health, Education and Welfare, the IRS has provided some "official" guidance as to what actions employers can take to remove barriers and thus qualify for tax credits under the law. In the absence of more specific guidance from either of the two primary federal enforcement agencies, employers should look to the following IRS guidelines in their efforts to make facilities accessible to handicapped applicants and workers. During compliance investigations, OFCCP hearings, and federal court cases, it would seem to be a valid argument for employers to insist on the applicability of the IRS standards to remove barriers, since both HEW and the Department of Labor refer to the tax credits as a means of reducing the expense of achieving compliance. This recommendation to use available tax credits would seem to constitute an implied endorsement of the following IRS guidelines by the two primary enforcement agencies.

Grading. The grading of ground, even contrary to existing topography, must attain a level with a normal entrance to make facilities accessible to individuals with physical disabilities.

Walks. A walk must be at least 48 inches wide and have a gradient no greater than 5 percent. In addition, a walk with a slope close to the maximum allowed and of considerable length must have level areas at regular intervals. Walks must also have a nonslip surface and cannot be interrupted by either steps or abrupt changes. If a walk crosses another walk, a driveway, or a parking lot, it must blend at a common level with the other elements. If the walk is inclined, it must have level platforms at the top and at the bottom. If a door swings out onto the platform toward the walk, the platform must be at least five feet deep and five feet wide. If a door does not swing onto a platform or toward a walk, then the platform need only be three feet deep and five feet wide. Platforms must extend at least one foot beyond the strike jamb side of any doorway.

Parking lots. There must be at least one parking space that is accessible to handicapped persons. The space must be close to an employer's facilities, set aside for the handicapped, and identified for such use. The space must be open on one side to allow room for people in wheelchairs or on braces or crutches to get in and out of an automobile onto a surface suitably level for wheeling and walking. If the space is placed between two conventional diagonal or head-on parking spaces, it must be at least 12 feet wide. The parking space must be positioned so that individuals in wheelchairs or on braces or crutches need not wheel or walk behind parked vehicles.

Ramps. A ramp cannot rise more than one inch in 12 inches. It must have at least one handrail that is 32 inches high measured from the surface of the ramp. The handrail must be smooth and extend one foot beyond the top and bottom of the ramp but not in a manner that in itself causes a hazard for the handicapped. The surface of the ramp must be of a nonslip nature. Ramps must have level platforms at the top and at the bottom. If a door swings out onto the platform or toward the ramp, the platform must be at least five feet deep and five feet wide. If a door does not swing onto the platform or toward the ramp, the platform must be at least three feet deep and five feet wide. A platform must extend at least one foot beyond the strike jamb side of any doorway. All ramps must have level platforms at every turn and a platform at least at every 30-foot interval. Curb ramps must be provided at intersections and cannot be less than four feet wide. Curb ramps cannot rise more than one inch in 12 inches.

Entrances. Every building must have at least one primary entrance that is usable by people in wheelchairs and is on a level accessible to an elevator.

Doors and doorways. Doors must have a clear opening of no less than 32 inches and must be operable by a single effort. The floor on the inside and outside of doorways must be level for a distance of at least five feet from the door in the direction in which the door swings. The level area must extend at least one foot beyond the strike jamb side of the doorway. Doorways cannot have sharp inclines or abrupt changes. The threshold must be flush with the floor. The door closer must be selected, placed, and set so as not to impair the use of the door by the handicapped.

Stairs. Stair steps must have round nosing with a radius of between one and one-half inches. Stairs must have a handrail 32 inches high, measured from the tread at the face of the riser. Stairs must have at least one handrail that extends at least 18 inches beyond the top and bottom steps. Steps must have risers that do not exceed seven inches.

Floors. All floors must have a nonslip surface. Floors on each story must be of a common level or must be connected by a ramp, as described earlier.

Toilet rooms. Toilet rooms must have sufficient space to allow traffic for individuals in wheelchairs. The toilet room must have at least one toilet stall that:

- Is at least 36 inches wide.
- Is at least 56 inches deep.
- Has a door, if any, that is at least 32 inches wide and swings out.
- Has handrails on each side 33 inches high and parallel to the

floor and 1½ inches in outside diameter, with 1½ inches clearance between rail and wall, and fastened securely at ends and center.

■ Has a water closet with a seat 19 to 20 inches from the finished floor and a center line located 18 inches from the side wall on which the handrail is located.

Toilet rooms must have lavatories with narrow aprons. Drain pipes and hot-water pipes under lavatories must be covered or insulated. A mirror and shelf above a lavatory must be no higher than 40 inches above the floor, measured from the top of the shelf and the bottom of the mirror.

A toilet room for men must have wall-mounted urinals with the opening of the basin 15 to 19 inches from the finished floor or floor-mounted urinals that are level with the main floor of the toilet room. Towel racks, towel dispensers, and other dispensers and disposal units must be mounted no higher than 40 inches from the floor.

Water fountains. A water fountain and a cooler must have up-front spouts and controls that can be hand-operated or hand- and foot-operated. A water fountain mounted on the side of a floor-mounted cooler must not be more than 30 inches above the floor. If a cooler is wall-mounted and hand-operated, then it must be mounted with the basin 36 inches from the floor. Water fountains cannot be fully recessed and cannot be set into an alcove unless the alcove is at least 36 inches wide.

Public telephones. A public telephone must be placed so that the dial and headset can be reached by individuals in wheelchairs. The telephone must be equipped for those with hearing disabilities and identified as such with appropriate instructions. Coin slots of public telephones must be no more than 48 inches from the floor.

Elevators. An elevator must be accessible to and usable by the handicapped worker or applicant at the levels used to enter the building and at other levels normally used. The cab size of the elevator must allow for the turning of a wheelchair and must measure at least 54 by 68 inches. The opening width of the door must provide a clearance of at least 32 inches. All essential elevator controls must be within 48 inches to 54 inches of the cab floor. The elevator controls must be usable by the blind and must be tactilely identifiable.

Controls. Switches and controls for light, heat, ventilation, windows, draperies, fire alarms, and all similar controls of frequent or essential use must be placed within the reach of individuals in wheelchairs. Switches and controls must be no higher than 48 inches from the floor.

Identification. Raised letters or numbers must be used to identify a room or office. Identifications must be placed on the wall to the right or left of the door at a height of 54 to 66 inches, measured from the finished floor. A door that might prove dangerous if a blind person were to exit or enter (for example, a door leading to a loading platform, boiler room, stage, or fire escape) must be tactilely identifiable.

Warning signals. An audible warning signal must be accompanied by a simultaneous visual signal for the benefit of individuals with hearing disabilities. A visual warning signal must be accompanied by a simultaneous audible signal for the benefit of the visually impaired.

Hazards. Hanging signs, ceiling lights, and similar objects and fixtures must be placed at a minimum height of 7 feet, measured from the floor.

International accessibility symbol. The symbol shown in Figure 4-9 must be displayed on routes to facilities and on routes to wheelchair-accessible entrances.

When employers are confused either about applying tax credits to their unique building requirements or about interpreting changing IRS regulations, they should consult with the Legislation and Regulations Division, Office of the Chief Counsel, Internal Revenue Service, 1111 Constitution Avenue, N.W., Washington, D.C. 20224.

Insuring the Handicapped Worker—Is There an Insurance Liability Myth?

One of the first reactions of employers toward hiring handicapped workers is fear that insurance costs will skyrocket. Normally, without statistics to support them, business executives claim there will be a never-ending spiral in their health, accident, hospitalization, and workers' compensation rates if they hire the handicapped.

Although many activist organizations as well as the federal government itself are claiming flatly that an employer's insurance rates won't change at all if handicapped individuals are hired, the fact is that insurance rates will vary depending upon a variety of factors. Nonetheless, the debate itself will probably prove to be inconsequential, since OFCCP and HEW's Office for Civil Rights have both stated clearly that insurance costs are *not* a legal reason for refusing to hire qualified handicapped persons. If an employer's insurance carrier refuses to underwrite a disabled individual, the employer may be expected to find a carrier who will.

Some studies, including one by E. I. du Pont de Nemours & Company, have shown that the physically handicapped are as good a risk on the job as their able-bodied coworkers. The du Pont study of 1,452 handicapped employees—including those with orthopedic disabilities, partial or total blindness, heart disease, amputations, paralysis, epilepsy, and partial or total deafness—covered a wide range of occupations. Many employers, like du Pont, have found that handicapped workers experience fewer disabling injuries on the job than other workers exposed to the same hazards. It has also been found by some companies that the handicapped have about the same number of minor injuries and are often more safety-conscious than their able-bodied workers. During its study, du Pont discovered, for instance, that 96 percent of its handicapped workers rated average or better in the area of safety. Among other things, the du Pont study of its handicapped employees illustrated that:

Adjustments in the work area were minimal.
Acceptance by other employees of handicapped workers was wholehearted.
Job performance was average or better.
Attendance was average or better.

A New York company employing only severely disabled persons reports that it pays standard rates for life insurance, hospitalization, disability benefits, and compensation insurance. If an individual missing one arm is hired by an employer and loses the other arm in a work-related accident, most states will reimburse employers for the difference between the compensation due the worker for initial loss and the award due for the substantially greater disability the worker actually suffers on the job. These extraordinary losses often are covered by states under a second-injury fund. Employers should check with their insurance carrier or the state insurance commissioner to determine the extent of such coverage in their state.

One prominent trade organization representing major U.S. companies, the National Association of Manufacturers, conducted a study of 279 members. This study revealed that 90 percent of the member companies experienced no increase in insurance costs as a result of hiring the handicapped.

As stated earlier, the question of insurance costs is a complex one, with many variables to be studied by employers. Some experts on the subject insist that the legal definition of a qualified handicapped individual (see Chapter 1), the kinds of handicapped persons actually employed, and the size of the employer are key factors in determining insurance costs. For example, individuals with "stabilized" handicaps (for example, blindness or deafness) do not require significantly greater medical treatment than able-bodied workers. But workers with progressive and degenerative diseases (for example, cancer and kidney failure) will need more than average medical care. The consequence of these distinctions can be great, particularly if a group health plan is rated according to claims experience.

Large corporations, like IBM, have stated that it is impossible to make a dent in insurance rates when a few high-claims cases are taken into account. IBM's analysis might, in part, account for du Pont's successful experience and attitude. If increases in insurance rates are to have any effect at all, it is generally agreed that medium-size and small employers (with enough workers to show a claims-related history) will feel the increases the most. The Health Insurance Institute, a trade group, has estimated that claims by handicapped workers will have an impact on premiums based on the dollar level and frequency of the claims made. The Institute has also stated that a group of 500 with typical major medical coverage could face a 3 percent increase in premiums the following year as a result of a single claim of $10,000. If the claim were $50,000, the increase in premium would probably be 20 percent. Before an employer gets caught up in the debate over whether insurance costs will be stable or higher, however, he should look at the requirements of the law. Section 503 states that employers cannot discriminate on "rates of pay or other compensation," while Section 504 prohibits discrimination in "rates of pay or any other form of compensation and changes in compensation" plus "fringe benefits available by virtue of employment, whether or not administered by the recipient." It is possible that some employers will be exempt from these requirements, however, if they can show that compliance will pose an undue hardship.

The basic concept of group insurance reveals a lot about how rates are established. Fundamentally, carriers are looking to reduce the risk and spread out the loss. Insurance costs will be determined by the following considerations: the degree of the risk, the value of the hazard proposed for coverage, the number of workers in the group plan, and the administrative expense of the carrier. Any event that affects directly these four basic considerations *must* affect the cost of the insurance.

Being profit-minded, the insurance industry operates on the basic principle that if losses result in higher claims, then premiums must rise. Who absorbs the cost? Does the employer pay it out of his own pocket? Can the increase be spread among all employees, or should the individuals causing the increases either pay the cost or be dropped from the plan? If the employer decides that the increase in insurance costs is unjustified or financially unmanageable, is he guilty of discrimination against handicapped workers? Unfortunately, the federal government has provided inadequate guidance on this subject. Employers are left with the immutable fact that the legal obligation of nondiscrimination is paramount. Unfortunately, the insurance industry, too, has provided employers with little clarification on how to control insurance costs while hiring a variety of handicapped persons.

Section 504 of the Rehabilitation Act in particular encourages

employers to look to insurance carriers to provide nondiscriminatory coverage. If an insurance plan is inherently discriminatory and
cannot be modified, then the employer is expected to secure
alternative insurance. It is conceivable, however, that an employer
acting in good faith could terminate one insurance plan only to find
that a replacement program is not available in the marketplace.
This problem for employers is compounded by the fact that insurance companies, by virtue of the state laws which regulate them,
have singular control over the risks which they wish to insure.

Most group policy rates apply for only one year at a time. If
there is a change in risks on the high side, certainly there must be
an increase in rates. A large number of claims by certain categories
of workers will force insurance rates up. Soaring health care costs
can make an already extraordinary risk under a group plan, for
example, a potential catastrophe for a small employer. The fact
that a few large claims go unnoticed by industrial giants like IBM
and du Pont, since they can "spread" the loss, is of little consolation
to the small federal contractor or grant recipient.

Some surveys of small employers have shown that insurance
companies will charge a higher rate for handicapped workers in a
group plan for coverage such as long-term disability, short-term
disability, medical insurance, and accidental death and dismem-
berment. As mentioned earlier, stabilized handicapping conditions
(for example, blindness) present less of a risk to insurers than
degenerative handicapping conditions (for example, heart disease).
It is evident that neither the federal government nor the insurance
industry has made a sophisticated study of the actual insurance
costs faced by employers hiring the handicapped. Perhaps ironi-
cally, one indication of this shortcoming can be seen in another
piece of federal legislation, the Age Discrimination in Employment
Act (ADEA). Under ADEA, employers have the option of hiring
older Americans and, at the same time, taking an exemption from
requirements that would inhibit their tendency to hire them. What
is the exemption? For agreeing to hire older Americans, employers
are released from the extraordinary expense of pension and insurance program increases! Why the Congress and federal enforcement officials recognized the insurance problem for older Ameri-

cans (many of whom are disabled) but not for the general category of handicapped persons should be perplexing to the business community.

HEW and DOL, in defending statutory requirements, have relied on scattered and inconclusive studies that show no increase in insurance rates for hiring the handicapped. The du Point study cited earlier is quoted frequently in government publications to defend the requirements of the law. However, a 1974 study by HEW entitled *Health Characteristics of Persons with Chronic Activity Limitations* clearly shows that certain conditions are limiting, such as heart condition, arthritis and rheumatism, hypertension without heart involvement, and, to a lesser degree, paralysis, visual impairment, and mental retardation. It can be assumed that some of these limitations will increase insurance rates.

What should also be disconcerting to employers is the apparent lack of interest in the insurance community to set realistic rates for the handicapped. In 1976, the American Council of Life Insurance and the Health Insurance Association of America admitted to HEW that certain types of health conditions have not been studied in a manner that allows statistically based insurance ratings. Conceivably, then, an employer will be denied insurance for all or certain categories of handicapped workers or will be forced to pay "package" rates with no factual base. Standardization of rates has its benefits, of course, as can be seen in the area of life insurance, where most of the individual applications are accepted at standard rates, therefore facilitating coverage of the handicapped in a group plan. However, group standardization is normally allowed only as long as the individual is *not* suffering from conditions such as heart disease or diabetes—two handicaps covered by federal law.

More than one observer of the equal employment opportunity scene has pointed out that the employers who take affirmative action—and therefore become visible—bear the brunt of criticism by the federal government and activists. Certainly, an effort at reasonable accommodation for a handicapped applicant or worker could backfire for an employer in the area of insurance coverage. For example, an employer who modifies his work schedule to accommodate a handicapped individual because the worker's health permits only part-time employment may be told by the insurance company that coverage can't be extended. In fact, the insurance carrier is likely to point out that the health problem that categorized the worker as a qualified handicapped person is the very condition which the insurance company wishes to avoid covering, since it represents an extraordinary risk. Now the employer is caught in the middle between compliance (making reasonable accommodation) and noncompliance (prohibition from providing equal benefits). It is doubtful, as we have seen, that by changing insurance companies an employer can solve this hypothetical problem. In the meantime, the company is in a very visible and highly vulnerable position.

While it can be hoped that Congress and federal officials will take a hard look at the insurance problems facing the business community, employers must proceed carefully in their affirmative action and reasonable-accommodation efforts for the handicapped. Discussions with insurance carriers should be initiated with the demand that explicit answers be given not only on the parameters of coverage for handicapped workers but also on specific costs and exemptions. If undue hardship is in fact a valid reason not to make reasonable accommodation (in the form of employee benefits), then employers must be prepared to defend their position. Employers may need to place coverage with additional insurance companies, particularly where existing carriers are not responsive to the demands of the law.

Federally Funded Training Programs

Several federal agencies, at the direction of Congress, have developed programs to encourage the training and employment of handicapped people in private industry. By subsidizing part of the cost of on-the-job training and supportive services, the federal government helps employers eliminate the extraordinary expense of employing handicapped people during their nonproductive period. Hopefully, the training subsidies will increase the representation of handicapped citizens in the private-sector workforce.

Employers should be cautioned, however, about the liability

inherent in accepting any kind of federal financial assistance, even indirectly, as the discussion of Section 504 regulations indicated in Chapter 1. The possibility exists that a contractor liable for compliance under Section 503 of the Rehabilitation Act (or Section 402 of the veterans law) could be exposed to further liability under Section 504 by accepting federal funds or participating in a federally funded training program. Unfortunately, agencies dispensing federal training funds (other than HEW) have not given a clear indication to recipients of how they intend to enforce antidiscrimination statutes protecting the rights of handicapped people.

What follows is a description of the more prominent federal training programs in which employers doing business with the federal government should consider participating. Programs are listed under the federal agency which administers them. The "Catch 22" for employers is that the disadvantages of participating in federally subsidized training and education programs (in particular, the greater compliance liability) must be weighed against the expressed obligation of contractors to hire, train, and advance in employment qualified handicapped persons and Vietnam-era veterans.

U.S. Department of Labor

As we have already discussed, CETA stands for the Comprehensive Employment and Training Act of 1973, as amended. Under CETA, the following programs can provide employers with funds to offset the extraordinary cost of hiring and training handicapped persons.

HIRE. HIRE stands for Help Through Industry Retraining and Employment. It is administered directly by the Labor Department's Office of National Programs and cosponsored by the National Alliance of Business (NAB).

Under HIRE, employers can enter into what have been termed "funding agreements" and be reimbursed one-half of a new worker's beginning hourly salary for up to six months of on-the-job training and vestibule instruction, provided the job pays at least $3.50 per hour. Vietnam-era and disabled veterans head the list of priority classes eligible to participate in the HIRE program. Eligibility is determined normally by the local office of the state employment service, which also conducts job referral; however, walk-in job candidates are eligible for HIRE under certain circumstances, and in all cases, the employer selects who is to be hired and trained. Employers should keep in mind that the state employment service is the same organization that cooperates with OFCCP in contractor compliance reviews. No hint at conspiracy needs to be made for employers to take note of the linkage between federal programs and agencies at all levels of government.

If the program is administered properly and the job candidates possess proper skills and motivations, HIRE can be an important tool in an employer's efforts to hire, train, and advance qualified handicapped persons. The cost savings themselves are significant.

Employers interested in HIRE should contact either the local or regional office of NAB listed in the telephone directory or contact directly the U.S. Department of Labor, Employment Training Administration, Office of National Programs, Patrick Henry Building, 601 D Street, N.W., Washington, D.C. 20213.

HIRE II. HIRE II is an offshoot of HIRE, with a few important differences. HIRE II funds have been allocated to what the Labor Department refers to as its CETA prime sponsors. These sponsors are normally municipal or county governments or, in the case of less densely populated areas, consortia of local governments.

Basically, the same guidelines apply under HIRE II as under HIRE, with the important exception that only veterans are eligible for the HIRE II program. Employers interested in HIRE II should contact the mayor's office, the county executive's office, or the local office of the state employment service.*

CETA prime sponsors. As we have seen, CETA prime sponsors are local governments or coalitions of them. They receive a variety of federal financial assistance such as special monies for the HIRE II training program. Under their normal revenue sharing allocations, however, CETA prime sponsors receive substantial funds for employment and training programs on the basis of the population

---

*In late 1979, the Labor Department was continuing with the plans to phase out the HIRE and HIRE II programs in favor of the Private Sector Initiative Program (PSIP) discussed later.

to be served as well as other factors. These sponsors have considerable discretion in the disbursement of their funds, and although (for political and other reasons) most spending occurs to enhance public-sector employment, agreements can be entered into with private employers in the manner of the HIRE and HIRE II programs.

For further information, contact the office of the mayor or county executive in your area.

Private Sector Initiative Program (PSIP). To encourage employer participation in PSIP, the Department of Labor will be making "promotional" grants to the National Alliance of Business and the Human Resources Development Institute (HRDI), the active manpower arm of the AFL–CIO discussed in Chapter 6. Under PSIP, Private Industry Councils (PICs) will be established in every major metropolitan area to decide how training funds should be allocated. Local interest groups, including veterans organizations and organizations for the handicapped, will also be pressing for the expenditure of PSIP monies serving their clientele.

Employers interested in obtaining PSIP funds to train handicapped workers should contact the office of the mayor or county executive nearest to their businesses.

Department of Health, Education and Welfare.

Under the 1978 amendments to the Rehabilitation Act of 1973, innovative programs were authorized to encourage the training of handicapped persons in the private sector.

Projects with Industry Program (PWIP). PWIP was set up under the direction of HEW's Rehabilitation Services Administration and should not be confused with the Labor Department's PSIP program. In consultation with state agencies, HEW will make funds available to employers to provide handicapped individuals with training and employment "in a realistic work setting." Additional goals of PWIP are the development and modification of jobs to accommodate the special needs of handicapped individuals, including job matching and job placement.

Echoing the section of the 1978 CETA amendments that authorizes cooperation between federal agencies on the goal of employment of the handicapped, the Rehabilitation Act amendments of 1978 direct the Department of Labor to work closely with the Rehabilitation Services Administration at HEW in identifying contractors subject to Section 503 and then notifying them of their possible eligibility for PWIP. In other words, PWIP can be "marketed" by the federal government with employers as a way to meet compliance obligations.

Employers interested in PWIP should contact the Rehabilitation Services Administration, Department of Health, Education and Welfare, 330 C Street, S.W., Washington, D.C. 20201.

Veterans Administration

On-the-job training. If a veteran served in the military between January 31, 1955, and January 1, 1977, he may be eligible for on-the-job training (including apprenticeship training) and education benefits if employed at qualifying companies. Generally, the military service must be at least 181 days of continuous active duty, any part of which occurred between the above dates.

The eligible veteran will receive a training allowance on a descending scale for up to 24 months. The wages paid by employers have no bearing on the veteran's training allowance.

The Veterans Administration is encouraging veterans to contact employers, unions, and their veterans representatives in the local office of the state employment service to learn about on-the-job training and apprenticeship programs of interest to them.

Since contractors and subcontractors are obligated to actively seek qualified disabled veterans and Vietnam-era veterans, one way to do so is under VA's OJT and apprenticeship programs, which themselves provide significant financial incentive for the worker to be productive.

For further information, employers should contact the nearest office of the VA or the veterans employment representative in the local office of the state employment service. A list of VA offices is included in Appendix J.

Vocational rehabilitation programs. Another way for employers to at least partially fulfill their affirmative action obligations as federal contractors or subcontractors is to participate in a veterans vocational rehabilitation program. Veterans benefits and services under this program include counseling, education, on-the-job training, special training assistance (for example, a reader service for the blinded veteran), medical and dental treatment, prosthetic aids, special equipment, and restorative services.

Basically, veterans in active service during or after World War II must complete vocational rehabilitation training within nine years of discharge. In certain cases, a four-year extension can be granted. Normally, training shouldn't exceed 48 months and can include school courses (trade/technical), business courses, on-the-job or apprenticeship training, or a combination of the above.

Employers interested in vocational rehabilitation programs should contact the sources mentioned in the prior discussion of VA on-the-job training programs.

Special Incentive Programs

Some of the following organizations and activities benefit from federal funds to carry out the government's goal of increasing employment opportunities for handicapped persons. Employers should keep in mind that participation in any of these programs may constitute the benefit of federal funds, thereby subjecting the recipient to the requirements of Section 504 of the Rehabilitation Act of 1973.

Human Resources Development Institute (HRDI). As we have seen, HRDI is the manpower arm of the AFL–CIO and is quite active in encouraging employers—and unions—to develop training programs for handicapped people.

In 60 cities nationwide, the HRDI staff has offered a wide variety of services to employers and unions, including technical compliance assistance, counseling of disabled workers, job placement, development of on-the-job training programs, design of affirmative action plans, and modification of restrictive employment practices. Clearly, HRDI's goal is to place handicapped people in union jobs providing union wages and fringe benefits. HRDI's additional goals for the handicapped include union membership, entrance into union apprenticeship programs, and job security.

HRDI is able to undertake this extensive outreach program

because of a grant from HEW under the PWIP program discussed earlier. With this fact in mind, along with the clear understanding that HRDI is seeking to increase union job placement of handicapped persons, employers may want to contact HRDI at 815 16th Street, N.W., Washington, D.C. 20006.

Epilepsy Foundation of America. The foundation's Training and Placement Service (TAPS) program is another activity sponsored by federal funds (in this instance under a CETA grant) to improve the training and employment opportunities of a specific protected class of handicapped individuals.

TAPS operates through the foundation's chapters in six cities at this time: Atlanta, Boston, Minneapolis/St. Paul, Cleveland, Portland, and San Antonio. TAPS staff will develop on-the-job training and supportive service programs for employers *after* the foundation provides epileptics with vocational counseling, job skills assessment, and interviewing improvement techniques. Follow-up services include additional counseling plus education programs for an employer's staff to increase understanding of the epileptic w.rker. The foundation indicates that more than 600 epileptics have been placed in jobs since the program began.

As an incentive to employers, TAPS has funds available (through CETA) to pay one-half of the first 160 hours of on-the-job training and one-fourth of the next 160 hours.

The foundation correctly points out that epilepsy is a very common condition that does not imply deficiency in intelligence, aptitude, or vocation potential. Epilepsy is an episodic disability covered under the definition of handicapped individual in the Rehabilitation Act of 1973. Pointing to a study by the Commission for the Control of Epilepsy and Its Consequences which indicated that unemployment among people with epilepsy is more than twice the national average and that, where it occurs, job placement is below the epileptic's ability and education level, the foundation has made it an urgent goal to eliminate this apparent inequity. It is not unreasonable to assume that the foundation is advising epileptics of their employment rights as well as of contractor obligation under federal law.

Employers interested in the TAPS program or in descriptive

literature on how to help a worker who is having a seizure should contact the Epilepsy Foundation of America, 1828 L Street, N.W., Suite 406, Washington, D.C. 20036.

National Association for Retarded Citizens (NARC). Like the Epilepsy Foundation of America, the National Association of Retarded Citizens (NARC) benefits from a federal training grant under Title III of the CETA legislation. Under the NARC project, an employer enters into an agreement to hire and train a mentally retarded person at the rate of pay offered nonretarded people in the same job category. In return, NARC will reimburse employers (using CETA funds) one-half of the starting salary for the first four weeks of employment and one-fourth of the starting wages for the next four weeks.

For most employers, the productivity of the retarded worker would most likely be more important than the federal stipend, and NARC seems to have made a concerted effort to ensure success. Local NARC chapters (there are 1,700 of them nationwide) screen all job applicants and certify that they're job-ready. NARC reaffirms the employer's absolute right of selection, training, and, if necessary, termination.

NARC makes a good case for hiring retarded persons in routine, repetitive occupations and backs up its claims with statistics and success stories. According to NARC, the mentally retarded person is far better suited for some jobs with which "quick thinkers" become bored and impatient. In fact, the routine character of certain occupations is precisely what makes the mentally retarded employee feel secure in his work. NARC clients have been holding jobs such as building maintenance man, mail clerk, laborer, office machine operator, warehouseman, stock clerk, food service worker, and keypunch operator.

NARC conducted a study of employers it has worked with in its OJT program and found that almost 75 percent of retarded people trained by employers under this program were retained by them. The list of employers participating in the program reads like a "Who's Who" of American business. It includes companies such as American Motors Corporation, Bally Manufacturing, Montgomery Ward, Newsday, Emerson Electric, Banquet Foods, Hyatt Corporation, Marriott Corporation, Coca-Cola Company, Rockwell International, Connecticut General Life Insurance Co., Grumman Aerospace Corp., and IBM. For further information, contact the National Association of Retarded Citizens, OJT Project, P.O. Box 6109, 2709 Avenue "E" East, Arlington, Texas 76011.

Goodwill Industries of America (GIA). GIA is one of the few organizations representing the handicapped that administers both Department of Labor and Department of Health, Education and Welfare programs to aid special groups of citizens. Under CETA and PWIP sponsorship, GIA has set up training, education, and job placement programs in Baltimore, Tacoma (Wa.), San Jose (Ca.), South Bend (In.), Colorado Springs, Columbus, Fort Worth, Miami, Winston-Salem (N.C.), Atlanta, Bridgeport (Ct.), Camden (N.J.), Detroit, Honolulu, Oakland, Pittsburgh, Portland, San Antonio, and Washington, D.C.

GIA emphasizes that training of the handicapped takes place in cooperation with industry *after* job needs in the community have been identified. In addition, employers assist GIA in structuring the training process so as to meet particular worksite needs. GIA boasts a high retention rate in private employment and encourages employers to return workers to the GIA workshop if further training is necessary.

GIA would like to expand its training and placement program to all of its 165 locations. For further information, contact GIA, 9200 Wisconsin Avenue, N.W., Washington, D.C. 20014.

Other Aids to Employers

In their communities, employers can identify a variety of programs and services designed to help handicapped individuals and veterans secure gainful employment. Described below are just a few of the organizations operating at the national level that can help employers develop local programs.

Blinded Veterans Association (BVA). Pointing to the successes of blinded or visually impaired veterans as television talk show hosts, ranchers, and state legislators, BVA encourages employers to give their members a job opportunity after BVA has given them counseling and training in the use of special equipment. For example, BVA has trained its members to use a made-for-the-blind office calculator, a computerized tape recorder, and a special video aid consisting of a closed-circuit television with a powerful lense.

Employers interested in listing job openings with the Blinded Veterans Association should contact the organization at 1735 De-Sales Street, N.W., Washington, D.C. 20036.

Registry of Interpreters for the Deaf. If an interpreter will be helpful to a deaf employee (HEW encourages this "reasonable accommodation"), employers may want to contact the Registry, which has more than 2,000 members and has chapters in several states. Write to the Registry of Interpreters for the Deaf, 814 Thayer Avenue, Silver Spring, Maryland 20910.

Paralyzed Veterans of America (PVA). PVA has set up a nationwide job placement service for its own members and for all people with substantial disabilities. By maintaining complete profiles on individuals in its computer system, PVA can match job candidates with prospective employers quickly and efficiently.

For employers interested in improving their affirmative action and recruitment/outreach programs, PVA can be contacted at 4330 East-West Highway, Suite 300, Washington, D.C. 20014. PVA's telephone number is 301-652-2135.

6
Can Employers Cope Effectively?

Studies conducted by the federal government and private consultants have revealed that employers are woefully ill prepared to meet their affirmative action requirements with regard to the handicapped. Most employers are either unaware of the regulations or, if acquainted with them, totally without the skills needed to achieve compliance.

Before discussing some strategies for coping with federal regulations and the discrimination charges that arise from lack of compliance, let us examine some of the reasons employers are facing difficulties in the handicapped community.

Activist Organizations

The handicapped population of the United States numbers somewhere between the broad range of 18 and 68 million, according to the U.S. General Accounting Office and depending on how you define handicapped. Whatever figure is chosen, it is generally agreed that the handicapped are no longer sitting at home timidly, if they ever did. Nor are they being shuttled off to work in sheltered workshops supported, in some cases, by the business community. Out of the burgeoning number of national, state, and local organizations representing handicapped persons has emerged a coalition of new activists demanding, among other things, equal opportunity in employment.

These organizations are not satisfied with what they consider the limited achievements of the Rehabilitation Act of 1973 and the Vietnam-Era Veterans Readjustment Assistance Act of 1974. For those employers who doubt their earnestness, how many would have predicted a sit-in demonstration in Washington, D.C., by handicapped citizens prior to the formulation of the Rehabilitation Act's Section 504 implementation rules? The sit-in did occur, with the wrath of handicapped activists directed against the federal bureaucracy.

Millions of handicapped persons will consider their legislative gains under the Rehabilitation Act and other federal statutes as minimal until they secure the general benefits contained in the Civil Rights Act of 1964. If the civil rights law is amended, all employers, not just federal contractors, subcontractors, and beneficiaries of federal financial assistance, will be subject to stringent equal opportunity rules protecting handicapped citizens. The trend both in Congressional action and in administrative rulings by federal agencies invested with the power to enforce legislation pertaining to the handicapped seems to be toward just such pervasive civil rights for handicapped persons.

The American Bar Association has endorsed vigorous enforcement of federal, state, and local architectural barrier laws. At least one traditional and prestigious law firm in Washington, D.C., has donated thousands of hours of legal counsel to disabled plaintiffs. Other law firms are expected to follow this lead.

Handicapped activists and their supporting organizations didn't appear overnight. Their growth has been encouraged by the federal government, foundations, and a number of community-minded groups. We will review some of the more prominent organizations representing handicapped persons and the kinds of programs they are instituting on behalf of their constituencies.

National Center for Law and the Handicapped (NCLH)

NCLH is a nonprofit organization headquartered in South Bend, Indiana, and affiliated with the University of Notre Dame Law School. The center receives funds from the Department of Health, Education and Welfare and other organizations in carrying out its activities as an advocate of the rights of handicapped persons.

In one court case, the center joined an ad hoc coalition of handicap advocacy groups to petition the federal government to strengthen the affirmative action obligation of recipients of federal funds. In a memorandum supporting the petition, NCLH insisted that despite federal laws and executive orders, "the promise of equal employment opportunity for the handicapped remains largely unfulfilled." On a number of occasions, NCLH has indicted the Department of Labor for laxity in enforcing Sections 503 and 504 of the Rehabilitation Act of 1973, which are discussed in detail in Chapter 1. Overall, NCLH has been urging OFCCP to enforce more stringently all components of the handicap legislation.

Among other activities, NCLH publishes *Amicus,* a bimonthly magazine. In one issue, *Amicus* summarized a round-table discussion with activist panelists on strategies for settling the employment grievances of handicapped persons. This particular issue is important to the business community, because it highlights a principle for handicapped activists referred to as "litigation strategy." Basically, the strategy focuses not only on suing employers for noncompliance but also on using (simultaneously) administrative agencies like OFCCP and HEW to conciliate disputes.

In almost every court case filed by activist attorneys, the strategy is to build a legal foundation for the favorable resolution of subsequent handicapped worker complaints. One panelist described the kind of employer he considered easily subject to "attack" for discrimination. Another discussed the advantages of suing in federal rather than state courts because the former are more sympathetic to constitutional and civil rights claims arising out of employment discrimination cases.

Decrying the lack of both litigation and lawyers in the handicap area, one panelist urged class action suits in every discrimination case filed so that a remedy for all persons similarly harmed can be secured. Another panelist, seeing potential roadblocks to class action suits on statutory grounds, argued that handicapped persons who are victims of discrimination should consider suing on the constitutional grounds of denial of due process and equal protection under the law, a tack already taken by some municipal as well as private employees.

Additional conclusions reached by the panelists included the need for increased surveillance of employers by activists' attorneys and the need to increase sympathy in the courts for the pleas of handicapped plaintiffs. The panelists also urged handicapped complainants not receiving a satisfactory response from a federal enforcement agency (for example, OFCCP) to request intervention by their congressmen and senators.

Clearly, NCLH is an astute and aggressive advocate of the rights of handicapped citizens and can be expected to speak out on important issues affecting its constituency.

American Coalition of Citizens with Disabilities (ACCD)

ACCD is headquartered in Washington, D.C. Its affiliated members include the National Association of the Deaf, the Paralyzed Veterans of America, and the National Association for Retarded Citizens. In one year, the coalition's membership of affiliated organizations for the handicapped grew from 17 to 62 while individual membership increased 300 percent.

In addition to conducting studies and lobbying Congress for stronger laws to aid the handicapped, the coalition enters lawsuits to further its members' goals. One such lawsuit resulted in the Department of Transportation mandating buses accessible for the handicapped. In another instance, the coalition joined the Department of Justice and became a plaintiff in a class action antitrust suit against the major U.S. manufacturer of wheelchairs.

In the opinion of many, ACCD is the lead advocacy organization in the United States for the rights of handicapped citizens.

Disabled American Veterans (DAV)

DAV is headquartered in Washington, D.C., and is a major veterans organization with more than 600,000 members.

DAV has a full-time national employment director on its staff, whose function is to assist disabled veterans with complaints arising out of alleged noncompliance by businesses in employment of disabled and Vietnam-era veterans. DAV has gone so far as to develop a special form for use by its members in filing employment discrimination complaints. The organization will even represent veterans in any necessary follow-up actions arising out of their complaints. Working through a field staff of 260 national service officers, DAV has the manpower to aid any disabled veteran in an employment discrimination case. These national service officers are stationed in every regional office of the Veterans Administration. DAV even has mobile field service units to assist veterans in remote areas.

As a self-appointed watchdog of Congress and the Department of Labor, DAV prods both organizations to implement tougher standards for industry to follow in hiring, training, and advancing disabled veterans and veterans of the Vietnam era. In addition to representing disabled veterans, DAV will make its advocacy services available to any individual who served in the military.

DAV has assisted in filing close to 200 complaints with the Labor Department on behalf of disabled veterans confronted with hiring discrimination. Also, DAV has filed complaints against a number of federal contractors who have failed to list job openings with the state employment service, a mandatory requirement under Section 402 of the veterans law discussed in Chapter 1.

In addition to its activist role on behalf of disabled veterans, DAV also consults with federal contractors on how they can meet their compliance obligations, particularly in the area of recruitment of qualified disabled and Vietnam-era veterans.

Legal Defense Fund of the National Association of the Deaf

The Legal Defense Fund was established in 1976 to handle significant lawsuits affecting the entire hearing-impaired community. Since that time, it has participated in over 100 court cases involving complaints of deaf clients in the areas of employment, education, insurance, and social services. In one case of interest to employers, the Legal Defense Fund represented a deaf man refused employment because the company had a standard policy not to hire the hearing-impaired. The court ordered the employer to change the discriminatory policy.

To further the civil rights of all deaf persons, the Legal Defense Fund publishes all its court cases in a series of reference books that are made available to other activist attorneys throughout the United States.

Mainstream, Inc.

Mainstream is a nonprofit organization headquartered in Washington, D.C., which encourages employers to comply with handicap legislation. Mainstream also assists handicapped individuals in resolving discrimination complaints and, to this end, has installed a toll-free "Call for Compliance Hotline." With this service, Mainstream consults with Labor Department officials to brief them on the complaint received and to aid in its resolution.

Other Mainstream activities include conducting compliance seminars for the business community and lobbying Congress for stringent handicap legislation. Clearly, Mainstream wears several hats in the compliance arena.

The Epilepsy Foundation of America

The foundation, also headquartered in Washington, D.C., is active on behalf of its particular handicapped constituency in a manner that appears to be conciliatory toward the business community. The foundation's goals are primarily educative and supportive of the various categories of epileptics. The foundation has released studies that indicate that two out of every 100 adults have epilepsy and that 80 percent of the people with epilepsy can work with no complications resulting from the disability.

Because the unemployment rate among people with epilepsy is reportedly more than twice the national average, the foundation has become actively involved in job placement in the private sector through its Training and Placement Service (TAPS) program. Because TAPS can assist an employer in fulfilling affirmative action requirements toward the handicapped, it is discussed in Chapter 5.

Human Resources Development Institute (HRDI)

Most employers, particularly those with union agreements, should be familiar with HRDI, the self-proclaimed "manpower arm" of the AFL–CIO in Washington, D.C. For years, HRDI has worked through its various affiliated unions to foster a variety of social causes in the area of employment and training. HRDI's activities involve job development and placement, apprenticeship outreach programs, skills upgrading programs, aid to ex-offenders, special assistance to veterans, and a relatively new program to help the handicapped secure meaningful employment.

Like the Epilepsy Foundation of America, HRDI receives federal grants and contracts to implement its handicap job placement program and is able to place at least subtle pressure on certain employers to fulfill statutory obligations to hire handicapped persons. HRDI, better staffed and funded than the Epilepsy Foundation, regularly surveys both union and nonunion employers in 60 cities nationwide to ascertain their compliance with handicap regulations. Some businesses might view the HRDI effort as an unofficial extension of the compliance review procedure of the Office of Federal Contract Compliance Programs (OFCCP) simply because both organizations pursue a similar compliance goal.

What should be of serious concern to employers is HRDI's efforts to foster participation of local bargaining agents in the development of affirmative action plans for the handicapped at companies where the union has representation. Under federal law, unions are required to participate in the development of such plans, and HRDI is urging them to do so. In short, the HRDI presence can be felt in many ways, including potential coercion of employers who fail to meet their equal employment obligations.

For employers with union agreements, HRDI can be of assistance in the implementation of an affirmative action plan for the handicapped. For this reason, their training and placement program is described in Chapter 5.

The American Council of the Blind

Headquartered in Washington, D.C., the American Council of the Blind serves as the lead agency for 43 active state groups as well as other special-interest organizations. The council defines itself as a research and advocacy organization on government affairs and federal legislation, always stressing the civil rights of blind persons. Echoing the sentiments of similar organizations, the council has bemoaned the "permissiveness" it sees in the implementation and enforcement of handicap legislation.

The National Association for Retarded Citizens (NARC)

NARC is an activist organization similar in operation to the Epilepsy Foundation of America. Headquartered in Arlington, Texas, NARC actively seeks to increase the employment of retarded persons in the private sector. To foster its efforts, NARC relies on funds provided by the Department of Labor. Considerable contact is made with private-sector employers to encourage the employment of NARC members. Because of the scope and apparent success of the NARC training and placement program, it is described in Chapter 5.

Paralyzed Veterans of America (PVA)

Headquartered in Washington, D.C., and much like the Disabled American Veterans, PVA serves veterans in the areas of advocacy and discrimination complaints. PVA has a membership of 11,000 out of a total of 20,000 paralyzed veterans, according to the Veterans Administration.

Through its 30 state and regional chapters, the PVA staff gives personal attention to the problems of its members. One critical problem, as PVA views it, is intentional and unintentional discrimination in employment faced by paralyzed veterans.

In its efforts to increase employment of paralyzed veterans in private industry, PVA has established a nationwide job placement service. Since employers can use such a service to enhance their affirmative action efforts under the law, the PVA placement program is described in Chapter 5.

Goodwill Industries of America

Headquartered in Washington, D.C., Goodwill has established several of what it terms "operation goals," a few of which imply stepped-up activity in the area of the rights of handicapped people. Goodwill has committed itself to improving the condition of the handicapped with regard to architectural barriers, employment, and training. Goodwill is particularly dedicated to eliminating discrimination in employment and will likely be working through its numerous local offices to do so. Goodwill offers some rather extensive training and employment placement services to employers. These activities are described in Chapter 5.

National Federation of the Blind

Headquartered in Washington, D.C., the federation represents thousands of blind or visually impaired persons.

In February 1979, the federation made news by petitioning the Secretary of Labor under the Administrative Procedures Act to limit the granting of subminimum wage certificates to private businesses and sheltered workshops. These certificates are granted for special categories of severely or multihandicapped individuals under the Fair Labor Standards Act (see Chapter 1).

The federation contended in its petition that subminimum wage certificates are not needed to spur employment of blind persons in competitive industry since Sections 503 and 504 of the Rehabilitation Act of 1973 already require businesses to give affirmative action preference to these persons. In fact, the federation charged private industry with using the subminimum wage exemption to secure cheap labor and to avoid the affirmative action provisions of the law, which require the active recruitment of qualified blind persons (among others) at full wages. In a related charge, the federation accused the business community with subcontracting work to sheltered workshops (whose workers can receive subminimum wages) to effect the same illegal goals.

In summary, the federation asked the Secretary of Labor to initiate special rule making to ensure equitable compensation not only for the 3,500 blind persons now being paid subminimum wages but also for the thousands who will follow after them.

Disability Rights Center (DRC)

With the help of Ralph Nader, DRC was set up in 1976 as a tax-exempt, nonprofit corporation chartered to further the civil rights of all disabled people.

On' of DRC's primary activities is the dissemination of material to disabled people on how to enforce their rights. DRC also trains the disabled in this area.

DRC regularly testifies before Congressional committees on legislation supporting the handicapped and petitions federal agencies on the development of new guidelines governing the enforcement of such legislation.

Like many activist organizations, DRC supports court cases that argue for a private right of action under Section 503 of the Rehabilitation Act of 1973, a subject that will be discussed later in this chapter.

The Office for Handicapped Individuals (OHI)

OHI was established in 1974 by an act of Congress to ensure consistency in the goals of more than 120 federal programs designed to benefit handicapped citizens.

OHI serves as an advisory arm to HEW and has no funding or enforcement authority. In effect, it acts as a sort of independent advocate for the causes and needs of the entire handicapped community. By evaluating the variety of federal programs available to assist the handicapped and disseminating information to all interested organizations, OHI is in a position to improve the delivery of services to this protected group.

Within OHI, there is a national Clearinghouse on the Handicapped. This clearinghouse responds to inquiries from handicapped individuals and from organizations which represent their interests both inside and outside the government.

In addition to the private advocacy groups discussed, the business community must contend with OHI as a publicly funded advocacy organization intent on improving the rights of the handicapped in every phase of American life, including employment in the private sector.

The National Easter Seal Society

One of the oldest organizations in the country serving the handicapped, the National Easter Seal Society has pioneered in providing rehabilitative services to thousands of Americans each year. The society has also continued its role as a staunch advocate of civil rights for handicapped citizens.

Operating through more than 1,100 state and local affiliates, the society provides physical, occupational, and speech therapy; audiological training; vocational counseling; and vocational evaluation. The society also serves as an advocate of equal rights for the handicapped at the federal, state, and local government levels. To help eliminate architectural and attitudinal barriers to the handicapped, the society conducts educational programs for several groups, including business organizations.

Public Interest Law Center (PILC)

PILC is a private, nonprofit law firm headquartered in Philadelphia that serves as an advocate for and counsel to groups such as the Paralyzed Veterans of America and the Pennsylvania Association of Retarded Citizens.

In *Drennan* v. *Philadelphia General Hospital,* a federal court case discussed later in this chapter, PILC won a judgment on behalf of epileptic job applicants. PILC boasts of having won all 18 employment discrimination court cases which it has handled and emphasizes that its future efforts in this area will focus on cases of exceptional legal impact.

PILC receives financial support from a broad range of public and private sources, including the Philadelphia Bar Association, the American Coalition of Citizens with Disabilities, the Paralyzed Veterans of America, and the Department of Health, Education and Welfare.

OFCCP Charges and Settlements

Despite frequent complaints about the lack of federal agency responsiveness, an increasing number of handicapped workers and applicants are filing discrimination charges with OFCCP before turning to the federal courts. The activist organizations discussed earlier in this chapter are a prime motivator of such actions.

According to the law, OFCCP must try to settle discrimination complaints against employers through conciliation and persuasion.

When a settlement can't be achieved amicably, however, and OFCCP feels that the charges against the employer have merit, then severe sanctions can be placed on the federal contractor or subcontractor. In many cases, the sanctions can have the impact of a federal court ruling.

What follows is a summary of discrimination complaints filed with OFCCP by handicapped workers and job applicants and the settlements that have been negotiated. Cases are described first by industry category and then by type of handicapping condition. Employers should take particular note of the diversity of disabling conditions that can qualify an individual as handicapped under federal law.

Airlines

In November 1978, American Airlines was accused by the OFCCP of discriminating against an epileptic worker who was suspended from his job as a fleet service clerk after suffering a seizure on the way to work. American Airlines was charged with failure to accommodate the employee's physical handicap at its Philadelphia location despite the size and variety of the airport workforce. The airline's contentions that it doesn't hire persons with seizures to operate motorized equipment and that the worker was continually absent were deemed by OFCCP to be irrelevant and inaccurate, particularly in light of the fact that the worker was offered an alternative job after eight months of suspension and that the new assignment would have required either relocation or commutation of nearly 200 miles a day. OFCCP said it tried unsuccessfully to "conciliate the dispute." American Airlines decided to contest the complaint and will go through the formal OFCCP hearing process.

In 1977, both Trans World Airlines and United Airlines were accused of discrimination under Section 503 of the Rehabilitation Act. TWA was charged with denying a former airline pilot a nonflying job after he recovered from a heart attack. TWA contended that the pilot was not qualified for the alternative job but said it was trying to find him another job in the company.

United was charged with improperly refusing employment to

an individual with a hearing impairment and an ankle injury. While United contended that the noise levels at the job site would aggravate the applicant's hearing condition and that it feared further injury to the ankle, the OFCCP investigation determined that the work was not performed in a high-noise area and that the ankle was completely healed.

To settle the complaint, United agreed to hire the person and pay over $13,000 in back pay compensation. The airline agreed further to discontinue the use of physical and mental job standards that tend to screen out qualified handicapped individuals and that are not related to specific job performance.

In 1979, Eastern Airlines was accused by OFCCP of discriminating against a diabetic. This was the first charge of its kind filed with the federal government. According to OFCCP, the diabetic was initially refused employment, was subsequently hired, and was then dismissed from a job as a ramp service employee. Eastern denied that it discriminates against persons with controlled diabetes and contended that the individual was fired for reasons unrelated to the handicap.

Construction Industry

E. E. Black, Ltd., a Department of the Army contractor in Honolulu, was cited for refusal to hire a worker with a spinal deformity despite the fact that he was cleared for heavy labor by previous medical examination. However, the company's pre-employment physical adjudged him a poor risk for work as a carpenter. OFCCP said that efforts to secure voluntary compliance through conciliation were unsuccessful. What followed is a textbook case for employers on the formal OFCCP hearing process.

When a Labor Department administrative law judge sided with E. E. Black, it appeared that the employer had prevailed. In March 1979, however, the Assistant Secretary of Labor overruled his own administrative law judge, finding that E. E. Black had discriminated against the applicant solely because of a perceived impairment and had thereby denied him a job for which he was fully capable at that time. Pointing to the company's medical opinions as the reason for disqualification, the Assistant Secretary ruled that E. E. Black had failed to prove that the individual couldn't perform immediate work as an apprentice carpenter. The complainant's condition had potential significance only in the future and not the present. The Assistant Secretary concluded also that E. E. Black's medical standards themselves illegally screened out the applicant. Thus the first administrative test of a key and controversial section of the definition of a qualified handicapped individual (that is, a person "perceived" as handicapped) resulted in coverage being extended by OFCCP.

E. E. Black was ordered to offer the complainant an apprentice carpenter position and to make a back pay settlement. When the company refused and decided to appeal the decision in federal court (the last recourse open to a federal contractor or subcontractor who wishes to challenge an OFCCP decision), the Department of Labor temporarily suspended enforcement of its ruling. E. E. Black asked the court to issue an injunction against enforcement of the DOL ruling and to affirm the company's right to practice what it called "preventive industrial medicine."

Black's position was supported by a friend-of-the-court brief filed by the Chamber of Commerce of the United States. The Chamber argued that the Labor Department ruling would force an employer "to hire an applicant that he knows has a particular medical condition which will cause him to be injured in the future."

In September of 1980, the United States District Court Judge Samuel P. King upheld the labor department's ruling that the construction worker was a "qualified handicapped individual."

Among other things, the court rejected E. E. Black's contention that only impairments defined by the American Medical Association are protected by the Rehabilitation Act, since such an interpretation would clearly go against the intent of congress to "protect a large number of people in a broad range of situations."

While agreeing with the company that the risk of future injury may be a legitimate factor to consider during the hiring process, the court stated that such concerns still cannot be used to "make an otherwise capable person incapable." Finally, the court's ruling pointed out that E. E. Black's hiring standards, in general, tended to "screen out" qualified individuals.

University

In November 1978, Northwestern University was the first university, as a federal contractor, cited by OFCCP for discrimination against the handicapped. The school dismissed a technical researcher in 1976 after she returned to work following mastectomy surgery. OFCCP charged that "equal opportunity was denied to a qualified employee because of an unrelated handicap." OFCCP stated further that no aspect of the cancer condition interfered with the worker's performance.

The university claimed the employee was not qualified for the position due to a lack of strong secretarial skills, but OFCCP found that such skills were not required in the employee's original job description. Also, the employee had received a satisfactory job evaluation when rated three months before undergoing the operation. The university was also charged with failure to take affirmative action to find the employee a similar professional position. OFCCP found evidence of jobs at the school for which she was qualified but not placed.

In October 1979, Northwestern settled with OFCCP without admitting a Section 503 violation. The university agreed to provide job counseling and other assistance to the complainant. Noting the school's commendable record in rehabilitative medicine, OFCCP decided that stronger measures weren't necessary.

Utilities Company

In May 1979, Virginia Electric and Power Company (VEPCO), the sole supplier of electrical power to the federal government in the state of Virginia, was charged with failure to hire a job applicant with a history of heart disease.

VEPCO denied the individual a job as a storeroom clerk, contending that the position was too strenuous for a person with a heart condition. The individual subsequently filed a complaint with OFCCP's regional office in Philadelphia.

After its investigation, OFCCP determined that the job was primarily sedentary in nature. The only physical activity involved was to climb two sets of stairs to deliver the mail each day. OFCCP ruled that VEPCO could have made a "reasonable accommodation" for the complainant by assigning the mail delivery responsibility to another worker. According to OFCCP, such an accommodation would *not* pose an "undue hardship" for VEPCO and was, in fact, the easiest type of modification any employer can make.

VEPCO challenged the OFCCP finding, claiming an "undue hardship," and requested a hearing before an administrative law judge.

Manufacturing

In 1977, General Dynamics Corporation refused an individual employment as a technical illustrator on the grounds that a previous back injury would be aggravated by the stress of working over a desk. The company also feared that his disability would increase its risk of liability. OFCCP charged that the job did not entail activities that would aggravate the condition, citing the fact that the man was employed shortly thereafter as a technical illustrator with another firm. The individual sought back pay for nine months of missed employment and received $5,063 in an OFCCP-negotiated conciliation agreement.

In 1977, Hercules, Inc., fired a man as "physically unsuitable" because of a disease causing periodic formation of growths that required surgical removal. An OFCCP investigation indicated that the individual was qualified to perform his assigned tasks and had, in fact, been working for the company successfully for more than one year before being terminated.

Copper Refinery

In April 1979, OFCCP charged ASARCO, an Arizona firm, with illegally dismissing two heavy-equipment operators with negative back X-rays. Both individuals were deemed unemployable by the company after being given mandatory physical examinations when returning to work from layoff status.

The attorney for both individuals described their conditions as a minor congenital deformity of the spine and a minor scarring from previous surgery. He claimed further that neither worker had a record of medical problems on the job.

OFCCP charged ASARCO with applying illegal physical job requirements and with using improperly the results of medical examinations. ASARCO contended that the physical requirements are validly job-related and has requested a hearing before a DOL administrative law judge. The ASARCO case marked the first multiparty complaint filed with OFCCP.

Appliance Company

In the summer of 1979, OFCCP charged the Frigidaire Sales Corporation with screening out a Vietnam-era veteran from an appliance servicing position in 1974 because he had received prior psychiatric treatment from a Veterans Administration hospital. This case marks the first time an administrative complaint was filed against an employer under Section 402 of the Vietnam-era Veterans Readjustment Assistance Act of 1974.

Municipal Government

The City of Los Angeles is the first municipal government charged with discrimination by OFCCP. The city's Department of Water and Power (DWP), by virtue of its $31-million annual contract with the U.S. Department of the Interior to operate the Hoover Dam, was accused under Section 503 of discrimination against a former mental patient.

The complainant is a 33-year-old Vietnam-era veteran who admitted during the application process that he had been hospitalized briefly for mental illness. After written and oral tests, the applicant was offered employment as an assistant tree trimmer, pending a medical examination. The physician disqualified the applicant, and the city's personnel department agreed that the individual was unsuitable on a psychological basis. When the Los Angeles Board of Civil Service Commissioners and the Medical Review Board sided with the city, the applicant filed a complaint with OFCCP's regional office in San Francisco.

The city's Medical Director stated that Los Angeles had a long-standing policy to automatically disqualify individuals with a history of severe mental illness from certain kinds of employment. Since the complaint was filed, however, Los Angeles has eliminated categorical disqualifications in an effort to comply with Sections 503 and 504 of the Rehabilitation Act.

In addition to charging discrimination against the complainant, OFCCP charged Los Angeles with general discrimination in its personnel practices. While the City was contesting the OFCCP charges, the Mental Health Association of Los Angeles County filed a class action suit against the City, alleging discriminatory hiring practices against those with a history of mental illness. The suit seeks an offer of employment for the complainant, an award of damages, and an order prohibiting any future discrimination by the city. Eventually, DOL dropped its administrative complaint against the city, citing information obtained through its investigatory process. OFCCP's action has no bearing, however, on the class action suit filed separately.

Miscellaneous OFCCP Back Pay Awards and Other Forms of Compensation

OFCCP continues to authorize wide-ranging awards to handicapped individuals as a result of complaints and follow-up investigations of contractors and subcontractors. Below are listed some awards made, by category of handicap.

Blind. A data processing technician received $19,797 in pay and accrued benefits from a Texas oil drilling company. The legally blind worker wore corrective lenses for his handicap but lost his job due to alleged poor performance. An OFCCP investigation found the company's allegation to be unfounded.

Manic depressive. A complainant received $2,631 from a Virginia electronic-equipment firm after he was refused employment because it was felt that he couldn't handle the pressure of a certain job. When the complainant's psychiatrist contended that the problem was controlled, the firm hired the individual in a different position but at the same rate in pay.

Hearing loss. A complainant received $4,624 from a Chicago heavy-equipment company which claimed that he couldn't perform the duties of the job satisfactorily. After an OFCCP investigation showed that the individual was qualified, he was reinstated. The settlement included back pay, retroactive seniority, and all accrued benefits.

Amputation. A complainant received $2,040 in severance pay from a New Hampshire engineering firm which had fired him. The individual was placed on recall and the company agreed to hire him in a comparable position.

Epilepsy. A complainant received $9,000 in back pay from a Massachusetts research company after it was determined that his epilepsy was under control. The company offered to rehire the complainant and agreed to pay a portion of Social Security for the period in question. The individual chose not to be reinstated.

Alcoholism. A bench assembly worker for an auto accessories company in Massachusetts received $3,500 in back pay plus a pension as of the date of his dismissal. The person was not reinstated and refused to be rehabilitated.

Spinal condition. A complainant in New York (also blind in one eye) received $1,500 in back pay and was reemployed by an insurance company. A complainant with a similar spinal condition received $7,000 from an economic-development corporation.

Back injury. A complainant in Pennsylvania received $5,446 in back pay from an air brake company. He was reinstated to his position with full seniority.

Disabled veteran. A 50 percent disabled complainant received $14,760 in lost wages and benefits from a food processing company in Pennsylvania. He was rehired at a higher salary with retroactive seniority.

Deaf. A complainant received $1,130 in back wages from a tire manufacturer in North Carolina. He declined a job offer.

Speech impairment. A complainant received $2,000 in back wages from a bottling company in Texas. The individual was offered reemployment but declined it.

Enlarged heart. A complainant received $4,840 in back wages from a trucking company in Colorado. He was also reinstated to his former position.

Kidney transplant. A complainant received $1,399 in back wages from a calculator manufacturer in Colorado. She declined an offer of re-employment with the company.

Veteran. A complainant with 20 years military experience was refused a job by a computer manufacturer in Arizona because he was "too military oriented." He received $14,000 in lost wages but declined an offer of employment.

High blood pressure. A complainant received $4,130 in back wages from a telephone company in Hawaii. The individual was reinstated, and job accommodations were made for him.

Mastectomy. A complainant received $3,946 in back wages from an electronics manufacturer in California. She was also reinstated to her former position.

Schizophrenia. A complainant received $3,625 in back wages from an aircraft company in the state of Washington. The individual was also hired as a structural engineer.

A few of the handicap categories discussed include veterans (one without any disability), since they are often eligible for substantially the same benefits as qualified handicapped individuals.

A number of other charges of discrimination against employers have been settled before intervention by OFCCP, to the benefit of handicapped persons. Clearly, employers faced a formidable task in taking on either the OFCCP or the persistent handicapped complainant.

Many employers feel that they are being victimized by frivolous charges of discrimination, yet they see no way to fight back effectively. Quite frequently, corporate lawyers opt for OFCCP settlements when the alternative is protracted and expensive litigation. The benefits of these "shortcut" settlements must be weighed against the damage done to the company's reputation *if* the complaint should have been challenged as unjustified. Fighting back against unjustified allegations of discrimination, however, will prove futile if employers don't have a proper "game plan" in operation long before the gauntlet is dropped. For these reasons, a carefully designed affirmative action plan for handicapped applicants and workers, as discussed in Chapter 7, is essential.

Activities in the Federal Courts

As we have just seen, with the encouragement of a number of activist organizations as well as on their own initiative, handicapped job applicants and workers are filing an increasing number of administrative complaints against employers. Most charges against federal contractors and subcontractors filed with the federal government result in the kinds of OFCCP settlements described in the previous section.

However, many handicapped complainants are not content to pursue OFCCP-sanctioned administrative remedies, citing the delays in processing complaints and the inadequacy of settlements. For these reasons, an increasing number of complaints are being filed in federal and state courts against employers.

Employers must remember that there is scant and inconsistent case history in this new area of personnel law, particularly as it affects the handicapped. Although more precise guidance is likely to be forthcoming, federal and state courts seem content now to approach the issue of handicapped discrimination on a rather individual basis. If there is precedent at all for some of the federal court decisions favoring either the handicapped individual or the employer, it has a foundation in the general area of employment discrimination against minorities and other protected classes. The following review of selected federal court cases will reveal a decided trend in favor of the handicapped individual's private right of action (in other words, the right to seek remedies in court) even when administrative remedies are available from OFCCP and HEW.

It is generally agreed that the U.S. Supreme Court decisions in *Griggs* v. *Duke Power Company* (1971) and *Albermarle Paper Company* v. *Moody* (1975) are two of the most important, if not the most important, cases in the history of equal employment opportunity law. These cases contain landmark decisions in that they broaden the scope of personnel law, clarify what employers are expected to do, and specify the potential financial penalties for noncompliance.

In *Griggs* v. *Duke Power Company,* the first case in which the Supreme Court interpreted Title VII of the Civil Rights Act of 1964, the central issue was the testing and selection procedures of an employer who had allegedly discriminated against minorities for years. Although the company contended that it had not intended to discriminate and that its testing and selection program met a "business necessity," the court turned to the Equal Employment Opportunity Commission's (EEOC) guidelines,* which indicated that any testing and selection program must be related to specific job requirements. Further, the EEOC's broad definition of test included "all formal, scored, quantified, or standardized techniques of assessing job suitability," such as evaluations of personal history, establishing educational requirements, scored interviews, and scored application forms. In deferring to EEOC guidelines, the court pointed out that Duke had not even attempted to validate its testing and selection procedures.

Thus in *Griggs,* the court clarified and expanded the definition of employment discrimination and brought into focus the issues of hiring, promotion, testing, and the business necessity of specific employment practices as they affect protected classes of workers. Some experts feel that the Griggs decision will eventually result in a requirement for all employers to avoid discrimination in these areas against an additional protected class, the handicapped.

In *Albermarle Paper Company* v. *Moody,* the issues raised by the plaintiff against the employer dealt with the seniority system, the pre-employment testing program, and, perhaps most important, the right to equitable financial relief for prior discrimination suffered.

In ruling against the employer in the Moody case, the court decided that back pay, in addition to being a proper means of compensating victims, should also be a financial incentive for the employer to end discrimination, regardless of whether or not the employer had acted in good faith. As in the Griggs case, the court also found that the employer's testing system did not meet a business necessity and that the burden was on the employer to prove that it did.

Two additional U.S. Supreme Court cases in the general area of employment discrimination, it is felt by many, will eventually have an affect on the rights of handicapped applicants and workers. In

---

*EEOC has jurisdiction over all employers (*except* federal contractors and subcontractors) with respect to employment discrimination. It is widely held, however, that court decisions involving general EEOC guidelines will have a direct impact on how the courts decide specific suits alleging discrimination against the handicapped.

McDonnell Douglas Corp. v. *Green,* the Supreme Court laid down the rules whereby an individual must establish his case for discrimination. First, the plaintiff must prove that he is a member of a protected class. He must next show that he applied for the job in question and was rejected despite being qualified. Third, rejection for the job despite qualification must be shown. Finally, it must be shown that the position in question remained open and applications were solicited by the employer after the plaintiff was rejected. If the plaintiff meets these four conditions, then the burden of proof shifts to the employer, who must set forth a nondiscriminatory reason for rejection of the applicant or for failure to promote a worker already on the job. Handicapped individuals meeting the four prima facie conditions discussed above could present a formidable obstacle to a federal contractor or subcontractor trying to defend his personnel practices.

Another important U.S. Supreme Court case, *Alexander* v. *Gardner-Denver Company,* centers on the question of arbitration decisions and the right to file an individual claim of discrimination (either simultaneously or later) even if the dispute is under arbitration. In this case, the court ruled that an employee can seek simultaneous remedies under his collective-bargaining agreement —administratively with the Equal Employment Opportunity Commission or via federal court action. It seems likely that the same rights affirmed in Gardner-Denver would be extended to a handicapped complainant, in which case the Office of Federal Contract Compliance Programs would replace the Equal Employment Opportunity Commission as the federal agency with administrative jurisdiction.

With these important decisions, the Supreme Court has laid the groundwork for other federal and even state courts to rule in a similar manner whenever protected classes of workers such as minorities or females are the victims of discrimination. Employers should not be surprised to find handicapped plaintiffs and even administrative agencies like OFCCP pointing to the Griggs and Moody decisions in particular to support their claims for back pay and other forms of redress.

Since the Supreme Court's Griggs and Moody decisions, federal court cases in which specific charges have been brought by handicapped persons against companies doing business with the federal government have been scattered and inconsistent. Looked at collectively, however, they seem to be leading toward expanded legal rights for the handicapped under Sections 503 and 504 of the Rehabilitation Act and Section 402 of the Vietnam-Era Veterans Readjustment Assistance Act.

In *Davis* v. *Bucher,* a U.S. district court ruled that the city of Philadelphia erred in not considering former drug addicts receiving methadone treatment as qualified handicapped individuals. The judge also ruled that the city had violated the equal protection clause of the Fourteenth Amendment. He then encouraged the filing of a class action suit on behalf of other handicapped individuals similarly discriminated against by the city. The judge ordered the city to cull its employment records and submit to the court lists of applicants denied employment since 1971 because they were former drug addicts. The city's employment practices were also declared unconstitutional.

In *Drennan* v. *Philadelphia General Hospital,* the federal district court ruled in favor of a plaintiff not hired as a laboratory technician because of her epilepsy. In addition to finding a cause of action under the Fourteenth Amendment, the court also found a private right of action to exist under Section 504. Applying the doctrine of primary jurisdiction, however, the court directed the plaintiff to pursue administrative remedies through OFCCP.

In another case, however, *Wood* v. *Diamond State Telephone,* a U.S. district court decided against a handicapped complainant, ruling that a private right of action is inconsistent with the legislation fashioned by Congress, in this instance the Rehabilitation Act of 1973, which emphasizes resolution of disputes by conciliation and persuasion.

In *Trageser* v. *Libbie Rehabilitation Center,* the U.S. Court of Appeals ruled that Title VI of the Civil Rights Act of 1964* does *not* provide the individual with a judicial remedy for employment discrimination by an institution receiving federal funds *unless* pro-

*Section 504 complaints are brought in federal court under the Civil Rights Act, since there is no expressed judicial review authority in the Rehabilitation Act.

viding employment is the primary objective of the aid or *unless* discrimination in employment necessarily causes discrimination against the primary beneficiaries of the federal aid. In June 1979, the Supreme Court refused to review the limited appelate court ruling.

In the Trageser case, a private corporation operating a nursing home received Medicare and Veterans Administration funds. The plaintiff, suffering from a visual impairment, was fired as director of nursing. In citing Section 504 of the Rehabilitation Act of 1973 and particularly the 1978 amendments to the law, the court held that it had only limited right to judicial review in employment cases of this nature.

If employers see the Trageser case as a victory for them against multiple and overlapping compliance responsibilities under Sections 503 and 504, they should also keep in mind the narrow court ruling which was handed down. For example, an employer participating in a federally subsidized training program under the Comprehensive Employment Training Act, in which the primary goal of the federal assistance is to foster permanent, full-time employment for the trainees, would presumably have been subject to court review under the Section 504 requirements. Also, the Trageser decision has not generated consistent interpretations by other federal courts, as will be seen shortly.

The Trageser case generated considerable critical comment by handicapped activists, HEW, and even members of Congress, who viewed the appellate court's literal ruling under Section 504 as a misinterpretation of legislative intent. Two senators wrote the U.S. Solicitor General urging him to seek the Supreme Court review which was eventually denied, arguing that the court in the Trageser case had unduly and inequitably restricted the intended civil rights protections of handicapped individuals.

Both the Fourth Circuit Court ruling in the Trageser case and the Supreme Court's decision not to review it have forced HEW's Office for Civil Rights (OCR) to modify its approach to enforcement of Section 504 in employment discrimination cases where federal financial assistance is not intended for employment purposes. But OCR is accepting the court's ruling as binding only in the states under the jurisdiction of the Fourth Circuit Court (that is, Maryland, Virginia, West Virginia, North Carolina, and South Carolina). In the meantime, employment discrimination cases will be accepted by OCR in other jurisdictions in the hope that a counter-ruling decision can be secured. If a favorable ruling can be obtained by OCR, an ultimate ruling on the extent of Section 504 coverage will likely be sought from the U.S. Supreme Court.

In September 1979, the U.S. District Court for Northern California ruled decisively in favor of private right of action under both Sections 503 and 504 of the Rehabilitation Act of 1973, pointedly disagreeing with the U.S. Fourth Circuit Court of Appeals' limited ruling in *Trageser* v. *Libbie Rehabilitation Center.*

In *Hart* v. *Alameda County,* the court ruled that a private right of action is supported by a Congressional decision to model Section 504 on Title VI of the Civil Rights Act of 1964, by Congress's decision (under the 1978 amendments to the Rehabilitation Act) to authorize the award of attorney's fees to prevailing parties under Section 504, and by the fact that existence of a private right of action is not likely to frustrate the purposes of Section 504.

The judge ruled in the Hart case that a private right of action under Section 504 is *not* limited to situations in which the primary objective of the federal financial assistance is to provide employment, even though the language of the federal statute seems to require such an interpretation. The judge looked beyond the limitation seen by the appellate court in the Trageser case to Congressional intent to expand, not restrict, Section 504 remedies under Title VI procedures. With regard to Section 503, the judge ruled that a right of private action was "assumed" to exist, even though administrative remedies through OFCCP might be available, since such a liberal interpretation will further the goals of the statute.

The plaintiff in the Hart case was a controlled epileptic who, after years as a volunteer counselor, applied for permanent employment in the Probation Department of Alameda County. The plaintiff passed the Civil Service examination and was placed on the eligibility list but never selected for the job. He contended that he was denied employment because of his handicap. The defense relied heavily on the argument that there was no private right of action under Section 503 or Section 504.

Since the court agreed with the defense that there was no expressed private right of action under either Section 503 or Section 504, it had to be determined whether such a remedy was *implied* in the statute. To do so, the court turned to *Cort* v *Ash* [422 U.S. 66, 78 (2975)] to apply four key factors:

1. Is the plaintiff one of the class for whose "especial" benefit the statute was enacted?
2. Is there an indication of legislative intent, explicit or implicit, either to create such a (private right of action) remedy or to deny one?
3. Is it consistent with the underlying purpose of the legislative scheme to imply such a remedy for the plaintiff?
4. Is the cause of action traditionally relegated to state law, so that it would be inappropriate to infer a cause of action based solely on federal law?

In finding that the plaintiff met all four conditions set forth in *Cort* v. *Ash,* the judge rejected the court's decision in the Trageser case as too narrow and restrictive. The judge saw good historical precedent for private right of action under Section 504 and, while agreeing that the courts are split on Section 503, reasoned that Congress "contemplated" such a private right of action. To assume such a right under Section 503, according to the court, causes no harm but rather fulfills legislative intent.

The court did rule, however, that a plaintiff must exhaust administrative remedies before assuming a private right of action. It was noted that the plaintiff in Hart had filed a complaint with OFCCP and apparently received no adequate response. In favoring supplemental court action, the judge also stated that administrative penalties, such as contract termination and debarment, "do not provide the kind of narrow, specific relief appropriate to remedy individual instances of discrimination."

The judge's decision in the Hart case more than hints at the inadequacy of OFCCP-type administrative remedies for handicapped complainants. In *Chaplin* v. *Consolidated Edison Company,* the

U.S. government came out and admitted for the first time its inability to process expeditiously all the Section 503 and Section 504 complaints it receives and, also for the first time, urged the court to rule in favor of a private right of action.

In a friend-of-the-court brief filed in the Chaplin case, which involved a claim of job discrimination by an epileptic, the departments of Justice, Labor (DOL), and Health, Education and Welfare (HEW) jointly argued that a private right of action was necessary to supplement Section 503 and Section 504 administrative remedies. Citing a burgeoning number of discrimination complaints backlogged in their enforcement agencies, the three federal departments argued that the handicapped deserved a "speedy resolution" of their complaints.

DOL pointed out that of almost 4,000 complaints received in 1978, only 1,760 had been resolved, with the situation worsening in 1979. In the court brief, the director of OFCCP stated that private lawsuits "would greatly assist the Department of Labor to enforce Section 503." HEW's Office for Civil Rights confessed to facing the same problem of being unable to resolve complaints expeditiously, even though HEW is operating under court order to resolve Section 504 complaints within 225 days of their receipt.

In January of 1980, the judge found in favor of a private right of action even when administrative remedies have not been exhausted, agreeing with the government that it could not make timely responses to complaints.

Thus in *Hart* v. *Alameda County* and *Chaplin* v. *Consolidated Edison Company,* employers can see examples of a seeming trend toward recognition of the right of handicapped individuals to press their cases in federal court.

In *Rogers* v. *Frito Lay,* the critical issue of private right of action was raised as well, with the complainant on the advocacy side and the employer on the opposing side. In 1979, the case reached the Fifth Circuit Court of Appeals in New Orleans, where it has been consolidated with a similar case, *Moon* v. *Roadway Express, Inc.*

In June 1977, the Rogers suit was dismissed by the U.S. District Court for the Northern District of Texas on the grounds that the court lacked jurisdiction. The judge ruled that Congress intended no private right of action when it enacted Section 503, since the law authorized the Department of Labor to investigate complaints against federal contractors and subcontractors. The U.S. District Court for the Northern District of Georgia reached the same conclusion in the Moon suit. The appellate court, however, agreed to answer the central question: is a private lawsuit a legal means of enforcing Section 503?

Friends-of-the-court briefs were filed in the Rogers/Moon consolidated case on behalf of the complainants by the Disability Rights Center of Washington, D.C., and the Public Interest Law Center of Philadelphia, two activist organizations discussed earlier in this chapter. These two activist organizations contend, among other things, that the 1978 amendments to the Rehabilitation Act of 1973 authorizing reasonable attorney's fees for "a violation of a provision" of the Rehabilitation Act imply that Section 503 complaints may be taken to federal court.

The employers in the Rogers/Moon case argued for the adequacy of OFCCP enforcement, declaring that the DOL–OFCCP administrative scheme is exactly the mechanism Congress intended under Section 503.

In February 1980, the appellate court affirmed the rulings of the two lower courts and held that handicapped individuals do not have a private right of action to sue under Section 503. The decision in this consolidated case marks the first time a federal appeals court has ruled on the issue of private right of action under Section 503 and points up, in light of other cases examined here, inconsistent interpretation of the handicapped legislation by federal courts throughout the United States.

The Fifth Circuit Court concluded that there was no "persuasive evidence in the legislative history" that Congress intended to confer a private right. Interpreting the law literally, the Court dismissed pro-private-right statements by some congressmen as "retroactive wisdom" which didn't change the language of Section 503 of the Rehabilitation Act.

In 1974, Bob Jones University of Greenville, South Carolina, attempted to avoid entirely the potential legal entanglements that result from participation in programs receiving federal financial assistance. Despite the fact that the school was not directly involved in any federally funded education programs, the district court noted that some enrolled students were receiving G.I. benefits and that the school was thus in fact participating, even if indirectly, in a federal program. Since the school refused to sign a compliance form as required under the Civil Rights Act of 1964, G.I. Bill payments to students attending Bob Jones University were stopped.

In almost every case cited in this section the civil rights of handicapped workers and applicants were affirmed by the courts, often in vigorous language. Clearly, many courts are giving a broad interpretation to the "intent" of Congress in writing Section 503 and Section 504 of the Rehabilitation Act of 1973. Members of Congress have even stepped forward and affirmed this broad intent.

With the federal government's own belated confession that it can't process expeditiously all the discrimination complaints it is receiving from handicapped applicants and workers, it seems likely that employers will face an increasing number of private lawsuits. With regard to the single issue of private right of action, employers operating in several states are faced with the perplexing problem of applying distinctly contrary district court decisions to their various operations until such time that the U.S. Supreme Court sets forth a new law of the land.

Employer Strategies for Coping

As we have seen, there are a number of activist organizations urging the handicapped either to file discrimination complaints with OFCCP or to pursue federal court remedies. Through its various compliance review procedures, OFCCP is also encouraging handicapped workers and applicants to "go public" with their discrimination charges. In many instances, the handicapped individual is simply no longer reluctant to file a charge of discrimination.

In view of this new activism, there are a number of companies for which there can be no effective strategy for coping with a discrimination complaint brought by a handicapped applicant or worker. By the time the charges reach the OFCCP review stage or result in a federal court case, defense efforts will prove to be futile. The futility arises out of a series of common employer mistakes, which often begin with management's failure to take compliance obligations seriously. Notwithstanding the business owner's frequent contention that only a sleuth could penetrate the labyrinthine network of federal handicap requirements, the hard fact of compliance responsibility remains unchallenged. What, then, can employers do to cope with the increasing legal demands of handicapped individuals?

Once top management commits itself to hiring and mainstreaming the handicapped, the compliance task is simplified greatly. Next, a series of "action-oriented" programs must be developed and communicated to all levels of management and supervisory personnel—and even to workers. The aggregate of these programs is commonly known as an affirmative action plan. By adapting (*not* adopting) the model affirmative action plan in Chapter 7 to its particular requirements, an employer is automatically preparing to meet the discrimination challenge. Frivolous or unfounded charges of employment discrimination have been known to result in substantial judgments against employers simply because the company was ill prepared to rebut the discrimination charge with irrefutable evidence of compliance. One common shortcoming is the failure to document personnel actions, no matter how routine or insignificant they might seem to be, which would bolster the employer's position.

As has been seen, both OFCCP and the courts, with the intent of the law clearly in mind, have insisted that employers "personalize" the affirmative action process.* Plans taken from another company's personnel manual or even from a government guide, for instance, cannot reflect the particular needs of any company. Location and type of facilities, nature of the industry, diversity of occupations, recruitment sources, transportation, availability of workers—all have a bearing on the responsiveness and effectiveness of an affirmative action plan.

Over the years, companies doing business with the federal

_____

*To comply with Section 504 requirements, unlike Section 503 requirements, an employer need *not* implement an affirmative action plan. HEW does require, however, that employers avoid discriminatory employment practices.

government have failed consistently in key areas on equal employment opportunity. These shortcomings include:

- Failure to analyze and respond to the total available workforce in the area.
- A tendency to define job categories and classes of workers (such as the handicapped) so narrowly that, intentionally or otherwise, individuals designated to receive preferential hiring treatment under the law are actually excluded from consideration.
- Failure to define accurately the deficiencies in the company's personnel system (in other words, not recognizing the under-utilization of handicapped persons or not placing qualified handicapped workers in certain preferred job categories).
- Failure to develop realistic hiring goals for protected classes of workers, thereby either raising expectations too high or leaving them too low (in either instance, the likelihood of a discrimination charge is enhanced).
- A tendency to rely on good-faith efforts to substantiate compliance when only a solid affirmative action plan and documentation will suffice.

By meeting head-on the complex and time-consuming demand to develop an adequate affirmative action plan—that is, by making affirmative action as much a business objective as marketing strategy or inventory control—employers can deflect unwarranted charges of discrimination. A solid plan reinforces the employer's verbal commitment to doing what is statutorily mandated. From a staunch business point of view, the affirmative action plan is not just an idealistic goal; it is "preventive maintenance" in the truest sense.

Once an employer has a workable affirmative action plan in operation, he is ready to challenge unfounded charges of discrimination filed either with OFCCP or with the courts. To date, few employers have chosen to do anything except acquiesce to OFCCP settlement demands. As discussed earlier, the U.S. Supreme Court decisions in the Griggs and Moody cases have established a precedent for favoring the rights of workers by throwing the burden of proof back on the shoulders of the employer when a charge of discrimination is made.

The recent surge in employee litigation has forced many companies to focus their attention on a single, realistic goal—staying out of court. This understandable goal must be balanced with the dangerous precedent established by hasty out-of-court settlements which, inexpensive on the surface, spawn additional unfounded charges involving considerable expense.

More and more frequently, employers are taking practical steps to stave off personnel problems. Many employers are still asking the fundamental question: what practical steps can I take? For one thing, all relevant personnel procedures can be put in writing. Before an employee is fired or refused a promotion (or an applicant is rejected), his qualifications should be studied objectively in relationship to other workers in comparable positions. Job descriptions should be rewritten so as to include only essential criteria. Above all, every personnel decision should be fully documented and then guarded as confidential. No longer can employee information be released to the public or even prospective future employees with impunity.

As we have seen, in trying to predict the intent of Congress in writing the handicap legislation, there is little specific case law on which the employer can rely for guidance. In addition, only one OFCCP charge of discrimination (against E. E. Black, Ltd., of Honolulu) has reached the administrative law stage, where the Assistant Secretary of Labor ruled ultimately in favor of the applicant and the company, in turn, sued in federal court. When U.S. district courts have sided with employers against handicapped complainants, it has normally been on a legal technicality rather than on the merit of the case. For example, in the *Wood* v. *Diamond State Telephone* case, cited earlier, the judge ruled that the court lacked jurisdiction to hear the case since Congress intended for complaints to be filed with OFCCP. As can be seen in the earlier discussion of OFCCP settlements, however, as well as in the review of state laws and court decisions in Chapter 2, most judicial rulings have been in favor of the handicapped complainant.

Unquestionably, every employer doing business with the federal government needs a personalized strategy for coping with discrimination charges by handicapped workers and applicants. Notwithstanding the confusion and uncertainty created in the last few years by conflicting court decisions and changing federal compliance guidelines, employers need to undertake a thorough analysis of their hiring and employment practices in the context of the statutes on the handicapped and veterans. Only after this analysis is completed can a workable strategy be developed.

A number of years ago, one major company that was also incidentally a federal contractor undertook just such an analysis of its personnel practices and its affirmative action efforts, attempting to reconcile its findings and business needs with the demands to accommodate various classes of citizens protected by federal law. What follows is the efforts of this one employer and its confrontation with federal compliance agencies after developing a strategy for coping.

In January 1979, the nation's largest retailer, Sears Roebuck & Company, filed suit in U.S. District Court in Washington, D.C., charging OFCCP, HEW, and a host of other federal agencies with issuing conflicting equal employment regulations, including those covering handicapped workers and applicants. Sears is appealing the dismissal of its suit by the U.S. District Court.

Sears asked the court for injunctive relief and for a ruling that federal agencies be required to establish uniform compliance guidelines for employers to follow. Employing the tactic of some handicapped complainants, Sears charged that its right to due process guaranteed under the Fourteenth Amendment had been abridged. Almost concurrently with the filing of its court brief, Sears charged that the Equal Employment Opportunity Commission (EEOC)* broke off negotiations with it when it was willing to settle discrimination charges amicably.

In October 1979, EEOC filed a series of lawsuits against Sears, charging sex and race discrimination in four states. Contending

---

*EEOC enforces general antidiscrimination statutes involving women, minorities, and other protected classes but has no authority over federal contractors and subcontractors, whose requirements to hire the handicapped are overseen by OFCCP. This division of enforcement authority and the confusion which results from it is a key component of the Sears case.

that the suits are without foundation, Sears cites EEOC pronouncements in 1969 and 1974 that the company was a leader in affirmative action efforts. The governments suits were brought under the Civil Rights Act and Equal Pay Act. They seek to enjoin Sears from future discriminatory practices, to require the establishment of affirmative action plans, and to force the award of back pay. It had been rumored that an EEOC internal memorandum advising against the suits, because of Sear's voluntary compliance efforts, was a major reason why the federal government didn't file a nationwide lawsuit but instead focused the complaint in four states.

What is behind Sears' unprecedented challenge to the federal government's authority to regulate the employment practices of private companies? What is Sears' strategy for coping? While some individuals and organizations have accused Sears of using the suit to counterattack against the EEOC, others see Sears' action as the culmination of years of frustration trying to comprehend and then comply with a maze of government employment requirements.

In looking at Sears' efforts over the years and at the company's analysis of the country's employment picture since World War II, other employers may see an articulate rendition of their own unspoken frustration. Sears, in its own words, does *not* question the principles of affirmative action and equal employment opportunity. While Sears asserts that it has spent millions of dollars over the years to comply with government employment regulations and has achieved acceptable results, EEOC and other federal agencies assert that the company's achievement is inadequate. Without choosing sides, however, we can examine Sears' effort over the last 30 years—from Sears' point of view— to determine ways in which other employers can meet the challenge of discrimination against the handicapped.

At the heart of Sears' case is the contention that the federal government itself has created, since World War II, an unbalanced workforce dominated by able-bodied white males. In conducting its own study, Sears found that the G.I. Bill of Rights, veterans preference laws, and a variety of federally financed vocational training programs since World War II have helped mold a workforce that practically eliminates minorities and women. How then, Sears asked, can the federal government demand that employers hire persons either not in or not prepared (through adequate training) to enter the workforce?

Faced with this apparent paradox, Sears insists that it declined to sit back and do nothing. For one thing, Sears set up a special Department of Equal Opportunity within its national personnel office in 1968. The director of this department reports directly to the vice president of personnel. Also in 1968, Sears voluntarily became a federal contractor, thereby subjecting itself to the nondiscrimination provisions of Executive Order 11246 (and subsequently a variety of handicap statutes). Between 1968 and 1978, Sears worked closely with the General Services Administration* (as it was required to do) in developing an affirmative action plan which would meet federal guidelines. According to Sears, GSA conducted over 2,000 compliance reviews of its facilities and failed to detect any major problems. (Note: in April 1979, Sears announced that it will no longer do business with the federal government, citing harassment from OFCCP. In Sears' view, OFCCP is retaliating for the retailer's court challenge.)

In the fall of 1968, Sears prepared a publication entitled "Guide for the Development of an Affirmative Action Plan." This guide was sent to more than 2,500 Sears facilities and was followed by visits from Sears executives to these same facilities to enhance the development of affirmative action plans.

In 1970, Sears prepared and issued to its retail stores a comprehensive affirmative action manual, setting down detailed recordkeeping procedures and requiring detailed progress reports. Goals and timetables for hiring various categories of protected workers were established and, as reinforcement, had to be verified in *written* communications to Sears executives and managers.

In 1971, to encourage compliance by its subcontractor suppliers, Sears held a 2½-day conference. The conference was designed to brief subcontractors on their legal obligations to take affirmative action and to communicate to suppliers Sears' efforts and commitment in this area.

Believing as far back as 1968 that only solid evidence could be

*Prior to consolidation of compliance authority with OFCCP, a variety of federal agencies monitored the activities of government contractors, depending on the goods or services provided the government.

used to defend its actions, Sears began statistical studies to document its improvement in the area of affirmative action. In 1973, Sears convened another meeting of top executives and managers to review progress and problems in the company's affirmative action program. Out of this meeting grew Sears' MAG Plan, which became effective in 1974. Standing for Mandatory Achievement of Goals, MAG became the newest linchpin in Sears' effort to ensure what it considered a quality affirmative action effort.

As further documentation of its affirmative action efforts, Sears published its consolidated EEO-1 report in its 1973 annual report to shareholders. This report must be submitted to the federal government, but Sears was the first corporation in the United States to "go public" with it, thereby making its equal employment efforts accessible to shareholders, employees, and all other interested persons. In the 1977 annual report, Sears devoted a full page to "Progress in Equal Opportunity."

This capsulization of Sears' position and its efforts should serve as both a guide and also a warning to other employers subject to handicap legislation. As a guide, it shows the kinds of careful, well-documented actions necessary to meet the compliance challenge; as a warning, it illustrates that even the most conscientious effort can meet with problems and suspicions. This situation presents more than a veiled warning to other employers that even "preventive maintenance" can lead to incalculable problems.

Employers can look to the Sears effort as a model in at least one respect. Top executives (and *not* the personnel staff operating autonomously and without authority) decided long ago that affirmative action would be treated like any other business objective. Thus a reporting system was set up to monitor the affirmative action program and measure its progress. In Sears' view, weaknesses were identified and corrected. Finally, Sears informed its executives, managers, and supervisors that performance with regard to the affirmative action program rated along with other business objectives in determining compensation and promotion.

In the end, whether or not Sears wins its court case or even whether or not Sears in fact practices discrimination in employment, is somewhat inconsequential to other employers. What is important is that Sears had a personalized strategy for coping with equal employment and affirmative action requirements. Without such a plan, Sears' challenge would have been a needless expenditure of resources in a pre-ordained losing cause.

Short of mounting a challenge of the magnitude of Sears', what else can employers do to cope with discrimination charges? For one thing, they can prepare, well in advance, a strategy for working through the federal agency hearing process. If a federal contractor is charged with discrimination by a handicapped individual, the complaint will be processed by OFCCP. If a recipient or beneficiary of federal financial assistance is so charged, HEW's Office for Civil Rights has jurisdiction.*

If a federal agency decides that the discrimination charges have merit but conciliation can't be achieved, the hearing process is invoked automatically. It is at this stage that the employer faces considerable obstacles without an excellent defense. If an employer's case hinges on the dim memory of a supervisor or incomplete personnel records, for instance, the chances of fighting effectively against even frivolous discrimination charges will be reduced significantly. In short, every prudent employer will have to develop a strategy for coping, whether it be for a court defense or for a federal agency challenge.

Using the Federal Agency Hearing Process

At HEW, hearings for Section 504 complaints are conducted in a formal manner according to the guidelines laid down in the Federal Administrative Procedures Act. Reasonable notice will be sent to employers by registered or certified mail, return receipt requested. At least 20 days notice will be given before a hearing is scheduled, but an employer can request additional time to prepare his defense.

Rather than appear in person, an employer can waive a hearing appearance and submit written information and argument "for the record." By failing to respond at all, an employer totally waives his rights and consents to any decision rendered on the evidence

*HEW has jurisdiction until the 30 other federal agencies finalize their enforcement mechanisms, as discussed in Chapter 1.

available during the hearing. Obviously, a well-prepared handicapped complainant, whether or not he is represented by an activist organization, poses a formidable challenge to the employer who views the charges against him as capricious or inconsequential.

The administrative hearing is conducted in a courtlike atmosphere with testimony under oath, cross-examination, exhibits, arguments, and briefs. Witnesses invited by the government to testify on its behalf will be paid expenses to do so. Opportunity is given both parties to refute facts and arguments advanced by the other side. All decisions are based on the hearing record.

A hearing examiner presides over the session and will make either an initial decision or certify the record (along with his recommendations) for a decision by the "reviewing authority" or the Secretary of HEW. The hearing examiner may even ask the parties to submit trial briefs. In any case, both the complainant and the employer will receive a copy of the examiner's findings and recommendations.

To challenge an initial decision by a hearing examiner, an employer must file his exceptions with the reviewing authority designated. In rare instances, a final review will be made by the Secretary of HEW. If an employer fails to file and document the exception, his administrative remedies may be exhausted, but he can still seek judicial review (as we have seen in the Sears case, where negotiations with EEOC were unsuccessful). A complainant has the same dual rights as the employer, and, as we have also seen, activist organizations are encouraging handicapped persons to seek both administrative remedies and court relief, often simultaneously.

A decision by HEW against an employer can result in termination or suspension of a federal financial assistance agreement. Assistance will be restored if and when compliance is documented with reasonable assurance that it will continue.

As mentioned in the discussion of the Freedom of Information Act in Chapter 1, employers can expect to have their personnel practices "laid bare" at administrative hearings. HEW states in its regulations that "all pleadings, correspondence, exhibits, transcripts of testimony, exceptions, briefs, decisions, and other documents" related to the hearing may be inspected and copied in its Office for Civil Rights in Washington, D.C. It is at this stage that an employer's inadequate affirmative action plan can come back to haunt him time and time again.

Perhaps in a signal to activist organizations, HEW has ruled that any interested person or organization can file a petition to participate in a hearing. However, an "amicus curia" cannot introduce evidence and is not a party to the hearing. Nonetheless, these friends of the court (as we have seen in our discussion of activist organizations earlier in this chapter) can be quite effective in their restricted roles. In a hearing, they can ask the examiner to propound specific questions to witnesses. The amicus curia can also submit briefs. In short, there is no substitute for an employer's careful preparation and solid documentation when defending against a charge of discrimination during an HEW administrative hearing.

Under Section 504, HEW also has the additional authority to refer complaint cases to the Civil Rights Division of the Department of Justice, where the decision to institute litigation can be made. This collateral authority poses increased problems for the employer, since it provides HEW with an option to use in those cases where the administrative hearing process is deemed inadequate.

At OFCCP, the hearing process is similar to HEW's. OFCCP handles complaints under both Section 503 of the Rehabilitation Act and Section 402 of the Vietnam-Era Veterans Readjustment Assistance Act. An administrative law judge presides over the formal hearing process and issues his recommendations for the settlement of all charges and disputes.

However, as was seen in the E. E. Black, Ltd., case discussed earlier, the administrative law judge can be overruled by a higher official in the Department of Labor. In the E. E. Black case, the Assistant Secretary for Employment Standards denied that he had violated either the Administrative Procedures Act or his own Department's regulations by interceding. The Assistant Secretary ruled that he had ultimate authority to judge discrimination disputes under Section 503.

Additional Strategies

As we have seen in this chapter, there is no substitute for a sound, workable affirmative action plan that adapts to changing times and necessities and has the ongoing support of top management, middle management, supervisors, and even workers. Whether confronted in court or in an administrative hearing, an employer can quite conceivably lose against a frivolous charge of discrimination simply because he was ill prepared or, even worse, took the potential problem lightly.

As a means of staying current with changing federal regulations that protect the rights of handicapped persons, employers should participate in business organizations that monitor and report on federal regulations affecting companies doing business with the federal government. (As we have seen, handicapped individuals are buttressed in their demands by a variety of knowledgeable activist organizations.) The National Association of Manufacturers, for instance, is a very active trade association representing some 12,000 manufacturers, many of whom do considerable business with the federal government. Headquartered in Washington, D.C., NAM has frequently taken the time to place before the federal government, in a sensible and well-thought-out fashion, the employer's dilemma and confusion in trying to comply with the requirements of Sections 503 and 504. The Equal Employment Advisory Council, also headquartered in Washington, D.C., has been similarly vocal on the myriad requirements faced by employers under the Rehabilitation Act and other laws and regulations protecting the rights of handicapped citizens.

Employers who are determined to stay current on the handicap legislation and the interpretative regulations promulgated by various federal agencies should consider active participation in trade organizations like NAM, EEAC, and the U.S. Chamber of Commerce. The President's Committee on Employment of the Handicapped includes representatives from the business community to articulate the problems faced by the private sector and can be an excellent source of information.

Employers can also benefit from a number of publications dealing with handicap requirements in addition to those listed in

Appendix O. For instance, the *Federal Register* contains all official announcements by the Department of Labor and HEW, including rulings on enforcement of the handicap laws. These two federal departments also publish a number of newsletters, explanatory brochures, and guides on their activities, all of which are available to employers.

In the private sector, the Bureau of National Affairs, Commerce Clearinghouse, and a number of law reviews publish journals on employment practices which include important updates on requirements pertaining to the handicapped.

When management stops and contemplates the adverse impact of a charge of discrimination made by a handicapped worker or applicant—whether it be disruption of the workforce, lowering of employee morale, deterioration of the community image, or expensive litigation—it must realize that there is no substitute for a well-planned strategy for coping.

7
Developing an Affirmative Action Plan

The principle of mandatory affirmative action plans for protected classes of citizens goes back at least as far as 1964 with
the passage of the Civil Rights Act. The Labor Department is just
one federal agency looking at the Civil Rights Act in formulating
regulations for the safeguarding of handicapped persons' rights.

Since 1964, employers (including government contractors) have
been seeking guidance in setting up and implementing their own
personalized affirmative action plans. The stories of government
regulators announcing complex compliance rules and then refusing to interpret or explain them are legendary in the business
community. For most conscientious and well-intentioned
employers, however, the critical question is not confusing at all but
is simply one of getting the affirmative action job done efficiently.
The confusion over Section 503 versus Section 504 requirements
exacerbates an already difficult task for employers but does not
remove the responsibility for taking positive affirmative action
steps. Where, then, employers have been asking, is the guidance
needed to comply with antidiscrimination laws?

At least a few federal agencies, including the Department of Labor, have endorsed guidelines prepared originally by the Equal Employment Opportunity Coordinating Council and have recommended that private employers follow them in setting up affirmative action plans. Although the council's guidelines were not prepared with the handicapped in mind, they do offer excellent direction for employers on the formulation of affirmative action plans.

The council was established in 1972 by an act of Congress and directed to develop and implement policies which would eliminate conflict and inconsistency among agencies of the federal government responsible for administering and enforcing antidiscrimination laws. As might have been anticipated, federal agency members of the council couldn't agree on which policies to endorse, and the council was eventually dissolved. However, the 1978 amendments to the Rehabilitation Act of 1973 authorized the establishment of an Interagency Council, with the parallel responsibility of ensuring consistency in the enforcement of the handicap statutes. Time will tell whether or not the new council will be able to carry out its Congressional mandate. The original council's recommendations have no direct bearing on the activities of private employers, nor do they specifically address the rights of handicapped workers or applicants. However, the principles of responsible affirmative action laid down by the original council should be of considerable guidance to employers required by federal law to hire and accommodate the handicapped.

Equal Employment Opportunity Coordinating Council

The council's quintessential statement was that "equal employment is the law of the land," a comment echoed by both Labor Secretary Marshall and HEW Secretary Califano in speeches on Section 503 and Section 504, respectively. This statement has been repeated and paraphrased so frequently by federal officials charged with enforcing handicap statutes that employers should accept it as an inexorable fact of business life. The council goes on to recommend the following:

■ Equal access to employment should be limited only by the ability to do the job.

■ The remedies for past and present discrimination are vigorous enforcement of the law and affirmative action by employers.

■ A systematic plan based on sound organization analysis and problem identification is crucial to the accomplishment of any affirmative action objective.

■ Results-oriented (not cosmetic) affirmative action plans must be developed and implemented.

■ The employer's workforce must be analyzed to determine whether specific classes (such as handicapped persons) in individual job classifications are substantially similar to the percentages of the same classes in the job market with job-related qualifications.

■ When disparities are found between classes and job categories, each element of the overall selection process should be examined to determine which elements create discrimination.

■ The selection process should be examined to determine each element's validity in predicting job performance, specifically with regard to recruitment, tests, job ranking, interviews, and recommendations for selection, hiring, and promotion.

■ Affirmative steps to remedy discrimination must take into account the availability of basically qualified persons in the relevant job market.

Principles of Affirmative Action

Nothing is more critical than the employer's *awareness* of the legal requirements for hiring and accommodating the handicapped. This awareness should lead to a carefully planned and responsive affirmative action effort. Over the years, a number of principles have been established which help employers in the general area of equal employment opportunity. These principles can be applied to a specific program for any protected class of citizens, such as the handicapped, and include:

■ Establishment of a long-term goal and timetable for specific job categories.

■ Establishment of short-range interim goals and timetables.

- A recruitment program designed to attract qualified members of the protected group to be served.

- A systematic effort to organize work and redesign jobs that provide opportunities for persons lacking skills and knowledge but who can, with proper training, progress in a career field.

- Revamping selection procedures that have not been validated so that exclusion of certain classes of persons is either discontinued or not initiated in the first place.

- Ensuring that qualified members of affected groups are included in the pool from which new employees are selected.

- Regular monitoring of the affirmative action program, with timely adjustments where effectiveness is not demonstrated.

- A systematic effort to provide career advancement training, both classroom and on the job, to employees locked in to "dead-end" jobs.

- A companywide goal of genuine equal employment opportunity for all qualified persons.

With this historical perspective in mind, the affirmative action plan at the end of this chapter has been designed as a model for employers who, with contracts of at least $50,000 and with at least 50 workers, have to comply with Section 503 of the Rehabilitation Act of 1973 and/or Section 402 of the Vietnam-Era Veterans Readjustment Assistance Act of 1974. As already discussed, although Section 504 does not explicitly require recipients of federal financial assistance to have an affirmative action plan, the language of Section 504 suggests that they do. Not every suggestion in the model will be appropriate or necessary for each employer. In fact, the federal government urges employers to make sure that every affirmative action plan responds to the particular need of the firm and the workforce to be served. Employers must remember that a number of activist organizations, the federal government, and even employees will be scrutinizing the plan. It is imperative that the plan reflect accurately not only company policy but also the actions which will be taken to carry out company policy.

Employers mustn't forget that information placed in the affirmative action plan may very well end up being examined by a host of other parties. Editing of the plan may be necessary to protect legitimately confidential information. However, "sheltering" of confidential data can't be allowed to stand in the way of the plan's overall effectiveness. Ample time should be devoted for training key personnel in the operation of the plan and the philosophy which underpins it. More than a few employers have been damaged in negotiations with OFCCP because executives, managers, and supervisors were unable to discuss their affirmative action plan intelligently and convincingly. In this respect, executives and managers should be informed that their work performance is being evaluated, at least in part, on how they contribute to the plan's success. This business approach to affirmative action will eliminate the frequent misunderstanding of management and personnel staff that the plan is some sort of voluntary social effort which doesn't affect either the company's profitability or their own compensation and promotion opportunities.

In all instances, documentation must be made of actions taken by the company to comply with the handicap laws. This documentation will be invaluable proof of the company's efforts in the event a complaint is filed with OFCCP by a handicapped worker or applicant.

Every conceivable internal and external company resource should be mustered to illustrate, not only to the federal government but also to employees and the community, that the affirmative action effort is genuine. Some employers have discovered that unexpected benefits can be derived from looking at the affirmative action obligation in a positive fashion. One company, for example, put its front-line supervisors through an awareness/sensitivity program to detect workers with alcohol- or drug-related problems. These workers were then referred to qualified counselors available from a community agency. Multiple benefits were realized by this enlightened approach: handicapped workers were handled properly (and legally); supervisor participation in solving employee problems was ensured; worker productivity and morale were improved; professional services available in the community were secured at virtually no cost; and the company's affirmative action effort was documented.

Some employers, again at no cost, work with various state

vocational rehabilitation agencies—and should work with vocational rehabilitation specialists of the Veterans Administration—to obtain specially adapted equipment and interpreters for their handicapped workers. In short, it is not inconceivable that an employer can make a virtue out of the affirmative action necessity.

Special Note: For employers required to comply with both the Rehabilitation Act of 1973 and the Vietnam-Era Veterans Readjustment Assistance Act of 1974, the terms "handicapped person" or "handicapped individual" as used in the model affirmative action plan which follows should be interpreted so as to include, where appropriate, "disabled veteran" or "Vietnam-era veteran."

Model Affirmative Action Plan for Handicapped Workers and Applicants

Statement of Intent

It is the policy of this Company not to discriminate against any qualified employee or applicant for employment in regard to any position because of a physical or mental handicap or Vietnam-era service.

Reasonable accommodation will be made wherever necessary for the handicapping conditions of all employees or applicants, provided that the individual is otherwise qualified to perform the assignments connected with the job and provided that any accommodations made do not interfere with the effective operation of this Company.

Administration and Implementation

John Smith is responsible for the affirmative action program at this Company and has the complete support of management in the implementation of this Plan. Mr. Smith will be responsible for the following functions:

- Development of policy statements, programs, and internal as well as external communications regarding our affirmative action program.
- Design and implementation of an audit system to measure the effectiveness of our affirmative action program and to detect problems that need to be solved.
- Regular discussions with managers, supervisors, and employees to ensure that the Plan is being followed.
- Determining the need for remedial action and designing programs to correct deficiencies in the Plan.

- Serving as liaison between this Company and enforcement agencies, handicapped persons, and organizations representing the handicapped.
- Keeping management informed of the latest developments in the entire affirmative action area.

Dissemination of Policy

This Company's policy on affirmative action will be made known to all appropriate individuals and organizations both within and without the Company, including recruitment sources, community agencies, applicants, supervisors, management, and workers.

The following actions will be taken to ensure proper dissemination of information about our affirmative action plan:

- Executives, managers, supervisors, and other employees will be notified about the affirmative action plan. [Note: one way to document efforts to improve employment opportunities for handicapped persons is through interoffice memos such as the sample shown later in this Plan.]

- Reasonable internal procedures to ensure dissemination and enforcement will be developed, including training sessions and briefings on the Plan for all employees.

- Recruitment sources will be contacted and briefed, including private employment agencies, the state employment service, the local veterans' employment representative, the nearest vocational rehabilitation agencies, sheltered workshops, college placement offices, state education agencies (for example, schools for the blind, deaf, and retarded), labor organizations, and other groups serving the handicapped.

- Applicants and employees who believe they are covered by and wish to benefit from our Plan are invited to identify themselves on a confidential basis either immediately or at any time in the future and are encouraged to make recommendations on their own placement and accommodation. (Our formal Company invitation is reprinted in two separate "notices" at the end of this Plan.)

- All subcontractors, vendors, and suppliers will be notified in writing of our affirmative action plan.

- Clauses entitled "Affirmative Action for Handicapped Workers" and "Affirmative Action for Disabled Veterans of the Vietnam Era" will be included in each of our covered government contracts and subcontracts, including modifications, renewals, and extensions to these contracts. (These clauses are reprinted at the end of our affirmative action plan.)

- Employment records will be reviewed regularly to determine the availability of handicapped persons, disabled veterans, and Vietnam-era veterans for promotion and to determine whether or not the present and potential skills of these individuals are being fully utilized and developed.

■ This Plan or parts of it will be printed in our Company's policy and personnel manuals as well as other Company publications such as newsletters, magazines, and annual reports.

■ Handicapped workers will be included when employees are pictured in consumer, promotional, or help-wanted advertising.

■ Articles on the accomplishments of handicapped workers will appear in Company publications.

■ This Plan will be reviewed and discussed in employee orientation sessions and in management training programs.

■ Nondiscrimination clauses will be included in all union agreements.

■ This Plan is available for inspection by employees and applicants in the Personnel Office during regular working hours. Announcements to this effect have been posted at all Company facilities.

■ This Company's nondiscrimination policy, along with a statement that we will not interfere with employee rights under the Rehabilitation Act of 1973 and the Vietnam-Era Veterans Readjustment Assistance Act of 1974, will be posted on all Company bulletin boards.

Nondiscrimination

It is Company policy not to discriminate against any qualified applicant or employee for any position because of a handicap or because of Vietnam-era service. This policy of nondiscrimination applies to all personnel and employment practices, including:

Hiring.
Upgrading.
Transfer.
Recruitment or recruitment advertising.
Layoff or termination.
Compensation of any kind.
Selection for training.
Educational programs.
Company-sponsored recreational and social activities.

Employment and Placement

This Company will review all personnel procedures to ensure that handicapped persons, disabled veterans, or Vietnam-era veterans are given careful consideration for employment when their job qualifications are studied. Actions to be taken to ensure the adequacy of our personnel practices include:

- Development of new procedures for evaluating job qualifications.

- A schedule for the review of mental and physical job requirements to ensure that they are consistent with business necessity and job safety and health, particularly where such requirements have tended to screen out qualified handicapped persons, disabled veterans, and Vietnam-era veterans.

- Determining the validity of all job requirements to ensure that they are indeed job-related.

- Gearing all physical examinations specifically to the job for which the applicant is being considered.

- Making reasonable accommodation except where business necessity or undue financial burden can be illustrated.

- Making a careful assessment of the job qualifications of known handicapped applicants and employees for job vacancies, promotions, and training opportunities.

Personnel Procedures and Policies

In carrying out our Company plan, the following actions will be taken:

- The application or personnel form of each known handicapped applicant will be annotated to identify each vacancy for which the applicant was considered; this form will be available for inspection by government compliance officials and by Company officials who audit our internal compliance activities.

- The personnel or application records of each known handicapped employee will include each promotion and each training program for which the individual was considered.

- All applicants will go through the normal interview process, and alternative sites for interviewing will be set up if the personnel office presents barriers to the mobility-impaired.

- When a handicapped employee or applicant is rejected for employment, promotion, or training, a statement of reasons will be appended to the personnel file or application form. This statement will include a comparison of the qualifications of the handicapped applicant or employee and the person actually selected and will include a description of the reasonable accommodation considered. The statement will be available to the applicant or employee upon request.

- When reasonable accommodations are undertaken to make it possible to hire, promote, or train a handicapped individual, a description of the accommodation will be placed in the personnel records or in the application form of the individual affected.

■ All job descriptions will be reevaluated to determine the difference between essential and nonessential tasks and between "skills" and "experience" which can be gained on the job. Vague requirements will be eliminated.

■ The total selection process will be evaluated (including training and promotion) to ensure freedom from stereotyping handicapped persons in a manner that limits their access to all jobs for which they are qualified.

■ Arrangements will be made for career counseling for known handicapped employees.

■ Job qualifications of a nondiscriminatory nature will be made available for review to all members of management involved in the recruitment, screening, selection, and promotion processes.

■ All personnel involved in recruitment, screening, selection, promotion, disciplinary, and related processes will be chosen for their assignments so as to ensure their commitment to implementation of this Plan.

■ Formal briefing sessions will be held with all recruitment sources (on the Company premises where possible) and, when feasible, will include plant tours, explanations of present and future job openings, job descriptions, worker specifications, explanations of the selection process, and distribution of recruitment literature.

■ Handicapped persons will be placed on the Company's personnel staff, where possible, but in any event will be consulted on appropriate nondiscriminatory personnel policies and recruitment practices.

■ Handicapped employees will be made available for participation in career days, youth motivation programs, and related activities in the community.

■ Recruitment efforts at schools will include special efforts to reach handicapped students.

■ Efforts will be made to participate in work study programs with rehabilitation facilities and schools, including Veterans Administration facilities, which specialize in training or educating handicapped persons.

■ Continued efforts will be made to maintain and establish Company on-the-job training programs and federally assisted apprenticeship programs.

Training

The Company will make every effort to ensure that all interested parties assist in implementation of the Plan. To this end, the Company will work with subcontractors, vocational rehabilitation facilities, labor unions, training organizations, and recruitment agencies, among other groups.

Recruiting

The Company will actively recruit qualified handicapped persons, disabled veterans, and Vietnam-era veterans and will request assistance in doing so from employment agencies as well as other organizations such as labor unions, particularly when revision of the collective-bargaining agreement is necessitated.

Recruitment practices of the Company will include the following:

■ All recruitment sources will be notified of the Company's nondiscrimination policy and its affirmative action plan.

■ Applicants will be recruited without regard to physical or mental handicaps that don't interfere with the ability to perform a specific job.

■ Sources likely to refer qualified handicapped and veteran applicants will be identified and included in all recruitment efforts.

■ An ongoing relationship will be established with organizations identified in this Plan under "Dissemination of Policy" when such organizations can help with the recruitment of handicapped persons, disabled veterans, and Vietnam-era veterans. [Note: active participation in veterans' "job fairs" is encouraged by OFCCP.]

Complaint Procedures

Any employee of this Company may personally or through an authorized representative file a written complaint alleging noncompliance with the Rehabilitation Act of 1973 or the Vietnam-Era Veterans Readjustment Assistance Act of 1974, provided that the complaint is filed within 180 days of the alleged violation, as required by the law. Complaints can be filed with the local veterans' employment service or with the nearest office of the U.S. Department of Labor's Office of Federal Contract Compliance Programs.

Before the complaint is processed, however, our internal review procedure, as outlined below, must be utilized in an effort to achieve expeditious and effective resolution of the complaint. If a satisfactory resolution cannot be achieved in this manner within 60 days, then the appropriate federal compliance agency will proceed with investigating the complaint.

No applicant or employee will be subject to coercion, intimidation, interference, or discrimination for filing a complaint or for assisting in an investigation of this Company for alleged violation of the above two federal laws.

Internal Review Procedure

Under our Plan, an internal review procedure has been set up to resolve discrimination complaints expeditiously.

Employers who are members of a labor union should file grievances with collective-bargaining agents. For other employees, discrimination complaints should be registered with one of the Company's Equal Employment Opportunity (EEO) counselors. In all cases, discrimination charges will be investigated and reviewed as quickly as possible.

Under no circumstances will the Company tolerate retaliatory actions against an individual who files a complaint either under the internal review procedure or with the federal government.

Sample Interoffice Memoranda

To: Vice President, Personnel
From: Office of the President
Date: January 12, 1981

Please follow through on previous discussions we have had regarding the expanded employment of handicapped persons, disabled veterans, and Vietnam-era veterans at all levels of the corporate headquarters and at our branch operations. Contact the appropriate recruitment sources and reaffirm our policy of nondiscrimination and equal employment opportunity. Make sure managers and supervisors in particular are briefed on Company policy in this respect.

I will expect a full report prior to next month's Board of Directors' meeting on the progress we're making and any obstacles you might be facing in carrying out the Company's affirmative action plan.

Company Notice to Handicapped Individuals

This employer is a government contractor subject to Section 503 of the Rehabilitation Act of 1973, which requires government contractors to take affirmative action to employ and advance in employment qualified handicapped individuals. If you have such a handicap and would like to be considered under the affirmative action program, please tell us. Submission of this information is voluntary and refusal to provide it will not subject you to discharge or disciplinary treatment. Information obtained concerning individuals shall be kept confidential, except that (1) supervisors and managers may be informed regarding restrictions on the work or duties of handicapped individuals and regarding necessary accommodations, (2) first-aid and safety personnel may be informed, when and to the extent appropriate, if the condition might require emergency treatment, and (3) government officials investigating compliance with the Act shall be informed.

If you are handicapped, we would like to include you under the affirmative action program. It would assist us if you tell us about (1) any special methods, skills, and procedures which qualify you for positions that you might not otherwise be able to do because of your handicap, so that you will be considered for any positions of that kind, and (2) the accommodations which we could make which would enable you to perform the job properly and safely, including special equipment, changes in the physical layout of the job, elimination of certain duties relating to the job, or other accommodations.

Company Notice to Disabled or Vietnam-Era Veterans

This employer is a government contractor subject to Section 402 of the Vietnam Era Veterans Readjustment Assistance Act of 1974 which requires government contractors to take affirmative action to employ and advance in employment qualified disabled veterans and veterans of the Vietnam era. If you are a disabled veteran covered by this program and would like to be considered under the affirmative action program, please tell us. This information is voluntary and refusal to provide it will not subject you to discharge or disciplinary treatment. Information obtained concerning individuals shall be kept confidential, except that (1) supervisors and managers may be informed regarding restrictions on the work or duties of disabled veterans, and regarding necessary accommodations, and (2) first-aid personnel may be informed, when and to the extent appropriate, if the condition might require emergency treatment. In order to assure proper placement of all employees, we do request that you answer the following question: If you have a disability which might affect your performance or create a hazard to yourself or others in connection with the job for which you are applying, please state the following: (1) The skills and procedures you use or intend to use to perform the job notwithstanding the disability and (2) the accommodations we could make which would enable you to perform the job properly and safely, including special equipment, changes in the physical layout of the job, elimination of certain duties relating to the job, or other accommodations.

Contractual Clause on Affirmative Action for Handicapped Workers

(a) The contractor will not discriminate against any employee or applicant for employment because of physical or mental handicap in regard to any position for which the employee or applicant for employment is qualified. The contractor agrees to take affirmative action to employ, advance in employment, and otherwise treat qualified handicapped individuals without discrimination based upon their physical or mental handicap in all employment practices such as the following: employment, upgrading, demotion or transfer, recruitment, advertising, layoff or termination, rates of pay or other forms of compensation, and selection for training, including apprenticeship.

(b) The contractor agrees to comply with the rules, regulations, and relevant orders of the Secretary of Labor issued pursuant to the Act.

(c) In the event of the contractor's noncompliance with the requirements of this clause, actions for noncompliance may be taken in accordance with the rules, regulations, and relevant orders of the Secretary of Labor issued pursuant to the Act.

(d) The contractor agrees to post in conspicuous places, available to employees and applicants for employment, notices in a form to be prescribed by the Director, provided by or through the contracting officer. Such notices shall state the contractor's obligation under the law to take affirmative action to employ and advance in employment qualified handicapped employees and applicants for employment, and the rights of applicants and employees.

(e) The contractor will notify each labor union or representative of workers with which it has a collective-bargaining agreement or other contract understanding, that the contractor is bound by the terms of Section 503 of the Rehabilitation Act of 1973, and is committed to take affirmative action to employ and advance in employment physically and mentally handicapped individuals.

(f) The contractor will include the provisions of this clause in every subcontract or purchase order of $2,500 or more unless exempted by rules, regulations, or orders of the Secretary issued pursuant to Section 503 of the Act, so that such provisions will be binding upon each subcontractor or vendor. The contractor will take such action with respect to any subcontract or purchase order as the Director of the Office of Federal Contract Compliance Programs may direct to enforce such provisions, including action for noncompliance.

Contractual Clause on Affirmative Action for Disabled or Vietnam-Era Veterans

(a) The contractor will not discriminate against any employee or applicant for employment because he or she is a disabled veteran or veteran of the Vietnam Era in regard to any position for which the employee or applicant for employment is qualified. The contractor agrees to take affirmative action to employ, advance in employment, and otherwise treat qualified disabled veterans and veterans of the Vietnam era without discrimination based upon their disability or veterans' status in all employment practices such as the following: employment upgrading, demotion or transfer, recruitment, advertising, layoff or termination, rates of pay or other forms of compensation, and selection for training, including apprenticeship.

(b) The contractor agrees that all suitable employment openings of the contractor which exist at the time of the execution of this contract and those which occur during the performance of this contract, including those not generated by this contract and including those occurring at an establishment of the contractor other than the one wherein the contract is being performed but excluding those of independently operated corporate affiliates, shall be listed at an appropriate local office of the state employment service system wherein the opening occurs. The contractor further agrees to provide such reports to such local office regarding employment openings and hires as may be required.

State and local government agencies holding federal contracts of $10,000 or more shall also list all their suitable openings with the appropriate office of the state employment service, but are not required to provide those reports set forth in paragraphs (d) and (e).

(c) Listing of employment openings with the employment service system pursuant to this clause shall be made at least concurrently with the use of any other recruitment source or effort and shall involve the normal obligations which attach to the placing of a bona fide job order, including the acceptance of referrals of veterans and nonveterans. The listing of employment openings does not require the hiring of any particular job applicant or from any particular group of job applicants, and nothing herein is intended to relieve the contractor from any requirements in Executive Orders or regulations regarding nondiscrimination in employment.

(d) The reports required by paragraph (b) of this clause shall include, but not be limited to, periodic reports which shall be filed at least quarterly with the appropriate local office or, where the contractor has more than one hiring location in a state, with the central office of that state employment service. Such reports shall indicate for each hiring location (1) the number of individuals hired during the reporting period, (2) the number of nondisabled veterans of the Vietnam era hired, (3) the number of disabled veterans of the Vietnam era hired, and (4) the total number of disabled veterans hired. The reports should include covered veterans hired for on-the-job training under 38 USC 1787. The contractor shall submit a report within 30 days after the end of each reporting period wherein any performance is made on this contract identifying data for each hiring location. The contractor shall maintain at each hiring location copies of the reports submitted until the expiration of one year after final payment under the contract, during which time these reports and related documentation shall be made available, upon request, for examination by any authorized representatives of the contracting officer or of the Secretary of Labor. Documentation would include personnel records respecting job openings, recruitment, and placement.

(e) Whenever the contractor becomes contractually bound to the listing provisions of this clause, it shall advise the employment service system in each state where it has establishments of the name and location of each hiring location in the state. As long as the contractor is contractually bound to these provisions and has so advised the State system, there is no need to advise the state system of subsequent contracts. The contractor may advise the state system when it is no longer bound by this contract clause.

(f) This clause does not apply to the listing of employment openings which occur and are filled outside of the 50 states, the District of Columbia, Puerto Rico, Guam, and the Virgin Islands.

(g) The provisions of paragraphs (b), (c), (d), and (e) of this clause do not apply to openings which the contractor proposes to fill from within his own organization or to fill pursuant to a customary and traditional employer-union hiring arrangement. This exclusion does not apply to a particular opening once an employer decides to consider applicants outside of his own organization or employer-union arrangement for that opening.

(h) As used in this clause: (1) "All suitable employment openings" includes, but is not limited to, openings which occur in the following job categories: production and nonproduction; plant and office; laborers and mechanics; supervisory and nonsupervisory; technical; and executive, administrative, and professional openings as are compensated on a salary basis of less than $25,000 per year. This term includes full-time employment, temporary employment of more than 3 days' duration, and part-time employment. It does not include openings which the contractor proposes to fill from within his own organization or to fill pursuant to a customary and traditional employer-union hiring arrangement nor openings in an educational institution which are restricted to students of that institution. Under the most compelling circumstances an employment opening may not be suitable for listing, including such situations where the needs of the government cannot reasonably be otherwise supplied, where listing would be contrary to national security, or where the requirement of listing would otherwise not be for the best interest of the government.

(2) "Appropriate office of the state employment service system" means the local office of the federal-state national system of public employment

offices with assigned responsibility for serving the area where the employment opening is to be filled, including the District of Columbia, Guam, Puerto Rico, and the Virgin Islands.

(3) "Openings which the contractor proposes to fill from within his own organization" means employment openings for which no consideration will be given to persons outside the contractor's organization (including any affiliates, subsidiaries, and the parent companies) and includes any openings which the contractor proposes to fill from regularly established "recall" lists.

(4) "Openings which the contractor proposes to fill pursuant to a customary and traditional employer-union hiring arrangement" means employment openings which the contractor proposes to fill from union halls, which is part of the customary and traditional hiring relationship which exists between the contractor and representatives of his employees.

(i) The contractor agrees to comply with the rules, regulations, and relevant orders of the Secretary of Labor issued pursuant to the Act.

(j) In the event of the contractor's noncompliance with the requirements of this clause, actions for noncompliance may be taken in accordance with the rules, regulations, or relevant orders of the Secretary of Labor issued pursuant to the Act.

(k) The contractor agrees to post in conspicuous places, available to employees and applicants for employment, notices in a form to be prescribed by the Director, provided by or through the contracting officer. Such notice shall state the contractor's obligation under the law to take affirmative action to employ and advance in employment qualified disabled veterans and veterans of the Vietnam era for employment, and the rights of applicants and employees.

(l) The contractor will notify each labor union or representative of workers with which it has a collective-bargaining agreement or other contract understanding, that the contractor is bound by the terms of the Vietnam-Era Veterans Readjustment Assistance Act, and is committed to take affirmative action to employ and advance in employment qualified disabled veterans and veterans of the Vietnam era.

(m) The contractor will include the provisions of this clause in every subcontract or purchase order of $10,000 or more unless exempted by rules, regulations, or orders of the Secretary issued pursuant to the Act, so that such provisions will be binding upon each subcontractor or vendor. The contractor will take such action with respect to any subcontract or purchase order as the Director of the Office of Federal Contract Compliance Programs may direct to enforce such provisions, including action for noncompliance.

Appendixes

A
Required Federal Poster

equal employment opportunity is the law

igualdad de oportunidad en el empleo es la ley

Private Industry, State, and Local Government

Title VII of the Civil Rights Act of 1964, as amended, prohibits job discrimination because of race, color, religion, sex or national origin.

Applicants to and employees of private employers, state/local governments, and public/private educational institutions are protected. Also covered are employment agencies, labor unions and apprenticeship programs. Any person who believes he or she has been discriminated against should contact immediately

The U. S. Equal Employment Opportunity Commission (EEOC)
2401 E St., N.W.
Washington, D. C. 20506

or an EEOC District Office, listed in most telephone directories under U. S. Government.

Industrias Privadas, Gobiernos Locales y Estatales

El Título VII de la Ley de Derechos Civiles de 1964, enmendado, prohibe la discriminación en el empleo por razón de raza, color, religión, sexo o nacionalidad de origen.

La ley protege a los empleados y solicitantes de empleo en empresas privadas, gobiernos estatales y locales e instituciones educacionales públicas y privadas. También abarca las agencias de empleo, sindicatos de trabajadores y programas de aprendizaje. Cualquier persona, tanto hombre como mujer, que crea que ha sido objeto de discriminación debe escribir inmediatamente a

The U. S. Equal Employment Opportunity Commission (EEOC)
2401 E St., N.W.
Washington, D. C. 20506

o a cualquier oficina regional de EEOC, las que se encuentran en las guías telefónicas locales bajo el nombre de: U. S. Government.

Federal Contract Employment

Executive Order 11246, as amended, prohibits job discrimination because of race, color, religion, sex or national origin and requires affirmative action to ensure equality of opportunity in all aspects of employment.

Section 503 of the Rehabilitation Act of 1973 prohibits job discrimination because of handicap and requires affirmative action to employ and advance in employment qualified handicapped workers.

Section 402 of the Vietnam Era Veterans' Readjustment Assistance Act of 1974 prohibits job discrimination and requires affirmative action to employ and advance in employment (1) qualified Vietnam era veterans during the first four years after their discharge and (2) qualified disabled veterans throughout their working life if they have a 30 percent or more disability.

Applicants to and employees of any company with a federal government contract or subcontract are protected. Any person who believes a contractor has violated its affirmative action obligations, including nondiscrimination, under Executive Order 11246, as amended, or under Section 503 of the Rehabilitation Act should contact immediately

The Employment Standards Administration Office of Federal Contract Compliance Programs (OFCCP)
Third and Constitution Ave., N.W.
Washington, D. C. 20210

or an OFCCP regional office, listed in most telephone directories under U. S. Government, Department of Labor. Complaints specifically under the veterans' law should be filed with the Veterans' Employment Service through local offices of the state employment service.

All complaints must be filed within 180 days from date of alleged violation.

Empleos En Compañías Con Contratos Federales

La Orden Ejecutiva Número 11246, enmendada, prohibe la discriminación en el empleo por razón de raza, color, religión, sexo o nacionalidad de origen y exige acción positiva para garantizar la igualdad de oportunidad en todos los aspectos del empleo.

La Sección 503 de la Ley de Rehabilitación de 1973, prohibe la discriminación en el empleo contra personas que sufran de impedimentos físicos o mentales y exige acción positiva en el empleo y promoción de personas que sufran de impedimentos físicos o mentales, siempre que reúnan las condiciones indispensables para el desempeño del empleo.

La Sección 402 de la Ley de 1974 de Asistencia para el Reajuste de los Veteranos de la Era de Vietnam, prohibe la discriminación en el empleo y exige acción positiva en el empleo y promoción de (1) veteranos de la era de Vietnam, durante los primeros cuatro años después de haber sido separados del servicio activo, siempre que reúnan las condiciones indispensables para el desempeño del empleo (2) ciertos veteranos que tengan un 30 por ciento o más de impedimentos físicos o mentales mientras puedan trabajar, siempre que reúnan las condiciones indispensables para el desempeño del empleo.

La ley protege a los solicitantes de empleo y empleados de cualquier compañía que tenga un contrato o subcontrato con el gobierno federal. Cualquier persona que crea que uno de estos contratistas no ha cumplido con sus obligaciones de tomar acción positiva, incluyendo la de no discriminar, bajo la Orden Ejecutiva 11246, enmendada, o bajo la Sección 503 de la Ley de Rehabilitación, debe escribir inmediatamente a

The Employment Standards Administration Office of Federal Contract Compliance Programs (OFCCP)
Third and Constitution Ave., N.W.
Washington, D. C. 20210

o a cualquier oficina regional de OFCCP, las que se encuentran en la mayoría de las guías telefónicas bajo: U. S. Government, Department of Labor. Las reclamaciones específicamente comprendidas bajo la ley de veteranos, deben de dirigirse a Veterans' Employment Service por medio de las oficinas locales del servicio de empleo del estado.

Todas las reclamaciones deben de ser registradas dentro de los 180 días subsequentes a la fecha del supuesto acto de discriminación.

U.S. Department of Labor
Employment Standards Administration
Office of Federal Contract Compliance Programs

OFCCP-1420
(October 1976)

☆U.S. GOVERNMENT PRINTING OFFICE: 1977 O—235-411

B
Helpful Organizations

American Association of Workers for the Blind, 1511 K Street, N.W., Washington, DC 20005, 202-347-1559. The Association has a number of active chapters throughout the United States and offers the handicapped and employers a national job exchange service.

American Council of the Blind, 1211 Connecticut Avenue, N.W., Suite 506, Washington, DC 20036, 202-833-1251. The Council provides a variety of services to blind persons and employers through its state and local chapters.

American Foundation for the Blind, 15 West 16th Street, New York, NY 10011, 212-924-0420.

American Institute of Architects, 1735 New York Avenue, N.W., Washington, DC 20006. AIA publishes a number of guides on the removal of architectural barriers to the handicapped.

American Mutual Insurance Alliance, 20 North Wacker Drive, Chicago, IL 60606. The Alliance provides rehabilitative services and insurance information to interested parties.

American National Standards Institute, 1430 Broadway, New York, NY 10018. ANSI develops standards for the elimination of architectural barriers which are cited as "official" guidelines by many federal agencies.

Architectural and Transportation Barriers Compliance Board, 330 C Street, S.W., Washington, DC 20201. The Board provides information to all interested parties on federal accessibility requirements.

Blinded Veterans Association, 1735 DeSales Street, N.W., Washington, DC 20036, 202-347-4010. The Association offers rehabilitation training, equipment adaptation, and job placement services.

Committee for the Handicapped/People to People Program, Suite 610, 1028 Connecticut Avenue, N.W., Washington, DC 20036, 202-223-4450.

Disabled American Veterans, 807 Maine Avenue, S.W., Washington, DC 20024, 202-554-3501. DAV assists employers in hiring and training disabled veterans and will assist in the mediation of disputes involving federal government compliance requirements.

Epilepsy Foundation of America, 1828 L Street, N.W., Washington, DC 20036, 202-293-2930. The Foundation, under a Department of Labor grant, runs a Training and Placement Service (TAPS) project in several cities, with the goal of increasing the employment of epileptics in private industry. Contact the Foundation for locations of TAPS programs.

George Washington University, Job Development Laboratory, Rehabilitation Research and Training Center, 2300 Eye Street, N.W., Room 240, Washington, DC 20037. The Center conducts bioengineering and job accommodation studies that demonstrate ways in which employers can meet the special needs of handicapped applicants and workers.

Goodwill Industries of America, 9200 Wisconsin Avenue, N.W., Washington, DC 20014, 301-530-6500. Goodwill, through a federal grant, offers a variety of vocational rehabilitation, job placement, training, and employment services to the handicapped and to employers. For a list of the Goodwill chapters participating in this program, write the national office.

Mainstream, Inc., 1156 15th Street, N.W., Washington, DC 20005, 202-833-1136. Mainstream provides information and publications to handicapped citizens and employers. Its toll-free "Hotline" number (800-424-8089) can be used by anyone with questions on compliance with handicap legislation.

National Association of the Physically Handicapped, 76 Elm Street, Loudon, OH 43140. The Association provides rehabilitative and other services to the handicapped through its local chapters.

National Association of Rehabilitation Professionals in the Private Sector, 1019 Hayse, Oak Park, IL 60302, 312-875-0570. A new organization which sprung up partly in response to federal legislation prohibiting discrimination against the handicapped in private employment, the Association fosters an exchange of ideas on compliance by managers and personnel specialists in private industry.

National Association of Retarded Citizens, 2709 Avenue E East, Arlington, TX 76011, 817-261-4961. NARC sets up on-the-job training programs for mentally retarded persons. Federal incentive funds are used to reduce the employer's training cost. Contact the Association for a list of chapters participating in this training program.

National Center for a Barrier Free Environment, Seventh Street and Florida Avenue, N.E., Washington, DC 20002. The Center serves as an information clearinghouse on barrier-free design.

National Easter Seal Society for Crippled Children and Adults, 2023 West Ogden Avenue, Chicago, IL 60612, 312-243-8400. The Society publishes an extensive array of literature on helping crippled individuals become fully participating members of the community.

National Institute for Rehabilitation Engineering, 97 Decker Road,

Butler, NJ 07405, 201-838-2500. The Institute provides a variety of rehabilitative training, prosthetic devices, and equipment to the severely and multiple handicapped.

National Paraplegia Foundation, 333 North Michigan Avenue, Chicago, IL 60601, 312-346-4779. The Foundation works to improve the physical and vocational rehabilitation of persons with spinal cord injuries. Job referral services are also provided.

National Technical Institute for the Deaf, Rochester Institute of Technology, 1 Lomb Memorial Drive, Rochester, NY 14623. The Institute provides educational and business training to deaf students to prepare them for employment in the private sector.

Paralyzed Veterans of America, 4330 East-West Highway, Suite 300, Washington, DC 20014, 301-652-2135. PVA works with employers to improve the job opportunities of paralyzed veterans.

President's Committee on Employment of the Handicapped, Washington, DC, 202-961-3401. The Committee makes available a variety of publications and aids on how the handicapped can be successfully hired and trained.

Registry of Interpreters for the Deaf, 814 Thayer Avenue, Silver Spring, MD 20910. Through its state chapters, the Registry has more than 2,000 members available to provide interpreting services to deaf workers.

Rehabilitation Services Administration, U.S. Department of Health, Education and Welfare, 330 C Street, S.W., Washington, DC 20201, 202-245-6726.

Seeing Eye, Inc., Morristown, NJ 07960. This organization trains attendees of its month-long courses in the use, care, and control of their dogs.

C
Federal Agencies with an Office for Civil Rights

Chief, Compliance Division
Small Business Administration
1411 L Street, N.W.
Washington, DC 20416

Office of the General Counsel
Legal Services Corporation
733 15th Street, N.W.
Suite 700
Washington, DC 20005

Office of the General Counsel
National Endowment for the
    Arts
2401 E Street, N.W.
Room 1418
Washington, DC 20506

Office of the General Counsel
National Endowment for the
    Humanities
806 15th Street, N.W.
Washington, DC 20005

Chief Counsel
Office of Revenue Sharing
Department of the Treasury
2401 E Street, N.W.
Washington, DC 20226

Office of the General Counsel
Federal Home Loan Bank
    Board
1700 G Street, N.W.
3rd Floor
Washington, DC 20552

Office of the General Counsel
National Science Foundation
1800 G Street, N.W.
Washington, DC 20550

Office of the General Counsel
Tennessee Valley authority
400 Commerce Avenue
Room A E-11-B-33
Knoxville, TN 37902

Office of Human Goals
Veterans Administration
810 Vermont Avenue, N.W.
Washington, DC 20424

Intergovernmental Personnel
  Programs
Office of Personnel Manage-
  ment
(formerly Civil Service Comm.)
1900 E Street, N.W.
Room 2305
Washington, DC 20415

Office of the General Counsel
Community Services Adm.
1200 19th Street, N.W.
Washington, DC 20506

Office of the General Counsel
Agency for International De-
  velopment
Room 6892–New State
Washington, DC 20523

Office of Equal Opportunity—
  Civil Rights Division
Department of Agriculture
14th Street and Independence
  Avenue, S.W.
Auditor's Building
Washington, DC 20250

Office of Civil Rights
Department of Commerce
Main Commerce Building
14th Street and Constitution
  Avenue, N.W.
Washington, DC 20230

Office of the Deputy Assistant
  Secretary for Equal Oppor-
  tunity
Department of Defense
The Pentagon, Room 3E326
Washington, DC 20301

Federally Assisted Programs
  Division
Office of Equal Opportunity
Department of Energy
20 Massachusetts Avenue, N.W.
Room 6105
Washington, DC 20545

Office for Equal Opportunity
Office of the Secretary
Department of the Interior
18th and C Streets, N.W.
Washington, DC 20240

Civil Rights Division
Federal Program Section
Department of Justice
10th Street and Pennsylvania
  Avenue, N.W.
Washington, DC 20530

Legal Advisor's Office
Department of State
LM5425A
Washington, DC 20520

Office of Civil Rights
A-105
Environmental Protection
  Agency
401 M Street, S.W.
Washington, DC 2046

Labor Relations and Civil Rights
Department of Labor
200 Constitution Avenue, N.W.
Washington, DC 20210

Equal Opportunity Staff (BH)
General Services Administration
1800 F Street, N.W.
Room 6013
Washington, DC 20405

Office of the General Counsel
National Aeronautics and Space
Administration
400 Maryland Avenue, S.W.
Washington, DC 20546

Office of the Assistant General
Counsel for Regulation and
Enforcement
Department of Transportation
400 7th Street, S.W.
Washington, DC 20590

Office of Compliance
ACTION
806 Connecticut Avenue, N.W.
Washington, DC 20525

Office of Executive Legal Director
Nuclear Regulatory Commission
MMB 9604
Washington, DC 20555

Office of the General Counsel
Rules and Legislation
Civil Aeronautics Board
1825 Connecticut Avenue, N.W.
Washington, DC 20428

Management Services Division
Water Resources Council
2120 L Street, N.W.
Washington, DC 20037

Office of Independent Living
for the Disabled
Department of Housing and
Urban Development
451 7th Street, S.W.
Washington, DC 20410

Office of the General Counsel
Department of Health, Education and Welfare
330 Independence Avenue, S.W.
Room 5300
Washington, DC 20201

D
Regional Offices of the U.S. Department of Labor, Wage and Hour Division*

Atlanta

1371 Peachtree Street, N.E.,
  Room 331
Atlanta, GA 30309
404-881-7015
(AL, FL, GA, MS, NC, SC, KY,
  TN)

Boston

John Fitzgerald Kennedy
  Federal Building
Government Center
Boston, MA 02202
617-223-5565
(CT, ME, MA, NH, RI, VT)

Chicago

Federal Building, 8th Floor
230 South Dearborn Street
Chicago, IL 60604
312-353-7246
(IL, IN, MI, MN, OH, WI)

Dallas

555 Griffin Square
Dallas, TX 75202
214-767-6884
(AR, LA, NM, OK, TX)

Denver

Federal Office Building
Room 1408
1961 Stout Street
Denver, CO 80294
303-837-5302
(CO, MT, ND, SD, UT, WY)

Caribbean Office

New Federal Office Building
Carlos Chardon Street, Room
  403
Hato Rey, PR 00918
Overseas Op. 9-472-6620

*The Wage and Hour Division, through its regional offices listed here, investigates complaints under the Fair Labor Standards Act and enforces the general provisions of this law, including those sections which permit the employment of certain classes of handicapped workers at subminimum wages in competitive industry.

Kansas City

2000 Federal Office Building
911 Walnut Street
Kansas City, MO 64106
816-374-5382
(IA, KS, MO, NE)

New York

1515 Broadway
New York, NY 10036
212-399-5633
(NJ, NY)

Philadelphia

Gateway Building, 15th Floor
3535 Market Street
Philadelphia, PA 19104
215-596-1195

San Francisco

450 Golden Gate Avenue,
    Room 10431
P.O. Box 36018
San Francisco, CA 94102
415-556-3663
(AZ, CA, HI, NV, GU)

Seattle

4097 Federal Office Building
909 1st Avenue
Mail Stop 407
Seattle, WA 98174
206-442-1914
(AK, ID, OR, WA)

E
Regional Offices for Civil Rights, U.S. Department of Health, Education and Welfare*

Region I

140 Federal Street, 14th Floor
Boston, MA 02110
(CT, ME, MA, NH, RI, VT)

Region II

26 Federal Plaza, 33rd Floor
New York, NY 10007
(NJ, NY, PR, VI)

Region III

P.O. Box 13716
Philadelphia, PA 19101
(DE, DC, MD, PA, VA, WV)

Region IV

101 Marietta Street, 10th Floor
Atlanta, GA 30323
(AL, FL, GA, KY, MS, NC, SC, TN)

Region V

300 S. Wacker Drive
Chicago, IL 60606
(IL, IN, MI, MN, OH, WI)

For Cleveland, OH, office:

Region V

Plaza Nine Building
55 Erieview Plaza, Room 222
Cleveland, OH 44114

Region VI

1200 Main Tower Building
Dallas, TX 75202
(AR, LA, NM, OK, TX)

Region VII

12 Grand Building
1150 Grand Avenue
Kansas City, MO 64106
(IA, KS, MO, NB)

*The Office for Civil Rights, through it's regional offices listed here, investigates complaints of discrimination by handicapped persons and enforces the Section 504 federal statutes of the Rehabilitation Act of 1973.

Region VIII

Federal Building
1961 Stout Street, Room 11037
Denver, CO 80294
(CO, MT, ND, SD, UT, WY)

Region IX

100 Van Ness Avenue, 14th
  Floor
San Francisco, CA 94102
(AZ, CA, HI, NV, GU, Trust
  Territory of the Pacific Isles,
  American Samoa)

Region X

1321 Second Avenue, Room
  5041 MS/508
Seattle, WA 98101

F
OFCCP Regional Offices, U.S. Department of Labor

Region I—Boston

Assistant Regional Administrator for OFCCP/ESA
U.S. Department of Labor
JKF Building, Room 1612-C
Government Center
Boston, MA 02203

States Covered
Maine
New Hampshire
Vermont
Massachusetts
Rhode Island
Connecticut

Area Offices
Boston, MA
Bridgeport, CT
Hartford, CT
Providence, RI

Region II—New York

Assistant Regional Administrator for OFCCP/ESA
U.S. Department of Labor
1515 Broadway, Room 3306
New York, NY 10036

States Covered	Area Offices
New York	Albany, NY
New Jersey	Buffalo, NY
Puerto Rico	Long Island, NY
Virgin Islands	Newark, NJ
	New York, NY
	San Juan, PR
	Syracuse, NY
	Trenton, NJ
	White Plains, NY

Region III—Philadelphia

Assistant Regional Administrator for OFCCP/ESA
U.S. Department of Labor
Gateway Building, Room 15434
3535 Market Street
Philadelphia, PA 19104

States Covered	Area Offices
Pennsylvania	Baltimore, MD
Maryland	Philadelphia, PA
Delaware	Pittsburgh, PA
Virginia	Reading, PA
West Virginia	Richmond, VA
District of Columbia	Washington, DC

Region IV—Atlanta

Assistant Regional Administrator for OFCCP/ESA
U.S. Department of Labor
1317 Peachtree Street, N.E.,
    Room 720
Atlanta, GA 30309

States Covered	*Area Offices*
North Carolina	Atlanta, GA
South Carolina	Birmingham, AL
Kentucky	Charlotte, NC
Tennessee	Columbia, SC
Mississippi	Jackson, MS
Alabama	Jacksonville, FL
Georgia	Louisville, KY
Florida	Memphis, TN
	Miami, FL
	Nashville, TN
	Orlando, FL
	Raleigh, NC

Region V—Chicago

Assistant Regional Administrator for OFCCP/ESA
U.S. Department of Labor
New Federal Building, Room 1614
230 South Dearborn Street
Chicago, IL 60604

States Covered	*Area Offices*
Ohio	Chicago, IL
Indiana	Chicago, IL
Michigan	Chicago, IL
Illinois	Cleveland, OH
Wisconsin	Cleveland, OH
Minnesota	Columbus, OH
	Detroit, MI
	Detroit, MI
	Gary, IN
	Grand Rapids, MI
	Indianapolis, IN
	Milwaukee, WI
	Minneapolis, MN
	Peoria, IL

Region VI—Dallas

Assistant Regional Administrator for OFCCP/ESA
U.S. Department of Labor
555 Griffin Square Building, Room 506
Dallas, TX 75202

States Covered	*Area Offices*
Louisiana	Albuquerque, NM
Arkansas	Dallas, TX
Oklahoma	Houston, TX
Texas	Little Rock, AR
New Mexico	New Orleans, LA
	San Antonio, TX
	Tulsa, OK

Region VII—Kansas City

Assistant Regional Administrator for OFCCP/ESA
U.S. Department of Labor
Federal Office Building, Room 2000
911 Walnut Street
Kansas City, MO 64106

States Covered	*Area Offices*
Missouri	Kansas City, MO
Iowa	Omaha, NB
Nebraska	St. Louis, MO

Region VIII—Denver

Assistant Regional Administrator for OFCCP/ESA
U.S. Department of Labor
14431 Federal Office Building
1961 Stout Street
Denver, CO 80202

States Covered
North Dakota
South Dakota
Montana
Wyoming
Colorado
Utah

Area Offices
Denver, CO
Salt Lake City, UT

Region IX—San Francisco

Assistant Regional Administrator of OFCCP/ESA
U.S. Department of Labor
Federal Building, Room 10341
450 Golden Gate Avenue
San Francisco, CA 94102

States Covered
California
Nevada
Arizona
Hawaii
Guam

Area Offices
Honolulu, HI
Los Angeles, CA
Phoenix, AZ
San Diego, CA
San Francisco, CA
San Jose, CA
Santa Ana, CA

Region X—Seattle

Assistant Regional Administrator for OFCCP/ESA
U.S. Department of Labor
Federal Office Building
909 First Avenue, Room 1023
Seattle, WA 98174

States Covered
Washington
Oregon
Idaho
Alaska

Area Offices
Anchorage, AL
Portland, OR
Seattle, WA

G
State Agencies for Vocational Rehabilitation

Alabama

Director, Division of
Rehabilitation and Crippled
Children
Department of Education
2129 East South Boulevard
P.O. Box 11586
Montgomery, AL 36111

Alaska

Director, Office of Vocational
Rehabilitation
Department of Education
Pouch F, Mail Sop. 0581
State Office Building
Juneau, AK 99811

Arizona

Chief, Rehabilitation Services
Bureau
Department of Economic
Security
1400 W. Washington
Phoenix, AZ 85007

Arkansas

Commissioner, Rehabilitation
Services Division
Department of Human Services
1401 Brookwood Drive
P.O. Box 3781
Little Rock, AR 72203

California

Director, Department of
Rehabilitation
Human Relations Agency
830 K Street Mall
Sacramento, CA 95814

Colorado

Director, Division of
Rehabilitation
Department of Social Services
1575 Sherman Street
Denver, CO 80203

Connecticut

Associate Commissioner,
   Division of Vocational
   Rehabilitation
State Board of Education
600 Asylum Avenue
Hartford, CT 06105

Director, Board of Education
   and Services for the Blind
170 Ridge Road
Wethersfield, CT 06109

Delaware

Director, Vocational
   Rehabilitation Services
Department of Labor
1500 Shallcross Avenue
P.O. Box 1190
Wilmington, DE 19899

Administrator, Bureau for the
   Visually Impaired
Division of Social Services
305 W. Eighth Street
Wilmington, Delaware 19801

District of Columbia

Chief, Bureau of Rehabilitation
   Services
Social Rehabilitation
   Administration
Department of Human
   Resources
Room 816, 122 C Street, N.W.
Washington, DC 20001

Florida

Program Staff Director, Office
   of Vocational Rehabilitation
Department of Health and
   Rehabilitative Services
1309 Winewood Boulevard
Tallahassee, FL 32301

Chief, Bureau of Blind Services
Department of Education
2751 Executive Center Circle
   East
Tallahassee, FL 32301

Georgia

Georgia Division of Vocational
   Rehabilitation
Department of Human
   Resources
610 State Office Building
47 Trinity Avenue, S.W.
Atlanta, GA 30334

Guam

Chief, Department of
   Vocational Rehabilitation
Board of Control for Vocational
   Rehabilitation
Department of Education
P.O. Box 10-C
Agana, Guam 96910

Hawaii

Administrator, Division of
   Vocational Rehabilitation
Department of Social Services
P.O. Box 339
Honolulu, HI 96809

Idaho

Director, Vocational
  Rehabilitation Service
State Board for Vocational
  Education
1501 McKinney Street
Boise, ID 83704

Director, Idaho Commission for
  the Blind
State House
Boise, ID 83720

Illinois

Director, Division of Vocational
  Rehabilitation
State Board of Vocational
  Education and Rehabilitation
623 East Adams Street
P.O. Box 1587
Springfield, IL 62706

Indiana

Administrator, Rehabilitation
  Services Board
1028 Illinois Building
17 West Market Street
Indianapolis, IN 46204

Iowa

Associates Superintentent and
  Director
Division of Rehabilitation
  Education and Services
Department of Public
  Instruction
507 Tenth Street, Fifth Floor
Des Moines, IA 50309

Director, State Commission for
  the Blind
Fourth and Keosauqua Way
Des Moines, IA 50309

Kansas

Director, Division of Vocational
  Rehabilitation
Department of Social and
  Rehabilitation Services
State Office Building, Fifth
  Floor
Topeka, KS 66612

Director, Division of Services
  for the Blind and Visually
  Handicapped
Department of Social and
  Rehabilitation Services
Biddle Building, First Floor
2700 West Sixth Street
Topeka, KS 66606

Kentucky

Assistant Superintendent,
  Bureau of Rehabilitation
  Services
Department of Education
Capital Plaza Office Tower
Frankfort, KY 40601

Director, Bureau of Blind
  Services
Education and Arts Cabinet
593 E. Main Street
Frankfort, KY 40601

Louisiana

Executive Director, Division of
  Vocational Rehabilitation
Department of Education
1755 Florida Boulevard
P.O. Box 44371
Baton Rouge, LA 70804

Maine

Director, Bureau of
  Rehabilitation Services
Department of Health and
  Welfare
32 Winthrop Street
Augusta, ME 04330

Maryland

Assistant State Superintendent
  in Vocational Rehabilitation
Division of Vocational
  Rehabilitation
State Department of Education
P.O. Box 8717
Baltimore–Washington
  International Airport
Baltimore, MD 21240

Massachusetts

Commissioner of Rehabilitation
Massachusetts Rehabilitation
  Commission
296 Boylston Street
Boston, MA 02116

Commissioner, Commission for
  the Blind
110 Tremont Street, Sixth Floor
Boston, MA 02108

Michigan

Associate Superintendent of
  Rehabilitation and
  Institutional Education
State Department of Education
P.O. Box 30010
Lansing, MI 48909

Director, Bureau of Blind
  Services
Department of Social Services
Commerce Center Bldg.
300 South Capitol Avenue
Lansing, MI 48926

Minnesota

Assistant Commissioner for Vocational Rehabilitation
Division of Vocational Rehabilitation
Department of Education
390 North Robert Street
St. Paul, MN 55101

Director, State Services for the
  Blind and Visually Handi-
  capped
Department of Public Welfare
1745 University Avenue
St. Paul, MN 55104

Mississippi

Director, Division of Vocational
  Rehabilitation
Department of Education
1304 Walter Sillers State Office
  Building
P.O. Box 1698
Jackson, MS 39205

Director, Vocational Rehabilitation for the Blind
Department of Public Welfare
P.O. Box 4872
Jackson, MS 39216

Missouri

Assistant Commissioner, Division of Vocational Rehabilitation
Department of Elementary and Secondary Education
3523 North Ten Mile Drive
Jefferson City, MO 65101

Chief, Services of the Blind
Division of Family Services
Department of Social Services
Broadway State Office Building
Jefferson City, MO 65101

Montana

Administrator, Rehabilitative Services Division
Department of Social and Rehabilitation Services
P.O. Box 4210
Helena, MT 59601

Administrator, Visual Services Division
Department of Social and Rehabilitation Services
P.O. Box 4210
Helena, MT 59601

Nebraska

Assistant Commissioner and Director
Division of Rehabilitation Services
State Department of Education
301 Centennial Mall, So., 6th Floor
Lincoln, NE 68509

Director, Division of Rehabilitation Services for the Visually Impaired
Department of Public Instruction
1047 South Street
Lincoln, NB 68502

Nevada

Administrator, Rehabilitation Division
Department of Human Resources
Kinkead Building, First Floor
505 East King Street
State Capitol Complex
Carson City, NV 89710

New Hampshire

Chief, Vocational Rehabilitation Division
State Board of Education
105 Loudon Road, Building #3
Concord, NH 03301

New Jersey

Director, New Jersey Division of
Vocational Rehabilitation
Department of Labor and In-
dustry
Labor and Industry Building,
Room 1005
John Fitch Plaza
P.O. Box 2098
Trenton, NJ 08625

Commission for the Blind
State Board of Control, De-
partment of Institutions and
Agencies
Newark Center Building
1100 Raymond Boulevard
Newark, NJ 07102

New Mexico

Assistant Superintendent for
Vocational Rehabilitation
Department of Education
231 Washington Avenue
P.O. Box 1830
Santa Fe, NM 87501

New York

Associates Commissioner,
Office of Vocational Re-
habilitation
State Education Department
99 Washington Avenue
Albany, NY 12230

Director, Commission for the
Blind and Visually Handi-
capped
State Department of Social Ser-
vices
Ten Eyck Office Building
40 North Pearl Street
Albany, NY 12207

North Carolina

Director, Division of Vocational
Rehabilitation Services
Department of Human Re-
sources
620 North West Street
P.O. Box 26053
Raleigh, NC 27611

Director, Division of Services
for the Blind
Department of Human Re-
sources
P.O. Box 2658
Raleigh, NC 27602

North Dakota

Executive Director, Department
of Vocational Rehabilitation
State Board of Social Services
1025 North Third Street
P.O. Box 1037
Bismarck, ND 58505

Ohio

Administrator, Ohio Rehabilitation Services Commission
4656 Heaton Road
Columbus, OH 43229

Oklahoma

Administrative Assistant, Re-
habilitative and Visual Ser-
vices
Oklahoma Public Welfare
Commission
Department of Institutions, So-
cial and Rehabilitative Ser-
vices
Sequoyah Memorial Office
Building
P.O. Box 25352
Oklahoma City, OK 73125

Oregon

Administrator, Vocational Rehabilitation Division
Department of Human Re-
sources
2045 Silverton Road, N.E.
Salem, OR 97310

Administrator, State Commission for the Blind
535 S.E. 12th Avenue
Portland, OR 97214

Pennsylvania

Director, Bureau of Vocational
Rehabilitation
Department of Labor and In-
dustry
Labor and Industry Building,
Room 1317
7th and Forster Streets
Harrisburg, PA 17120

Commissioner, Office for the
Visually Handicapped
Department of Public Welfare
300 Capitol Associates Building
901 North 7th Street
P.O. Box 2675
Harrisburg, PA 17120

Puerto Rico

Secretario Auxiliar, Rehabilita-
cion Vocacional
Estado Libre Asociado de
Puerto Rico
Departmento de Servicios
Sociales
Division de Rehabilitacion Vo-
cacional
Apartado 1118
Hato Rey, PR 00919

Rhode Island

Administrator, Division of Vocational Rehabilitation
Social and Rehabilitative Services
40 Fountain Street
Providence, RI 02903

Administrator, Services for the
Blind
Social and Rehabilitative Ser-
vices
46 Aborn Street
Providence, RI 02903

South Carolina

Commissioner, Vocational Rehabilitative Department
301 Landmark Center
3600 Forest Drive
P.O. Box 4945
Columbia, SC 29240

South Dakota

Secretary, Department of Vocational Rehabilitation
State Office Building
Illinois Street
Pierre, SD 57501

Tennessee

Assistant Commissioner, Division of Vocational Rehabilitation
Department of Education
1808 W. End Building, Room 1400
Nashville, TN 37203

Director, Services for the Blind
Department of Human Services
303 State Office Bldg.
Nashville, TN 37219

Texas

Commissioner, Texas Rehabilitation Commission
7745 Chevy Chase Drive
Austin, TX 78752

Executive Director, State Commission for the Blind
Stokes Building
314 W. 11th Street
P.O. Box 12866
Austin, TX 78711

Trust Territory of the Pacific Islands

Chief, Vocational Rehabilitation Services
Office of the High Commissioner
Trust Territory of the Pacific Islands
Saipan, Mariana Islands 96950
Cable Address: HICOTT SAIPAN

Utah

Administrator, Division of Rehabilitation Services
State Board of Education
250 East 5th South
Salt Lake City, UT 84111

Administrator, Services for the Visually Handicapped
309 East First South
Salt Lake City, UT 84111

Vermont

Director, Vocational Rehabilitation Division
Department of Social and Rehabilitation Services
Agency of Human Services
81 River Street
Montpelier, VT 05602

Director, Division of Services
for the Blind and Visually
Handicapped
Department of Social and Re-
habilitation Services
Agency of Human Services
81 River Street
Montpelier, VT 05602

Virgin Islands
Director, Division of Vocational
Rehabilitation
Department of Social Welfare
P.O. Box 539
Charlotte Amalie
St. Thomas, VI 00801

Virginia
Commissioner, Department of
Vocational Rehabilitation
State Board of Vocational Re-
habilitation
4615 W. Broad Street, Room
314
P.O. Box 11045
Richmond, VA 23230

Director, Virginia Commission
for the Visually Handicapped
3003 Parkwood Avenue
Richmond, VA 23221

Washington
Director, Division of Vocational
Rehabilitation
Department of Social and
Health Services
State Office Building #2 (OB-
31C)
Olympia, WA 98504

Chief, Office of Services for the
Blind N-17-8
Department of Social and
Health Services
Community Services Division
P.O. Box 18379
Seattle, WA 98118

West Virginia
Director, Division of Vocational
Rehabilitation
State Board of Vocational Edu-
cation
P & G Building
2019 Washington Street East
Charleston, WV 25305

Wisconsin
Administrator, Division of Vo-
cational Rehabilitation
Department of Health and So-
cial Services
State Office Building
1 West Wilson Street
Madison, WI 53702

Wyoming
Director, Division of Vocational
Rehabilitation
Department of Health and So-
cial Services
Hathaway State Office Building,
Room 327
Cheyenne, WY 82002

H
Governors' Committees on the Handicapped

Alabama

Governor's Committee
2129 East South Boulevard
Montgomery, AL 36111

Alaska

Governor's Committee
P.O. Box 3-7000
Juneau, AK 98801

Arizona

Governor's Committee
P.O. Box 6123
Phoenix, AZ 85005

Arkansas

Governor's Committee
P.O. Box 2981
Little Rock, AR 72203

California

Governor's Committee
800 Capital Mall, Room 2077
Sacramento, CA 95814

Colorado

Governor's Committee
214 State Social Services
   Building
Denver, CO 80203

Connecticut

Governor's Committee
2550 Main Street
Hartford, CT 06120

Delaware

Governor's Committee
801 West Street
Wilmington, DE 19801

District of Columbia

Mayor's Committee
5602 Chillum Place, N.E.
Washington, DC 20011

Florida

Governor's Committee
77 Caldwell Building
Tallahassee, FL 32304

Georgia

Governor's Committee
270 Washington Street, S.W.
Atlanta, GA 30334

Hawaii

Governor's Committee
250 S. King Street, Room 603
Honolulu, HI 96813

Idaho

Governor's Committee
P.O. Box 7189
Boise, ID 83707

Illinois

Governor's Committee
188 W. Randolph Street
Chicago, IL 60601

Indiana

Governor's Committee
1330 W. Michigan Street
Indianapolis, IN 46206

Iowa

Governor's Committee
Grimes State Office Building
Des Moines, IA 50319

Kansas

Governor's Committee
401 Topeka Avenue
Topeka, KS 66603

Kentucky

Governor's Committee
332 Sickle Court
Frankfort, KY 40601

Louisiana

Governor's Committee
P.O. Box 44094
Baton Rouge, LA 70804

Maine

Governor's Committee
P.O. Box 309
Augusta, ME 04330

Maryland

Governor's Committee
1100 N. Eutaw Street, Room
  608
Baltimore, MD 21201

Massachusetts

Governor's Committee
C. F. Hurley Employment
  Security Building
Boston, MA 02114

Michigan

Governor's Committee
300 E. Michigan Avenue
Lansing, MI 48913

Minnesota

Governor's Committee
527 Jackson Avenue, Room 227
St. Paul, MN 55101

Mississippi

Govenor's Committee
P.O. Box 1698
Jackson, MS 39205

Missouri

Governor's Committee
P.O. Box 59
Jefferson City, MO 65101

Montana

Governor's Committee
Vacancy

Nebraska

Governor's Committee
P.O. Box 94600
State House Station
Lincoln, NB 68509

Nevada

Governor's Committee
500 E. Third St.
Carson City, NV 89701

New Hampshire

Governor's Committee
177 State Street
Portsmouth, NH 03801

New Jersey

Governor's Committee
Labor & Industry Building
Trenton, NJ 08625

New Mexico

Governor's Committee
P.O. Box 1928
Albuquerque, NM 87103

New York

Governor's Committee
270 Broadway, Room 2410
New York, NY 10007

North Carolina

Governor's Committee
215 Hillsborough Street
Raleigh, NC 27603

North Dakota

Governor's Committee
State Capitol Building, 13th
    Floor
Bismark, ND 58501

Ohio

Governor's Committee
4656 Heaton Road
Columbus, OH 43229

Oklahoma

Governor's Committee
301 Will Rogers Memorial
   Office Building
Oklahoma City, OK 73105

Oregon

Governor's Committee
402 Labor & Industry Building
Salem, OR 97310

Pennsylvania

Governor's Committee
7th and Forster Streets
Harrisburg, PA 17121

Puerto Rico

Governor's Committee
P.O. Box A-E
Rio Piedras, PR 00928

Rhode Island

Governor's Committee
24 Mason Street
Providence, RI 02903

South Carolina

Governor's Committee
P.O. Box 1406
Columbia, SC 29202

South Dakota

Governor's Committee
104 S. Lincoln, #101
Aberdeen, SD 57401

Tennessee

Governor's Committee
201 Capitol Towers
Nashville, TN 37219

Texas

Governor's Committee
TEC Building
Austin, TX 78778

Utah

Governor's Committee
136 E. South Temple Street
Salt Lake City, UT 84111

Vermont

Governor's Committee
Employment Security Building
Montpelier, VT 05602

Virginia

Governor's Committee
P.O. Box 1358
Richmond, VA 23211

Virgin Islands

Governor's Committee
P.O. Box 630
St. Thomas, VI 00801

Washington

Governor's Committee
P.O. Box 367
Olympia, WA 98501

West Virginia

Governor's Committee
301 Nelson Building
Charleston, WV 25301

Wisconsin

Governor's Committee
P.O. Box 2209
Madison, WI 53701

Wyoming

Governor's Committee
P.O. Box 2760
Casper, WY 82601

I
State Employment Security Offices

Alabama

State Employment Security
  Office
Industrial Relations Building
Montgomery, AL 36104

Alaska

State Employment Security
  Office
P.O. Box 3-7000
Juneau, AK 99801

Arizona

State Employment Security
  Office
P.O. Box 6123
Phoenix, AZ 85005

Arkansas

State Employment Security
  Office
P.O. Box 2981
Little Rock, AR 72203

California

State Employment Security
  Office
800 Capitol Mall
Sacramento, CA 95814

Colorado

State Employment Security
  Office
1210 Sherman Street
Denver, CO 80203

Connecticut

State Employment Security
  Office
Connecticut Employment
  Security Division
Hartford, CT 06115

Delaware

State Employment Security
  Office
801 West Street
Wilmington, DE 19801

District of Columbia

State Employment Security
  Office
14th and E Streets, N.W., Room
  220
Washington, DC 20004

Florida

State Employment Security
  Office
Caldwell Building
Tallahassee, FL 32304

Georgia

State Employment Security
  Office
State Labor Building
Atlanta, GA 30334

Hawaii

State Employment Security
  Office
825 Mililani Street
Honolulu, HI 96813

Idaho

State Employment Security
  Office
P.O. Box 7189
Boise, ID 83707

Illinois

State Employment Security
  Office
165 N. Canal Street, Room 200
Chicago, IL 60606

Indiana

State Employment Security
  Office
10 N. Senate Avenue
Indianapolis, IN 46204

Iowa

State Employment Security
  Office
1000 E. Grand Avenue
Des Moines, IA 50319

Kansas

State Employment Security
  Office
401 Topeka Avenue
Topeka, KS 66603

Kentucky

State Employment Security
  Office
New Capitol Annex Building
Frankfort, KY 40601

Louisiana

State Employment Security
  Office
P.O. Box 44094
Baton Rouge, LA 70804

Maine

State Employment Security
  Office
20 Union Street
Augusta, ME 04330

Maryland

State Employment Security
Office
1100 N. Eutaw Street
Baltimore, MD 21201

Massachusetts

State Employment Security
Office
C. F. Hurley Employment
Security Building
Boston, MA 02114

Michigan

State Employment Security
Office
7310 Woodward Avenue
Detroit, MI 48202

Minnesota

State Employment Security
Office
390 N. Robert Street
St. Paul, MN 55101

Mississippi

State Employment Security
Office
P.O. Box 1699
Jackson, MS 39205

Missouri

State Employment Security
Office
421 E. Dunklin Street
Jefferson City, MO 65101

Montana

State Employment Security
Office
P.O. Box 1728
Helena, MT 59601

Nebraska

State Employment Security
Office
P.O. Box 94600
State House Station
Lincoln, NB 68509

Nevada

State Employment Security
Office
500 E. Third Street
Carson City, NV 89701

New Hampshire

State Employment Security
Office
32 S. Main Street
Concord, NH 03301

New Jersey

State Employment Security
Office
P.O. Box V
Trenton, NJ 08625

New Mexico

State Employment Security
Office
P.O. Box 1928
Albuquerque, NM 87103

New York

State Employment Security
  Office
State Office Building Campus
Albany, NY 12201

North Carolina

State Employment Security
  Office
P.O. Box 489
Raleigh, NC 27602

North Dakota

State Employment Security
  Office
P.O. Box 1537
Bismarck, ND 58501

Ohio

State Employment Security
  Office
P.O. Box 1618
Columbus, OH 43216

Oklahoma

State Employment Security
  Office
Will Rogers Memorial Office
  Building
Oklahoma City, OK 73105

Oregon

State Employment Security
  Office
403 Labor & Industry Building
Salem, OR 97310

Pennsylvania

State Employment Security
  Office
7th and Forster Streets
Harrisburg, PA 17121

Puerto Rico

State Employment Security
  Office
414 Barbosa Avenue
Hato Rey, PR 00917

Rhode Island

State Employment Security
  Office
24 Mason Street
Providence, RI 02903

South Carolina

State Employment Security
  Office
P.O. Box 995
Columbia, SC 29202

South Dakota

State Employment Security
  Office
607 N. Fourth Street
Aberdeen, SD 57401

Tennessee

State Employment Security
  Office
Cordell Hull State Office
  Building
Nashville, TN 37219

Texas

State Employment Security
Office
TEC Building
Austin, TX 78778

Utah

State Employment Security
Office
P.O. Box 11249
Salt Lake City, UT 84111

Vermont

State Employment Security
Office
P.O. Box 488
Montpelier, VT 05602

Virginia

State Employment Security
Office
P.O. Box 1358
Richmond, VA 23211

Virgin Islands

State Employment Security
Office
P.O. Box 1092
St. Thomas, VI 00801

Washington

State Employment Security
Office
P.O. Box 367
Olympia, WA 98501

West Virginia

State Employment Security
Office
State Office Building
Charleston, WV 25305

Wisconsin

State Employment Security
Office
P.O. Box 1607
Madison, WI 53701

Wyoming

State Employment Security
Office
P.O. Box 760
Casper, WY 82601

J
Veterans Administration Offices*

Alabama

Aronov Building
474 S. Court Street
Montgomery, AL 36104

Alaska

VAO
Loussac-Sogn Building
429 D Street
Anchorage, AK 99501

Arizona

3225 N. Central Avenue
Phoenix, AZ 85012

Arkansas

Federal Office Building
700 W. Capitol Avenue
Little Rock, AR 72201

California

Federal Building
West Los Angeles
11000 Wilshire Boulevard
Los Angeles, CA 90024

USVAC
East Los Angeles Service Center
929 N. Bonnie Beach Place
East Los Angeles, CA 90063

2022 Camino Del Rio North
San Diego, CA 92108

211 Main Street
San Francisco, CA 94105

Colorado

Denver Federal Center
Denver, CO 80225

*The offices listed in this Appendix are either Veterans Administration Offices (VAO), Veterans Assistance Centers (USVAC), or Veterans Administration Centers (VAC).

341

Connecticut

450 Main Street
Hartford, CT 06103

Delaware

VAC
1601 Kirkwood Highway
Wilmington, DE 19085

District of Columbia

941 N. Capitol Street, N.E.
Washington, DC 20421

Florida

VAO
Post Office and Courthouse
   Building
311 W. Monroe Street
Jacksonville, FL 32201

VAO
Room 100
51 Southwest First Avenue
Miami, FL 33130

P.O. Box 1437
144 First Avenue South
St. Petersburg, FL 33731

Georgia

730 Peachtree Street, N.E.
Atlanta, GA 30308

Hawaii

P.O. Box 3198
680 Ala Moana Boulevard
Honolulu, HI 96801

Idaho

Federal Building and U.S.
   Courthouse
550 W. Fort Street, Box 044
Boise, ID 83724

Illinois

P.O. Box 8136
2030 W. Taylor Street
Chicago, IL 60680

Indiana

575 N. Pennsylvania Street
Indianapolis, IN 46204

Iowa

210 Walnut Street
Des Moines, IA 50309

Kansas

VAC
5500 East Kellogg
Wichita, KS 67218

Kentucky

600 Federal Place
Louisville, KY 40202

Louisiana

701 Loyola Avenue
New Orleans, LA 70113

Maine

VAC
Togus, ME 04330

Maryland

Federal Building
31 Hopkins Plaza
Baltimore, MD 21201

Massachusetts

John Fitzgerald Kennedy
   Federal Building
Government Center
Boston, MA 02203

Michigan

P.O. Box 1117A
801 W. Baltimore Street at 3rd
   Avenue
Detroit, MI 48232

Minnesota

VAC
Federal Building, Fort Snelling
St. Paul, MN 55111

Mississippi

VAC
1500 E. Woodrow Wilson
   Avenue
Jackson, MS 39216

Missouri

VAO
Federal Office Building
601 E. 12th Street
Kansas City, MO 64106

Federal Building, Room 4705
1520 Market Street
St. Louis, MO 63103

Montana

VAC
Fort Harrison, MT 59636

Nebraska

220 South 17th Street
Lincoln, NB 68508

Nevada

1201 Terminal Way
Reno, NV 89502

New Hampshire

497 Silver Street
Manchester, NH 03103

New Jersey

20 Washington Place
Newark, NJ 07102

New Mexico

500 Gold Avenue, S.W.
Albuquerque, NM 87101

New York

VAO
Leo W. O'Brien Federal
   Building
Clinton Avenue and North
   Pearl Street
Albany, NY 12207

Federal Building
111 W. Huron Street
Buffalo, NY 14202

252 7th Avenue at 24th Street
New York, NY 10001

VAO
Federal Office Building and
  Courthouse
100 State Street
Rochester, NY 14614

VAO
Gateway Building
809 S. Salina Street
Syracuse, NY 13202

North Carolina

Wachovia Building
301 North Main Street
Winston-Salem, NC 27102

North Dakota

VAC
Fargo, ND 58102

Ohio

VAO
Federal Office Building, Room
  1024
550 Main Street
Cincinnati, OH 45202

Federal Office Building
1240 East Ninth Street
Cleveland, OH 44199

VAO
360 South 3rd Street
Columbus, OH 43215

Oklahoma

2nd and Court Streets
Muskogee, OK 74401

VAO
Federal Building
200 Northwest 4th Street
Oklahoma City, OK 73102

Oregon

1220 Southwest 3rd Avenue
Portland, OR 97204

Pennsylvania

VAC
P.O. Box 8079
5000 Wissahickon Avenue
Philadelphia, PA 19101

1000 Liberty Avenue
Pittsburgh, PA 15222

VAO
19-27 North Main Street
Wilkes-Barre, PA 18701

Puerto Rico

VAC
Barrio Monacillos
Rio Piedras
San Juan, PR 00921

Rhode Island

Federal Building, Kennedy
  Plaza
Providence, RI 02903

South Carolina

1801 Assembly Street
Columbia, SC 29201

South Dakota

VAC
Sioux Falls, SD 57101

Tennessee

110 9th Avenue, South
Nashville, TN 37203

Texas

VAO
U.S. Courthouse and Federal
 Office Building
1100 Commerce Street
Dallas, TX 75202

2515 Murworth Drive
Houston, TX 77054

VAO
Federal Building and U.S.
 Courthouse
1205 Texas Avenue
Lubbock, TX 79401

VAO
410 South Main Street
San Antonio, TX 78285

1400 North Valley Mills Drive
Waco, TX 76710

Utah

125 South State Street
Salt Lake City, UT 84138

Vermont

VAC
White River Junction, VT
 05001

Virginia

211 West Campbell Avenue
Roanoke, VA 24011

Washington

915 Second Avenue
Seattle, WA 98174

West Virginia

502 Eighth Street
Huntington, WV 25701

Wisconsin

342 North Water Street
Milwaukee, WI 53202

Wyoming

VAC
2360 East Pershing Boulevard
Cheyenne, WY 82001

K
State Vocational Rehabilitation Programs Serving the Blind and the Visually Impaired

Arizona Department of
  Economic Security
Rehabilitation Services Bureau
Section of Rehabilitation for the
  Blind and Visually Impaired
1640 North Grand Avenue
Phoenix, AZ 85007

Arkansas Department of Social
  and Rehabilitation Services
Office for Blind/Visually
  Impaired
411 Victory Street, P.O. Box
  3237
Little Rock, AR 72203

Connecticut Board of
  Education
Services for the Blind
170 Ridge Road
Wethersfield, CT 06109

Delaware Department of Health
  and Social Services
305 W. Eighth Street
Wilmington, DE 19801

Florida Department of
  Education
Office of Blind Services
2571 Executive Center Circle,
  East
Howard Building
Tallahassee, FL 32301

Idaho Commission for the
  Blind
Statehouse
Boise, ID 83720

Iowa Commission for the Blind
Fourth and Keosauqua
Des Moines, IA 50309

Kansas Department of Social
  and Rehabilitation Services
Services for the Blind and
  Visually Handicapped
Biddle Building
2700 West 6th Street
Topeka, KS 66606

Kentucky Bureau for the Blind
State Office Building Annex
High Street
Frankfort, KY 40601

Louisiana Health and Human
  Resources
Office of Rehabilitation Services
Blind Services Program
1755 Florida Street
Baton Rouge, LA 70802

Massachusetts Commission for
  the Blind
110 Tremont Street, 6th Floor
Boston, MA 02108

Michigan Department of Social
  Services
Office of Services for the Blind
300 S. Capitol Avenue
Lansing, MI 48926

Minnesota Department of Social
  Services
Services for the Blind and
  Visually Handicapped
1745 University Avenue, First
  Floor
St. Paul, MN 55104

Mississippi Board of Education
Vocational Rehabilitation for
  the Blind
P.O. Box 4872
Jackson, MS 39216

Missouri Department of Social
  Services
Division of Family Services
Broadway State Office Building
Jefferson City, MO 65101

Montana Department of Social
  and Rehabilitation Services
Visual Services Division
P.O. Box 1723
Helena, MT 59601

Nebraska Department of
  Education
Division of Rehabilitation
  Services for the Visually
  Impaired
1047 South Street
Lincoln, NB 68502

New Jersey Commission for the
  Blind and Visually Impaired
1100 Raymond Boulevard
Newark, NJ 07102

New York Commission for the
  Visually Handicapped
Department of Social Services
Ten Eyck Office Building
40 North Pearl Street
Albany, NY 12207

North Carolina Department of
Human Resources
Division of Services for the
Blind
410 N. Boylan Avenue
P.O. Box 2658
Raleigh, NC 27602

Oregon Commission for the
Blind
535 S.E. 12th Avenue
Portland, OR 97214

Pennsylvania Department of
Public Welfare
Bureau for the Visually
Handicapped
P.O. Box 2675
Harrisburgh, PA 17120

Rhode Island Department of
Social and Rehabilitation
Services
Services for the Blind and
Visually Impaired
46 Adorn Street
Providence, RI 02903

South Carolina Commission for
the Blind
P.O. Box 11738, Capitol Station
Columbia, SC 29211

Tennessee Department of
Human Services
303–304 State Office Building
Nashville, TN 37219

Texas Commission for the
Blind
314 W. 11th Street
P.O. Box 12866
Austin, TX 78711

Utah Department of Social and
Rehabilitative Services
Services for the Blind and
Visually Handicapped
309 East First South
Salt Lake City, UT 84111

Vermont Department of Social
and Rehabilitative Services
Division for the Blind and
Visually Handicapped
Vocational Rehabilitation
Division
State Office Building
Montpelier, VT 05602

Virginia Commission for the
Visually Handicapped
3003 Parkwood Avenue
Richmond, VA 23221

Washington Department of
Social and Health Services
Office of Services for the Blind
3411 South Alaska Street
Seattle, WA 98118

L
State Statutes Prohibiting Discrimination in Employment*

*Published by *Amicus,* September/October 1978, a publication of the National Center for Law and the Handicapped. Reprinted with permission.

	ALASKA Stat. § 18.80.220 (Cum. Supp. 1976)	CALIFORNIA Cal. Lab. Code § 1413 (h), 1420 (a), 1432.5 (West. Supp. 1976)	COLORADO Rev. Stat. Tit. 24, §§24-34-801—24-34-802 (1977)
ADMINISTRATIVE ENFORCEMENT			
Enforcement Authority	State Commission for Human Rights	California State Fair Employment Practice Commission	Colorado Civil Rights Commission
Deadline for Reporting Alleged Violation	Within 300 days.	Within one year.	
Enforcement Authority of Administrative Agency	Fine of no more than $500 or imprisonment for no more than 30 days, or both.	Misdemeanor punishable by fine of no more than $500, or imprisonment for no more than six months, or both.	Misdemeanor punishable by fine of no more than $100, or imprisonment for no more than 60 days, or both.
INDIVIDUAL RECOURSE			
Private Right of Action	Complainant may file with superior court for relief.	Civil action, if no accusation is issued within 150 days or if commission earlier determines that no accusation will issue. Must be brought within one year of commission notification.	
Remedies	Relief including cash settlement.		
DEFINITIONS			
Employer	Anyone employing one or more persons within the state. Excludes not-for-profit organizations that are exclusively social and fraternal, and charitable, educational, or religious associations.	The state and all state and municipal agencies, and anyone employing five or more persons. Excludes religious associations and not-for-profit corporations.	The state, its political subdivisions, the public schools, and all other employment supported in whole or in part by public funds.
Handicap	A physical handicap.	Any physical impairment which requires special education or related services. Excludes mental illness, mental retardation, or behavior disorders stemming from alcoholism or drug addiction.	Blindness, deafness, or other physical disability which does not prevent performance of work in question.
COVERAGE OF LABOR ORGANIZATIONS	Not included	Included	Not included
SPECIAL PROVISIONS		Reasonable accommodation is not required.	

CONNECTICUT Conn. Gen. Stat. §§1-1f, 31-122 to 31-128 (Supp. 1977)	DISTRICT OF COLUMBIA Regulation No. 73-22 (Nov. 11, 1973)	FLORIDA Fla. Stat. Ann. § 413.08 (West. Supp. 1977)	GEORGIA Act 807, Georgia Laws 1978, Sec. 1-29
State Commission on Human Rights and Opportunities	District of Columbia Commission on Human Rights	Florida Commission on Human Relations	Office of Fair Employment Practices
Within 180 days.	Within one year.	Within 180 days.	Within 180 days.
Complaints in equity, in cases where an employer has 50 or more workers. Temporary injunctive relief, including restraining order.	Civil action leading to temporary restraining order and preliminary injunction. Cease and desist order, and affirmative action, including awarding of compensatory damages, reasonable attorney's fees, and hearing costs.	Affirmative relief, including reasonable attorney's fees.	
Complainant may obtain judicial review in county superior court by filing written petition with the court clerk within two weeks of receiving final notice from the state commission.	Complainant may seek damages and other remedies in any court of competent jurisdiction within one year of alleged violation	Civil action, if commission fails to conciliate or take final action within 180 days of filing.	Complainant may seek judicial review in county superior court.
Temporary relief or restraining order.	Damages or other remedies.	Affirmative relief, including reasonable attorney's fees.	
Anyone employing three or more persons, including the state and its agencies.	Anyone who employs an individual for compensation, except as domestic labor.	Any person employing 15 or more persons for 20 or more calendar weeks.	Any state agency employing 15 or more persons within the state for 20 or more calendar weeks.
Any chronic physical infirmity of congenital nature, or resulting from bodily injury organic changes or illness.	A bodily or mental disablement which may be the result of injury, illness, or congenital condition for which reasonable accommodation can be made.		A physical or mental impairment which substantially limits one or more major life activities. Physical handicap must not substantially interfere with the job. Mental impairment must be medically shown to have been removed.
Included	Included	Included	Not Included

	HAWAII Haw. Rev. Stat. §§ 378-1 to 378-10 (1978)	**ILLINOIS** III. Rev. Stat. Ch. 48 §§ 851-867 (1976)	**INDIANA** Ind. Code Ann. §§ 22-9-1-1 to 22-9-1-13 (Burns Cum. Supp. 1976)
ADMINISTRATIVE ENFORCEMENT **Enforcement Authority**	State Department of Labor and Industrial Relations	Illinois Fair Employment Practices Commission	Indiana Civil Rights Commission
Deadline for Reporting Alleged Violation	Within 90 days.	Within 180 days.	Within 90 days.
Enforcement Authority of Administrative Agency	Affirmative action, such as reinstatement with or without pay. Fine of no more than $500 or imprisonment for not more than 90 days, or both.	Fine of no more than $2,000, imprisonment of no more than 30 days, or both.	
INDIVIDUAL RECOURSE **Private Right of Action**	Complainant may seek judicial review.	Complainant may seek judicial review.	
Remedies	Cost of action, including fees of any nature and reasonable attorney's fees.	Damages, any order granting employment, or other relief.	
DEFINITIONS **Employer**	Anyone employing one or more persons.	The state and its agencies and anyone employing 15 or more persons during 20 or more calendar weeks.	The state, its agencies, and anyone employing six or more persons within the state. Excludes not-for-profit fraternal or religious organizations, religious institutions, and not-for-profit social organizations.
Handicap	A substantial physical impairment verifiable by medical evidence, which appears likely to continue throughout the individual's lifetime without substantial improvement.	Any physical or mental impairment demonstrable by medically acceptable clinical or laboratory diagnostic techniques, which constitutes a substantial limitation to one or more of a person's major life activities.	A physical or mental condition constituting a substantial disability, but which is unrelated to the person's ability to engage in a particular occupation.
COVERAGE OF LABOR ORGANIZATIONS	Included	Included	Included
SPECIAL PROVISIONS		Affirmative action is required of all contractors, subcontractors, and labor organizations furnishing services to state or municipal agencies.	Discrimination by contractors and subcontractors of state is prohibited. Modification of physical facilities or administrative procedures to accommodate handicapped persons is not required.

IOWA	KANSAS	KENTUCKY	MAINE
Iowa Code Ann. § 601A.1 to 601A.16 (1975)	Kan. Stat. § 44-1001 (Supp. 1976)	Ky. Rev. Stat. § 207.130 (Cum. Supp. 1976)	Me. Rev. Stat. Ann. Tit. 5 § 4553.7-a, 4572 (1977)
Iowa State Civil Rights Commission	Kansas Commission on Civil Rights	Kentucky Department of Labor	Maine Human Rights Commission
Within 120 days.	Within six months.	Within 180 days.	Within six months.
		Appropriate temporary relief, including restraining order.	Temporary injunction.
Complainant may seek judicial review.	Complainant may seek court review by trial *de novo*.	Complainant may seek judicial review or may file civil action in circuit court.	Complainant may file concurrent civil action in superior court.
		Damages, costs of lawsuit, and reasonable attorney's fees.	
The state, all state agencies, and anyone who employs workers within the state.	The state and all state agencies, as well as anyone in the state employing four or more persons. Excludes not-for-profit organizations.	Anyone employing eight or more workers within the state for 20 or more calendar weeks.	Anyone in the state employing any number of workers anywhere, and anyone outside the state employing persons who work in the state. Excludes not-for-profit religious or fraternal associations.
A physical or mental condition which constitutes a substantial disability.	A physical condition of congenital nature, or acquired by injury or disease, which constitutes a substantial disability.	Any physical condition which constitutes a substantial disability and is demonstrable by medically acceptable clinical diagnostic tests. Conditions not medically diagnosable, including alcoholism, drug addiction, and obesity, are excluded.	Any physical or mental disability which constitutes a substantial handicap as determined by physician, psychiatrist, or psychologist, as well as impairment which requires special education, vocational rehabilitation, or related services.
Included	Included	Included	Included
Reasonable accommodation and adaptation of preemployment tests are required. Every effort must be made to retain, reassign, and rehabilitate employees who become disabled.		Modification of physical facilities is not required. Preemployment inquiries are permitted concerning an applicant's handicapping condition.	

	MARYLAND Md. Ann. Code Art. 49b, § 18 (g), 19, 20 (1977)	MASSACHUSETTS Mass. Ann. Laws Ch. 149, § 24 (k) (Michie Law Co-op 1977)	MICHIGAN Mich. Stat. Ann. § 395.301 (1976)
ADMINISTRATIVE ENFORCEMENT **Enforcement Authority**	Commission on Human Relations		Michigan Civil Rights Commission
Deadline for Reporting Alleged Violation	Within six months.		Within 100 days.
Enforcement Authority of Administrative Agency		Fine of no less than $25, no more than $200.	
INDIVIDUAL RECOURSE **Private Right of Action**			Complainant may seek trial *de novo* in the circuit court of the county where alleged violation took place.
Remedies			Reasonable attorney's fees.
DEFINITIONS **Employer**	The state and anyone in business employing 15 or more persons for 20 or more calendar weeks.		Anyone employing four or more persons. Includes contractors and subcontractors who furnish material or perform work for a state agency.
Handicap	Any physical disability, or any mental impairment which may have required remedial or special education.		A determinable physical or mental characteristic of an individual which may result from disease, injury, congenital condition, or functional disorder. Also includes mental retardation.
COVERAGE OF LABOR ORGANIZATIONS	Included	Not Included	Included
SPECIAL PROVISIONS			Reasonable accommodation required.

MINNESOTA	MISSISSIPPI	MISSOURI	MONTANA
Minn. Stat. Ann. § 363.01 (West. 1977)	Miss. Code Ann. § 43-15 (1977)	Revised Statutes Ch. 296, § 296.010 to 296.070 (1978)	Mont. Rep. Code Ann. § 64-305 and 316 (1977)
Department of Human Rights		Missouri Commission on Human Rights	Montana Commission for Human Rights
Within six months.	Within 180 days.		Within 180 days.
		Misdemeanor sentence.	Appropriate temporary relief, including a restraining order.
Civil action within 45 days after commission has determined there is no probable cause, or between 25 days to one year after filing a complaint, if commission has not taken action.		Complainant may seek judicial review within 30 days of notice of commission's final decision.	Complainant may bring action in the state district court. Administrative remedies need not be exhausted in order to take judicial recourse.
Anyone employing one or more persons.		Anyone employing six or more persons or acting in the interest of an employer, directly. Excludes religious or sectarian corporations or associations.	Anyone employing one or more persons. Excludes fraternal, charitable, or religious associations, if such organizations are not for profit.
A mental or physical condition which constitutes a disability.		A physical or mental impairment resulting in a disability unrelated to the person's ability to perform the duties of a particular job.	Any physical disability which is caused by bodily injury, birth defect, or illness.
Included	Not Included	Included	Included

	NEBRASKA Neb. Rep. Stat. § 48-1102 and 1108 (1974)	NEVADA Nev. Rev. Stat. § 613.330 (1975)	NEW HAMPSHIRE N.H. Rev. Stat. § 354-A:3 (Supp. 1975)
ADMINISTRATIVE ENFORCEMENT			
Enforcement Authority	Nebraska Equal Opportunity Commission	Nevada Commission on Equal Rights of Citizens	New Hampshire Commission for Human Rights
Deadline for Reporting Alleged Violation	Within 180 days.	Within 180 days.	Within 90 days.
Enforcement Authority of Administrative Agency			
INDIVIDUAL RECOURSE			
Private Right of Action	Complainant may appeal commission's order in the district of the county where alleged violation occurred. Appeal must be made within 30 days of the date of commission's order.	Complainant may file a complaint with district court.	Complainant may obtain judicial review within 30 days of final order from commission.
Remedies			
DEFINITIONS			
Employer	Anyone who employs 15 or more persons for 20 or more calendar weeks. Excludes the United States, a corporation owned by the federal government, Indian tribes, and private clubs.	Anyone with 15 or more employees for 20 or more calendar weeks. Excludes the United States or any corporations owned by the federal government, Indian tribes, and private clubs.	Anyone employing six or more persons. Excludes fraternal, charitable, or religious associations, if such organizations are not for profit.
Handicap	Any physical or mental condition which is caused by bodily injury, birth defect, or illness.	A physical handicap, Including visual handicaps.	Any physical or mental disability other than illness.
COVERAGE OF LABOR ORGANIZATIONS	Included	Included	Included
SPECIAL PROVISIONS			

NEW JERSEY N.J. Stat. Ann. § 10:5-4 (West. 1976)	NEW MEXICO N.M. Stat. Ann. § 4-33-2 (a) (1974)	NEW YORK N.Y. Exec. Law § 292, 296 (McKinney 1976)	NORTH CAROLINA N.C. Jen. Stat. Ch. 168, §§ 128-15 (Supp. 1977)
Division on Civil Rights	New Mexico Human Rights Commission	New York Division of Human Rights	Office of State Personnel
Within 180 days.	Within 90 days.	Within a year.	
		Fine of no more than $500, or imprisonment for no more than one year, or both.	
	Complainant may obtain trial *de novo* in county district court by filing appeal within 30 days of commission's order.	Complainant may seek judicial review in any court of appropriate jurisdiction.	
Excludes not-for-profit clubs of a social, fraternal, charitable, educational, or religious nature.	Anyone employing four or more persons.	Anyone employing four or more persons.	
Any physical disability which is caused by bodily injury, birth defect, or illness.	Any physical or mental disability unrelated to a person's ability to perform a particular job.	Any physical or mental impairment resulting from an anatomical, physiological, or neurological condition which prevents normal bodily functions.	
Included	Included	Included	Not Included
		Equal opportunity must be provided by all contractors who are awarded state projects of $50,000 or more.	

	OHIO Ohio Rev. Code Ann. § 4112 (Page Supp. 1976)	OREGON Or. Rev. Stat. § 659.400 (1975)	PENNSYLVANIA Pa. Stat. Ann. Tit. 43, § 954 (Purdon Supp. 1976)
ADMINISTRATIVE ENFORCEMENT			
Enforcement Authority	Ohio Civil Rights Commission	Bureau of Labor	Pennsylvania Human Relations Commission
Deadline for Reporting Alleged Violation	Within six months.	Within one year.	Within 90 days.
Enforcement Authority of Administrative Agency			Fine of no less than $100, no more than $500, or imprisonment for no more than 30 days, or both.
INDIVIDUAL RECOURSE			
Private Right of Action	Complainant may seek judicial review.	Civil suit in circuit court, if the commission has been unable to obtain a conciliation agreement within one year. Suit must be filed within 90 days of the notice from the commission.	Court action upon commission notification that the complaint is being dismissed or that no agreement has been reached. Commission must give notice within one year.
Remedies		Compensatory damages. or $200. whichever is greater, and punitive damages not to exceed $2,500.	
DEFINITIONS			
Employer	The state, its agencies, and anyone employing four or more persons within the state.	Anyone employing six or more persons, including state and municipal agencies, with the exception of the Oregon National Guard.	The state and its agencies, and anyone employing four or more persons within the state. Excludes religious, fraternal, charitable, or sectarian associations except when they are supported by government funds.
Handicap	A medically diagnosable condition expected to continue for a considerable length of time, which can reasonably be expected to limit the person's functional ability.	A physical or mental disability including but not limited to sensory disability.	Any disability which does not substantially interfere with the ability to perform the essential functions of the position for which the handicapped person applies or in which that person is employed.
COVERAGE OF LABOR ORGANIZATIONS	Included	Included	Included
SPECIAL PROVISIONS	Discrimination in public works contracts is prohibited. Written complaints should be filed within 30 days of alleged violation with appropriate agency official or the Division of Equal Employment Opportunity for State Personnel.		Uninsurability or increased insurance costs under a group or employee insurance claim do not render a disability job-related.

RHODE ISLAND R.I. Gen. Laws Tit. 28, Ch. 5, § 28-5-6 (Supp. 1976)	TENNESSEE Tenn. Code Ann. § 8-4131 (Supp. 1976)	TEXAS Tex. Rev. Civ. Stat. Ann. Art. 4419e (Vernon 1976)	VERMONT Vt. Stat. Ann. Cit. 21, § 498 (Supp. 1976)
Rhode Island Commission for Human Rights			
Within one year.			
	Misdemeanor sentence.		
Complainant may obtain judicial review.			Complainant may bring civil action for damages, or apply for equitable relief or both.
			Damages or equitable relief, or both.
The state and its agencies, and anyone within the state employing four or more individuals.			
Any physical disability which is caused by bodily injury, birth defect, or illness.	Any physical or mental disability.	A mental or physical disability, including mental retardation.	A physical handicap.
Included	Not Included	Not Included	Included

VIRGINIA	WASHINGTON	WEST VIRGINIA	WISCONSIN
Va. Code § 40.1-28.7 (1976)	Wash. Rev. Code § 4.60.180 (1976)	W. Va. Code 5-11-3 (Supp. 1976)	Wisc. Stat. Ann. § 111.32 (1974)
	Washington State Human Rights Commission	West Virginia Human Rights Commission	Department of Industry, Labor and Human Relations
Within 90 days.	Within six months.	Within 90 days.	
		Fine of no less than $100, no more than $500, or imprisonment for no more than 30 days, or both.	
Complainant may file suit with any circuit court within 90 days of alleged violation.	Complainant may obtain review by the superior court of the county in which the alleged violation occurred. Petition must be filed within two weeks of the final order of the commission.		
	Damages, including reasonable attorney's fees.		
	Anyone with eight or more employees. Excludes not-for-profit religious organizations.	The state and its agencies, and anyone employing 12 or more persons within the state. Excludes private clubs.	The state and its agencies. Excludes not-for-profit social, fraternal, or religious associations.
A physical handicap.	A mental or physical handicap.	Blindness. A person shall be considered blind only if visual acuity does not exceed 20/200 in the better eye with correcting lenses.	
Not Included	Included	Included	Included

M
Activist Organizations*

American Coalition of Citizens
  with Disabilities
1346 Connecticut Avenue,
  N.W., Suite 308
Washington, DC 20036
(202-785-4625)

Disability Rights Center
1346 Connecticut Avenue,
  N.W., Suite 1124
Washington, DC 20036
(202-223-3304)

Disabled American Veterans
807 Maine Avenue, S.W.
Washington, DC 20024
(202-554-3501)

Goodwill Industries of America
9200 Wisconsin Avenue, N.W.
Washington, DC 20014
(301-530-6500)

Human Resources
  Development Institute
AFL–CIO National Office
815 16th Street, N.W.
Washington, DC 20006
(202-638-3914)

Mainstream, Inc.
1200 15th Street, N.W.
Washington, DC 20005
(202-833-1136)

National Association of the Deaf
  Legal Defense Fund
7th Street and Florida Avenue,
  N.E.
P.O. Box 1793
Washington, DC 20002
(202-651-5461)

*These organizations are generally involved in the following activities: lobbying Congress for more stringent nondiscrimination laws; legal defense of handicapped complainants; advocacy in the community for the rights of the handicapped; and development of information and aids for the handicapped.

National Center for Law and
the Handicapped
2111 W. Washington Street,
Suite 1900
South Bend, IN 46601
(219-288-4751)

National Easter Seal Society for
Crippled Children and
Adults
2023 West Ogden Avenue
Chicago, IL 60612
(312-243-8400)

Paralyzed Veterans of America
4330 East–West Highway, Suite
300
Washington, DC 20014
(301-652-2135)

Public Interest Law Center
1315 Walnut Street
Philadelphia, PA 19107
(215-735-7200)

N
Building Survey to Develop Guides for the Handicapped*

Name of Building_____Phone Number_____

Street Address _____City_____ State_____

Person Interviewed _____Title_____

Circle YES or NO
(Complete answer
in space provided
when necessary)

1. OFFSTREET PARKING

  a. Is an offstreet parking area available adjacent to building? .... Yes   No

  b. If adjacent offstreet parking is not available identify and give location of nearest
     and most convenient parking area_____

  c. Are parking area and building separated by a street? .... Yes   No

  d. Is the surface of the parking area smooth and hard (no sand, gravel, etc.)?.................. Yes   No

2. PASSENGER LOADING ZONE

  a. Is there a passenger loading zone? .... Yes   No

  b. If yes, where is it located in relation to selected entrance? _____
_____

3. APPROACH TO SELECTED ENTRANCE

  a. Which entrance was selected as most accessible ? _____

  b. Is the approach to the entrance door ground level? .... Yes   No

  c. Is there a ramp in the approach to or at the entrance door?........................... Yes   No

  d. If there are any steps in the approach to or at the entrance door, give total
     number of steps.. _____

  e. If there are steps, is there a sturdy handrail on at least one side or in the center?.... Yes   No

4. ENTRANCE DOOR

  a. What is the width of the entrance doorway (with door open)? .... _____

  b. Is the door automatic? .... Yes   No

  c. Are there steps between entrance and main areas or corridor? .... Yes   No

  d. If yes, what is the total number of steps?... _____

  e. If there are steps, is there a sturdy handrail in the center or on at least one side?......... Yes   No

5. ELEVATOR

  a. Is there a passenger elevator?... Yes   No

  b. Does it serve all essential areas?.. Yes   No

6. ESSENTIAL AREAS (See instructions for explanation) Area 1_____

  Area 2 _____ Area 3_____

*Published by the National Easter Seal Society for Crippled Children and Adults, 2023 W. Ogden Ave., Chicago, IL 60612, 1961. Reproduced with permission.

363

7. ACCESS FROM ENTRY TO ESSENTIAL AREAS   (1)   (2)   (3)

    a. Is the usable width of corridors and aisles at least 32"? .... Yes   No   Yes   No   Yes   No

    b. Is the narrowest clear doorway with door open 28" wide or more? Yes   No   Yes   No   Yes   No

    c. If not, what is the width? .... _____   _____   _____

8. INTERIOR OF ESSENTIAL AREAS

    a. Are there any steps between essential areas not served by elevator? Yes   No   Yes   No   Yes   No

    b. Does each flight of steps have a sturdy handrail on at least one
       side or in the center? .... Yes   No   Yes   No   Yes   No

9. PUBLIC TOILET ROOMS   **MEN**   **WOMEN**

    a. Where are toilet rooms located?   Men_____

                                    Women_____

    b. Would one need to go up or down steps to get to toilet room? .... Yes   No   Yes   No

    c. If so, how many? .... _____   _____

    d. If there are steps, does each flight of steps have a sturdy handrail on
       at least one side or in the center? .... Yes   No   Yes   No

    e. What is the width of toilet room entrance doorway (with door open)? _____   _____

    f. Is there free space in the room to permit a wheelchair to turn? .... Yes   No   Yes   No

    g. What is width of widest toilet stall door? .... _____   _____

    h. Does this stall have handrails or grab bars? .... Yes   No   Yes   No

10. MOTEL OR HOTEL GUEST ROOMS

    a. What is width of the entrance door to guest room (with door open)? .... _____

    b. What is width of entrance door to bathroom (with door open)? .... _____

    c. Are there handrails or grab bars near the toilet? .... Yes   No

    d. Are there handrails or grab bars for the bath or shower? .... Yes   No

11. PUBLIC TELEPHONE

    a. Where is the most accessible phone located? _____

    b. What type (booth, wall, desk)? _____

    c. If phone is in a booth, what is width of booth door (with door open)? .... _____

    d. Is the handset 48" or less from the floor? .... Yes   No

    e. Does the phone have amplifying controls for the hard of hearing? .... Yes   No

12. INTERIOR (Auditorium, Church, Restaurant, etc.)

    a. What is the distance from floor to edge of restaurant table? .... _____

    b. If there are booths, can a wheelchair be placed at the open end of booth? .... Yes   No

    c. In theaters, public halls, churches, etc. can persons remain in wheelchairs? .... Yes   No

    d. If yes, where? _____

    e. Can arrangements be made to reserve wheelchair space? .... Yes   No

13. ASSISTANCE AND AIDS AVAILABLE

    a. Is there an attendant who will take cars? .... Yes   No

    b. Is there help available for those needing assistance in entering? (doorman, porter)? Yes   No

    c. If not, is help available for those needing assistance if arranged for in advance? .... Yes   No

    d. Who to call in advance for assistance_____

    e. Telephone Number_____

    f. Are wheelchairs available? (at airports, hotels, museums, etc.)? .... Yes   No

Surveyor_____Date_____

O
Publications Helpful to Employers

Guide to the Evaluation of Permanent Impairments, American Medical Association, 535 N. Dearborn Street, Chicago, IL 60610.

Amicus (a bimonthly periodical), National Center for Law and the Handicapped, 211 W. Washington Street, South Bend, IN 46601.

Building Without Barriers for the Disabled, The American Institute of Architects, 1735 New York Avenue, N.W., Washington, DC 20006.

American National Standard Specifications for Making Buildings and Facilities Accessible to and Usable by the Physically Handicapped, American National Standards Institute, Inc., 1430 Broadway, New York, NY 10018.

Architectural Barriers: Bibliography, Reference Section, Division for the Blind and Physically Handicapped, Library of Congress, Washington, DC 20542.

Building for the Handicapped, The Architects Collaborative, 46 Brattle Street, Cambridge, MA 02138.

Construction Details: Planning for the Handicapped, Committee to Eliminate Architectural Barriers in Westchester County, 202 Mamaroneck Avenue, White Plains, NY 10601.

Handicapping America—Barriers to Disabled People, by Frank Bowe, New York: Harper & Row, 1978.

Federal Contract Compliance Manual, Superintendent of Documents, U.S. Government Printing Office, Washington, DC 20402.

INDEX

366